ASSIMILATING

NEW LEADERS

ASSIMILATING NEW LEADERS

The Key to Executive Retention

DIANE DOWNEY

with TOM MARCH

and ADENA BERKMAN

AMACOM

American Management Association

New York • Atlanta • Boston • Chicago • Kansas City • San Francisco • Washington, D. C.

Brussels • Mexico City • Tokyo • Toronto

This publication is designed to provide accurate and authoritative
information in regard to the subject matter covered. It is sold with the
understanding that the publisher is not engaged in rendering legal,
accounting, or other professional service. If legal advice or other expert
assistance is required, the services of a competent professional person
should be sought.

Library of Congress Cataloging-in-Publication Data

Downey, Diane.
    Assimilating new leaders: the key to executive retention / Diane Downey,
Tom March, Adena Berkman.
      p.   cm.
    Includes bibliographical references.
    ISBN 0-8144-0645-9
    1. Leadership.   2. Executive ability.   3. Employee retention.   I. March,
Tom.   II. Berkman, Adena.   III. Title.

HD57.7 .D69 2001
658.4'0714—dc21

2001022183

Printing Number

10 9 8 7 6 5 4 3 2 1

Contents

Acknowledgments

Although the cover indicates that this book was written "with" Tom March and Adena Berkman, they were genuine intellectual partners throughout the process of researching and writing this book. As DAI consultants and writing partners, they contributed key concepts and were responsible for writing large parts of the book.

Tom has collaborated on a number of new leader assimilation programs for DAI clients during his two years at the firm. His experience as a writer had an enormous impact on the shape and direction of the book. In addition to his work on new leader assimilation, he has assisted DAI clients in the design and delivery of change interventions in both the profit and nonprofit sectors. Prior to joining DAI, he taught at Fordham University, St. John's University, and Rutgers University–Newark. He completed his doctorate at New York University.

Adena's knowledge and experience identifying and addressing turnover issues while a consultant in the office of retention at Ernst & Young Australia added significantly to the depth and richness of our ideas. Adena's logical thinking and commitment to providing structure proved invaluable to the refinement and enhancement of our writing. Before joining DAI, Adena worked as a consultant with a number of multinational organizations in such areas as HR transformation and change management. Adena has an M.A. in Clinical Psychology from Yeshiva University and an M.A. in Organizational Psychology from Columbia University.

We wish to thank our colleagues at Downey Associates International, Inc. As with most DAI projects, this was truly a team initiative. The senior consultants contributed their client experiences and others assisted in researching and editing. We particularly want to thank Sheila Oh for helping to rewrite several chapters; Glen Alcantara for his creative contribution and critical thinking; Jenny Martel for her hours of research and tracking of obscure references; Navid Rahmanim for his computer expertise and development of our assimilation Web site, accessible at executiveassimilation.com or newleaderassimilation.com; and Mark Watson for his administrative support and dedication to the details.

We are particularly indebted to Joel Ospa, Managing Director at Goldman Sachs Investment Management Division, for his insights and ideas. We also thank the following colleagues who have offered their insight to us throughout the process of writing this book: Lourine Clark, Linda Crill, Jim Dickinson, Michele DiMartino, Paul Erickson, Inez Janger, Pat Lammers, Margaret Llamas, Les Martel, Rob Reid, David Rodriguez, Martha Sherman, Dennis Shiel, and Scott Stanley. Thank you to Adrienne Hickey, our editor, for her patience and guidance.

We are grateful to the many senior executives and HR professionals who shared their stories with us, and to our clients, from whom we continue to learn.

Some of this material first appeared in Executive Talent, a journal published by Kennedy Information, Fitzwilliam, N.H. The first article, "Comfortable Fit: Assimilating New Leaders" appeared in the Summer 2000 issue, pp. 68–76. The second, "Don't Let Changes in Leadership Derail Teams," appeared in the Fall 2000 issue, pp. 80–88. Both are by Diane Downey and Tom March.

INTRODUCTION

What Is "Successful Assimilation"?

May the road rise to meet you and the wind be always at your back.

—Traditional Irish blessing

Two wishes lie at the heart of this traditional blessing: one for future success and the other for fair traveling conditions to propel you forward. The road should lead you effortlessly toward your goal, with no potholes along the way into which you might stumble. It's a nice way to begin thinking about how we'd like new leaders to be able to enter organizations—the teams they lead, their peer groups, and the project teams that rely on their expertise.

We have observed that assimilation of new leaders occurs in roughly four stages over the course of two to three years. Assimilation begins at the point of hire and is complete when the individual becomes a full contributor and is no longer considered an outsider. A successful assimilation is one in which both the individual and the organization are transformed for the better and are able to leverage each other's strengths to achieve mutually beneficial goals. For this reason, the individual and the organization share responsibility for the success of this process—they travel down this road together.

> We go to great lengths to hire senior players. Only about a fifth of them stay two years.

In our experience, the process works best when the organization and the new leader shift the focus of their activities at each stage to incrementally expand the new leader's knowledge and influence. These activities build on each other across each stage of the process, focusing on relationships with individuals, team members, peers, and ultimately incorporating the organization as a whole. Moving too fast or neglecting an activity can compromise the strength of the foundation upon which successful assimilation depends. Small disconnects and misunderstandings become amplified over time. As Exhibit I-1 shows, the impact of neglected activities—or those that are attempted too soon or with little success—increases in severity over time. This makes subsequent stages of the assimilation process increasingly difficult.

Exhibit I-1. The impact of neglected assimilation actions over time.

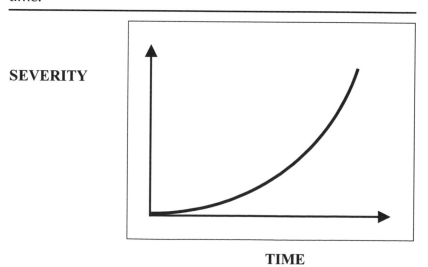

SEVERITY

TIME

For example, acting prior to fully understanding the new terrain and without building appropriate networks jeopardizes a new leader's likelihood of implementing an agenda in the future. Former President Clinton's health care initiative is a classic example. This large-scale intervention was attempted with neither appropriate stakeholder input nor strong support coalitions. Although the issue was well researched, the proponents of the plan failed to anticipate and plan for the strength of people's reactions to the proposed changes. The stigma attached to the key players reduced their credibility in such a way that they were not able to readdress that issue at a later time.

It would be nice if the entry process resembled the road of the Irish proverb cited above—with a clear goal, a well-defined path, and the support of the organization driving the new leader forward. The reality is that it is often a difficult road for everyone involved. For the new leader, the road is a series of intersections, each presenting choices that could lead away from desired goals. It's littered with potholes that can slow the process down—and the wind is almost always bearing down upon his face. On the organizational side, there is much more movement at the top than ever before. It is in the organization's best interest to support the assimilation process in order to get the best out of new placements as quickly as possible without destabilizing the rest of the organization.

> There is only a 50 percent chance that when someone takes a new job at a new company, he will remain with the company for more than two years.

A major factor contributing to assimilation difficulty is that it is a study in contrasts and apparent contradictions. The leader's task is to focus on both ends of the spectrum simultaneously and to obtain just the right balance for the situation. Exhibit I-2 identifies a few of the most common polarities that new leaders must engage in order to be successful.

Determining the right balance takes a great deal of careful thought, planning, and judgment. New leaders often feel like they're being asked to walk across a minefield. Even if the first several steps are safe, there is a risk of misstep around every corner. The assimilation journey is a continuous negotiation between various extremes. Deliberate decision making greatly increases the likelihood of success. The more

Exhibit I-2. Assimilation polarities: Achieving the right balance.

Assimilation Polarities		
	while...	
Being patient	←→	Becoming productive
Setting your own pace	←→	Following the organization's pace
Trusting your "intuition"	←→	Making deliberate criteria-based decisions
Pleasing your stakeholders	←→	Ensuring you can meet your own priorities
Implementing change	←→	Respecting the history and culture of the organization
Demonstrating competence	←→	Seeking advice and help when you need it
Building relationships based on trust	←→	Testing assumptions about others
Intervening appropriately	←→	Waiting until you have enough information
Drawing on past experience	←→	Not letting past experience blind you to new realities
Acting with authority	←→	Staying in learning mode
Not leading with your ego	←→	Displaying confidence
Making your position clear	←→	Seeking input and feedback
Affiliating with people	←→	Maintaining professional boundaries

awareness new leaders have about assimilation pitfalls prior to encountering them, the clearer their paths will be. By increasing this awareness and establishing a structured assimilation process, the organization—represented by the human resources department and hopefully the hiring manager—can have an enormous impact on the new leader's success.

New leaders need help determining which elements of their past experience will be most relevant and how to apply those elements within a new context. Researchers have discovered that learning is largely situational, that the rules and realities that one learns to rely on in one job may not apply to the next. Some researchers, most notably Abraham and Edith Luchins in their "water jar" experiment,[1] have used the term *negative transfer* to describe how relying on past learning and experience is never enough and often *hinders* assimilation into a new situation. The Luchins's water jar experiment tested the ways in which people developed solutions based on their methods for solving past problems that appeared to be similar. People were asked to obtain particular volumes of water using three different sized jars. The Luchins found that people being tested were constrained by the problem-solving methods they developed while solving the earlier problems. The superimposition of past rules and standards impedes adaptation and leads to errors in judgment. This difficult balance between drawing from experience and learning new paradigms is one with which all new leaders struggle.

THE AUDIENCE FOR THIS BOOK

Throughout this book, we speak directly to the person in the organization who has primary responsibility for hiring and shepherding a new leader through the assimilation process. Although we believe that it takes everyone's involvement and commitment to ensure that an individual is able to truly become a successful "insider," we have found that the responsibility for designing and implementing an assimilation strategy typically resides in the HR department. However, depending on the size and organization of the company, the assimilation process can also be led by the hiring manager, a mentor, or a member of senior management who is not part of HR.

We suggest the designation of an "HR Touchstone" to partner with the new leader through the process of assimilation. This HR professional may come from corporate HR or from the HR organization supporting the new leader's line of business. As a high-priority business need, the development of an assimilation process is an excellent opportunity for HR to impact the bottom line and to become a strategic partner with its businesses. As with most HR activities, the "touchstone" role requires that HR both act as advocate for the individual and ensure that the objectives of the organization are being met. Throughout the process, the HR Touchstone initiates a series of interventions to:

- Raise awareness as the new leader assesses himself and the organizational environment.
- Coach the new leader as well as his boss.

- Facilitate relationships between the new leader and his boss, peers, reports, and other stakeholders.
- Develop and implement an assimilation strategy.

We understand we have depicted an idealized version of what "could be." It is our intention to provide a vision of the future of HR as it becomes increasingly embedded in the business it supports, something to aspire toward. We acknowledge that given the many demands on an HR professional's time, there may not be ample opportunity to accomplish all that we are recommending. The tactics presented in this book are intended to provide a focus and make the reader better prepared and more effective in this role.

THE NEW LEADERS

New leaders, as we use the term in this book, include those who run a function or a business, and who operate as part of an organization's or division's senior leadership team. We refer to them using the terms *senior leaders* and *executives* interchangeably. Although the focus of this book is primarily on leaders from outside the organization, it is important to note that even those promoted or transferred from within an organization encounter many of the same difficulties, in spite of the organizational knowledge that they already possess.

We characterize our new leaders as "he" and "she" interchangeably. Our language is meant to represent people of all genders and ethnicities. However, it is important to note that women and minorities face unique problems and issues that compound the degree of difficulty they experience in the assimilation process. Those unique issues are evidence that the glass ceiling still exists, and they deserve greater attention than we can provide within the scope of this book.

WHY WE WROTE THIS BOOK

There is a great need for organizations to adopt a systematic approach to assimilating not just their CEOs, but *all* of their new leaders. CEO turnover has received a lot of attention lately—in a three-month period of 2000 alone, 350 chief executives in the United States left their jobs.[2] These are public figures with public names and faces, and their departures are almost always destabilizing. But what about the leaders who report to the CEO, or those who report to them? Most senior leaders do not have fame, nor are they the topic of discussion at cocktail parties. Nevertheless, they play an enormous role in determining an organization's fate, and the war for talent is really fought within their ranks.

So why do so many organizations leave them to fend for themselves, offering minimal assimilation assistance? We believe that having a structured assimilation process for senior-level leaders is a critical, and often overlooked, factor in executive retention. It is our hope that our readers will become assimilation-savvy, better able to navigate successfully through the churn and change of the assimilation period.

This book is intended to fill some gaps in the existing literature related to how new leaders experience and can proactively manage the assimilation process. Many have written about orientation and socialization for entry-level and midlevel employees. However, very few have addressed what senior leaders experience throughout an extended assimilation process. The difficulty of encountering a new environment is compounded by the fact that senior leaders must assimilate as they *enter into multiple teams* that immediately rely on their input and competence in order to succeed.

Research conducted over the past twenty years by Porter, Mowday, Jablin, and Hackman, among others, serves as a foundation upon which to consider the senior management entry process. The military, starting with Perry M. Smith's *Taking Charge: A Practical Guide for Leaders*,[3] has done a great deal of thinking about the issue of maximizing the effectiveness of leadership transitions. Similarly, in his 1987 book *The Dynamics of Taking Charge*,[4] John J. Gabarro compared the experiences of seventeen successful and unsuccessful senior managerial successions, and theorized about the kinds of change new managers can implement over time. Twelve years later, in *Right from the Start*,[5] Ciampa and Watkins expanded on Gabarro's research to focus on what new leaders can do during the *recruiting* phase, but they follow only the first six months of the new leader's progress.

The organizational landscape has changed dramatically and will continue to change. Senior executives now come and go with greater frequency and no longer have the strong affiliations with their organizations that used to be the norm when people "grew up" in an organization alongside a relatively stable group of peers. Many researchers and organizations overlook the link between assimilation and executive retention in spite of the overwhelming evidence we have observed.

While there is a large body of literature on leadership that we've drawn from, available resources offer little insight on the relative impact of primacy on the effect of new leaders' initial actions. The pressure of "firsts" weighs heavily on a new leader. First actions, first decisions, and first encounters significantly define how others in the organization will view the new leader for years to come. And the residue of first impressions becomes the filter through which others interpret all subsequent actions. This book focuses on these "firsts" and provides examples of things that can go wrong. However, it's also important to remember that these "firsts" represent *opportunities*—for redefining oneself, one's style, and one's status in a new situation. Entering a new organization or taking a new position allows new leaders to begin anew.

So how can a book prepare new leaders for something they can best learn by actually going through the assimilation process? People usually learn from experience or from observing others' experience. However, most people will not have had enough direct experience with entry into new organizations to discern patterns or to anticipate the predictable feelings or behaviors they will encounter. The stories and cases in this book, drawn from interviews and our experiences with assimilating leaders, provide you with an opportunity to learn by "observing" best practices as well as others' mistakes. The lessons you learn will help you to prepare your new leaders for the unavoidable challenges of assimilation, as well as provide them with the knowledge that will help prevent them from hitting "potholes" along the way. Our goal is to raise awareness about the choices available at each stage in the assimilation process, to present actions and methods that seem most likely to affect achieving results, to provide support in entry planning and management, and to lay out a facilitated process to introduce a new hire into management and professional teams.

Over the past fifteen years, consultants at Downey Associates International, Inc. have worked as assimilation strategists and coaches with numerous individuals and organizations to support them through their assimilation process. During that time we have been fortunate enough to work with a diverse range of organizations including Citigroup, MetLife, Ernst and Young Management Consulting Services, Marriott International, AT&T, Deutsche Bank, Fleet Bank, The Ford Foundation, Fidelity, Cadbury/Mott's, Bank of New Zealand, Société Générale, Shell Oil, TIAA-CREF, and many others. Although we use examples and case studies, in most cases we do not mention specific names, companies, or business problems, out of respect for our clients' confidentiality.

This book approaches new leader assimilation through the lens of our own experience with senior leaders as well as current research in social psychology, human behavior, socialization, influence, and other relevant fields. This integrative approach reflects our fundamental assumptions about organizational development—that addressing the complexities of organizational life requires a multidisciplinary approach that respects and accounts for the multitude of factors that influence human interaction.

For additional information, you can access our assimilation Web site at executiveassimilation.com, leaderassimilation.com, or newleader assimilation.com.

THE STRUCTURE OF THIS BOOK

This book is intended as a resource for those in the organization who support new leaders as well as for new leaders themselves, and it is divided in the following way:

- *Part One* explains the importance of leader assimilation and introduces the process. Chapter One examines the business case for focusing on the assimilation of senior leaders. Chapter Two introduces the "reciprocal impact" model of the assimilation process, including individual and organizational inputs, and the transformation process that *is* assimilation. Chapter Three, while not designed as a "how to" for the interview process, outlines the issues that both organizations and individuals should be aware of in order to set the stage for a successful assimilation. The data considered during the interview and assessment process have the greatest effect on a new leader's success or failure at assimilation.

- *Part Two* outlines each of the four stages of the assimilation transformation process in detail. In the beginning of the process, assimilation is a responsibility shared equally between the individual and the organization. Their roles and activities remain discrete. As time goes on, the organization's role decreases as the new leader masters the organizational challenges. This is happening as the actions of the organization and the individual converge. We reflect this shift visually in the beginning of each of the four chapters. In Chapters Four to Seven, the emphasis is on organizational assimilation actions that are divided into four categories: *raising awareness, facilitation, support/coaching,* and *intervention*. These categories reflect the different roles that the organization can play to assist in the assimilation process. Throughout these chapters, there are assimilation goals that build upon each other and have different relative emphasis from chapter to chapter.

- *Appendix A, The New Leader's Handbook,* is directed to the new leader himself. It focuses on actions that the individual can take in the initial stages of the assimilation process. Reading this material will give you greater insight into the thoughts and emotions of the new leader. You can also give the material to the new leader to help him deal with the issues he is likely to encounter during these phases of assimilation.

- *Appendix B* consists of organizational checklists that provide an opportunity to monitor each of the four stages of the assimilation process. This and all other activities and worksheets are designed to be used independently or in combination in the following ways:
  - Handouts to be given to all new leaders during an orientation forum
  - Discussion tools for use during coaching sessions
  - A way to inform the new leader's boss about what the new leader is experiencing
  - A way to help structure the support the hiring manager and the rest of the organization should provide

Our scope is broad in order to provide access to as many experiences and solutions as possible—solutions that have been proven in a variety of organizational settings. We realize that many of the challenges we identify and actions we recommend are situationally dependent. We trust that you as readers will choose those that are most relevant to your current situation. The most successful new leaders are those who recognize that, in spite of their experience and expertise, entering a new organization presents new challenges as well as new opportunities.

Notes

1. Abraham S. Luchins and Edith Hirsch Luchins. *Rigidity of Behavior: A Variational Approach to the Effect of Einstellung.* Eugene, Oreg.: University of Oregon Books, 1959.

2. According to a study by Challenger, Gray, and Christmas, cited in R. Abelson, "A Growing Corporate Challenge: The Empty Executive Suite." *New York Times,* 16 November 2000.

3. D. K. Smith. *Taking Charge of Change: Ten Principles for Managing People and Performance.* Reading, Mass.: Addison-Wesley, 1996.

4. J. J. Gabarro. *The Dynamics of Taking Charge.* Boston: Harvard Business School Press, 1987.

5. D. Ciampa and M. Watkins. *Right from the Start: Taking Charge in a New Leadership Role.* Boston: Harvard Business School Press, 1999.

Part One

SETTING THE STAGE
FOR SUCCESSFUL
ASSIMILATION

CHAPTER ONE

The Business Case for
Executive Assimilation

ACCELERATED EXECUTIVE TURNOVER

The "war for talent" has become part of today's business lexicon, describing organizations' obsession with the question: "How do we retain our top executives?" According to an article in the *Harvard Business Review*, 80 percent of a pool of 150 senior executives changed employers within two years.[1] Another study reports that 47 percent of executives appointed as presidents of public U.S. companies left their respective employers within four years.[2] In 1997, having surveyed twenty-five companies, the Corporate Leadership Council reported that an average of 50 percent of newly hired executives quit or were fired within their first three years.[3]

In addition to replacing the employees that have left, organizations are still adding new employees. On December 24, 2000, the *New York Times* reported that in its survey of middle managers and professionals, Management Recruiters International found a significant increase in projected hiring for the first half of 2001. Of the nearly 3,500 executives in the semiannual survey, 58.8 percent indicated plans to add to their middle management, upper management, and professional staffs, up 5.6 percentage points from the last half of 2000.[4]

Executive turnover is just the tip of the iceberg. In our experience working with Fortune 500 companies across a range of industries, we have seen increasing levels of turnover at all senior levels, not just among chief executive officers. One of our clients recently conducted a study of ninety resumes it received from applicants seeking leadership positions from 1999 to 2000. For each of the 359 positions listed on the applicants' resumes, the company tracked the length of time the applicant had remained in previous jobs. As Exhibit 1-1 shows, *68 percent of the time, people had been in their previous positions for twelve months or less!*

Drawing from our research and practical experience in developing strategies for retention and new leader assimilation, we have found that:

- *Any examination of organizational retention needs to transcend an examination of "why people leave."* Retention, like any other organizational change element, is fluid and dynamic and can be influenced by various factors at different stages of the organizational life cycle.

- *New leaders are most likely to leave when they lack the support they need to do their best work.* Within the current job market, senior executives are finding that they can pick and choose where they want to be. For senior hires, attrition is usually the result of the inability to make the contribution they were hired to make, and of difficulties negotiating cultural differences. For instance, Lubatkin, Schweiger, and Weber report that experiencing a loss of autonomy—in addition to percep-

Exhibit 1-1. Length of time in the job.

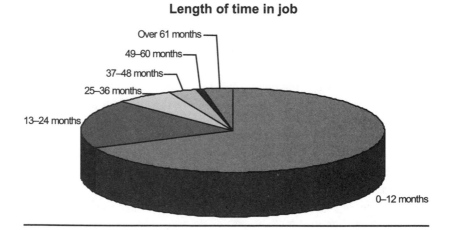

Length of time in job

Over 61 months
49–60 months
37–48 months
25–36 months
13–24 months
0–12 months

tions of cultural difference—accounts for 50 percent of variance in first-year turnover of executives in acquired companies.[5] The common occurrence of such negative experiences, particularly the perception of lessened self-efficacy, places greater pressure on organizations to provide a supportive environment.

- *Leaders are more likely to stay when they feel a deep commitment and affiliation with an organization.* This type of organizational commitment, one of the key elements of ensuring any type of employee retention, can't be built quickly using a snazzy, off-the-shelf orientation program. Adopting assimilation as a core competence helps organizations facilitate the development of this commitment by increasing new leaders' tenure in their jobs and decreasing the occurrence of unnecessary assimilation hardships.

THE DIRECT COSTS OF EXECUTIVE TURNOVER

The direct cost of replacing new leaders is well known. Bradford Smart suggests a breakdown of costs for those who make between $100,000 and $250,000 in salary per year. Smart estimates that "for average companies, the costs of mis-hires are perhaps . . . forty times base for those earning $100,000 to $250,000,"[6] when you consider the cost of recruiting, actual compensation expenditures, severence, and the additional cost of lost productivity, the time it takes for someone to become productive, business mistakes, and missed opportunities, among other factors.

Research conducted by Sibson & Company in four high-turnover industries found that employee turnover replacement costs have reduced earnings and stock prices by an average of 38 percent.[7] This estimated financial cost of replacing a new employee would have to be multiplied at least threefold to begin to understand the cost and impact of replacing a new leader who has failed or left an organization. The U.S. government estimates that between 1998 and 2008, the total number of positions for general managers and senior executives "due to growth and net replacements" is expected to increase by 16.4 percent.[8] The larger number of available leadership positions, coupled with an increase in positions available due to attrition, suggests that the costs of recruitment will rise dramatically over the next ten years. The bottom line is that, while the cost of leadership recruitment is likely to increase quite substantially over the next ten years, the bigger issue is that the cost to organizations exceeds the financial cost of replacement, assuming a replacement can be found.

THE INDIRECT COSTS OF EXECUTIVE TURNOVER

The effects of losing a leader ripple throughout an organization. The loss of an executive affects an organization's competitive position not only because it creates a leadership vacuum but also because it:

- Triggers turnover at other levels throughout the organization
- Creates a loss of intellectual and developmental resources
- Disrupts and weakens customer relationships

According to a principal of Sibson, "employee turnover has a significant effect on companies' bottom lines by inhibiting their ability to keep current customers, acquire new ones, increase productivity, and pursue growth opportunities."[9] Our experience with a wide range of clients supports the underlying assumptions of this statement. The uncertainty and struggles new leaders may experience in the entry process are felt across the organization—by the team; by peers; and ultimately, if not quickly corrected, by the customers. The implication is clear: How quickly and adeptly new leaders are able to adjust and reach their potential within an organization impacts the organization's competitive advantage, team output, and performance—and ultimately customer satisfaction and bottom-line profitability.

AN IMPACT ON TURNOVER AT EVERY OTHER LEVEL

"People don't quit companies, they quit bosses."[10]

Starting with the assumption that leaders—whether old or new—have a tremendous influence on the behaviors, attitudes, and performance of their teams, it is clear that one of the most destabilizing effects of leader turnover on an organization is increased turnover at all other levels of the organization.

Numerous studies have indicated a high correlation between employee job satisfaction and the relationship between the employee and direct supervisors and managers. According to the Corporate Executive Board, 41 percent of "high-value employees" who intend to leave their organization are dissatisfied with the quality of their managers.[11] Similarly, a Gallup study, based on recently conducted interviews with 2 million employees at 700 companies, found that there were strong links between employee tenure and the quality of employee-supervisor relationships.[12] The relationships new leaders develop with their teams become an important factor in whether their staff decide to stay with the organization or leave to seek opportunities elsewhere. Furthermore, if we start from the assumption that the cohesiveness and effectiveness of a team rests on the working alliances between supervisor and employee, loss of faith in the efficacy of leadership and the loss of a clear sense of continuity may reduce team members' job satisfaction and organizational commitment.

When teams experience a succession of leaders, they lose a sense of their organizational affiliation as the norms and expectations they have established for working together are placed in limbo. Disruption of norms and expectations have the potential to compromise a team's ability to be effective and achieve results. This is exacerbated when a leader's tenure is short-lived, as working alliances are often not in place long enough to support the attainment of change.

LOSS OF INTELLECTUAL AND DEVELOPMENTAL RESOURCES

A leader's involvement with peers and projects throughout the organization, beyond her own team, creates an intraorganizational dependence on her contributions. A recent article[13] in the *New York Times* examined how many companies are confronting leadership vacuums at the top of the house. The disrupting effects of leadership turnover outlined in this article are more than confirmed by our own experience with organizations that encounter assimilation difficulties—disrupted succession plans, lost institutional memory, lost connections to customers and others in the industry, and a shortage of mentors for the organization's potential future leaders. When new leaders enter a new organizational situation, they join multiple teams:

- The functional team they lead—their direct reports
- The executive team—the team of senior leaders who collaboratively have responsibility for enterprisewide direction
- The project-related cross-functional teams to which they contribute

A leader's success or failure has an impact on the productivity of each of these groups. Losing a leader decreases productivity because no one is quite sure whether or how to go forward. Without an executive in place to set priorities and strategically delegate responsibilities, resources are not coordinated. Furthermore, without a leader to set an agenda, teams become tentative, and informal leadership structures arise that can create barriers to the assimilation of the next new leader once he or she arrives. Such barriers set the stage for a prolonged, if not failed, assimilation of the new leader who does eventually join the team. *When leader turnover is high, working alliances across the organization are not in place long enough to embed any changes that are introduced.*

An organizational assimilation strategy can minimize the effects of the instability on the organization during a leadership transition, and therefore minimizes the potential destabilizing effects on the customer.

WEAKENED CUSTOMER RELATIONSHIPS

Drawing on the work of J. L. Heskett and others on the three-pronged relationship between service and profit—or the "service-profit chain"[14]— it is clear that there is a link between destabilization at the senior level and the loss of customer relationships, team effectiveness, and profitability. With disrupted leadership comes dissatisfaction from those employees left behind, whose feelings will inevitably become apparent to their (internal and external) customers. The lack of confidence in their organization's leadership may place the relationships between your remaining employees and your customers at risk. These relationships are another manifestation of the direct impact a leader's departure has on the bottom line.

The service disruptions caused by a leader's departure are potentially devastating. Customer relationships often take years to build and become profitable. Once disrupted, they are often difficult if not impossible to reestablish. Perceptions of discontinuity and inconsistency greatly influence customers' opinions of a company's reliability. In *The Loyalty Effect*, Frederick F. Reichheld cites a 1991 proprietary study of a property-casualty insurance company that was able to document a drop in customer satisfaction level from 75 percent to 55 percent when a service worker left. Similarly, Reichheld found that a 10-percentage-point improvement in broker retention would increase a broker's value by 155 percent.[15] These examples provide an important reminder that loyalty is easier to establish with an individual than with an inanimate entity like a corporation. Customers' relationships with their contacts at your organization form a large portion of their loyalty to the company itself.

ASSIMILATION IS NOT ANOTHER ORIENTATION PROGRAM

Many organizations mistakenly view "orientation" and "assimilation" as one and the same thing. Orientation programs usually focus on providing basic information to a new hire to introduce that person to the business, the organization's history, its structure, and who's who in the organization. These programs are often very time-bound—implemented over a few days to start new hires on the right track—rather than designed to help new hires succeed over time. In addition, these programs are usually geared toward *more midlevel and junior staff.* In fact, according to a search of the American Society for Training and Development's database, fewer than 5 percent of the orientation programs profiled are targeted at senior-level hires or the executive role in orientation and training. Organizations place a great deal of resources on recruiting senior leaders but spend very little time or money helping them once they arrive. Surprisingly, we've found that most people assume that senior leaders need *less* help assimilating than entry-level hires—even though this is the time when leaders need the most help, both in breaking out of their old paradigms and in resisting the urge to superimpose the lessons of their past experience onto situations in which they might not apply.

In contrast to orientation, assimilation is a *process* whose purpose is to ensure that leaders will adapt and become full contributors in the new organization faster, better, and with fewer destabilizing effects to the individual and the organization. An effective assimilation strategy acknowledges the difficulties of entry into a new organization, legitimizes an individual's adjustment period, and builds in multifaceted supporting mechanisms at an institutional level (e.g., peer supports, tips on bridging organizational knowledge, and learning gaps) to assist the new leader through the process. It begins with the assumption that organizational commitment, the degree to which an individual identifies with an organization, is developed as a sum total of experiences and interactions with the organization. An individual's relationship and identification with an organization—whether it is affiliation with the organization's mission and goals, social and affinity networks, organizational value and culture—begins to be shaped and formed the minute the individual interacts with the organization at any level. The initial job interview begins this process, and it is further shaped, tested, and developed upon entry into the organization by the interactions with one's supervisors, work group, and peers.

The process of assimilation takes a long time, longer than one might expect. Most of the executives we have worked with don't anticipate the void created by the absence of these supports. For the organization, this time period before the organizational bonds have actually solidified is both the window of vulnerability and the window of opportunity. This is the critical juncture in which an assimilation-savvy organization can step in, provide bridges that will facilitate the bonding process, and foster organizational commitment.

ASSIMILATION-SAVVY ORGANIZATIONS HAVE A COMPETITIVE ADVANTAGE

BUILDING ASSIMILATION AS A CORE COMPETENCE

Companies compete on the basis of core competencies—the combinations of skills and technologies that they can leverage across businesses, independent of the current product set and unique enough to provide a competitive advantage.[16] In order to maintain and continually reinvent competitive advantage, it is often necessary to "buy" leading-edge competencies—either technology or people—from the outside.

Given the "war for talent," we believe the most successful organizations in today's competitive market are those that use their assimilation strategies to build competitive advantage by increasing leadership retention. People will join a successful organization with a reputation as an industry leader, but they stay with an organization that they feel commitment to, *one that meets their emotional as well as intellectual needs.* If we assume, with John Gabarro, that it can take up to three years for new leaders to acquire and translate their in-depth understanding of the business and organizational environment into organizational impact, then retaining new executives at least this long is critical in order to get the maximum return on investment from these hires. Considering the projected increase in senior-level hires, this issue is going to become increasingly important. Assimilation-savvy organizations—those that support and embed a structured and formal assimilation process that enables senior leaders to navigate the cultural, intellectual, and emotional challenges of entering a new organization—*increase retention and help senior leaders become more productive in less time.* Having an organizationwide understanding of the process is the key driver for building individual commitment and a faster, smoother, and more effective transition for both the individual and the organization.

Assimilation-savvy organizations will gain competitive advantage by becoming leaders in hiring, acculturating, and utilizing talent from diverse sources. An organization that builds assimilation as a core competence ensures that the entire organization understands and works to support this process. This requires developing skills in selecting the best candidates, as well as defining and shaping formal and informal pathways that enable and accelerate this process. These organizations do not approach the entry of a new leader with a "sink or swim" mentality but with an understanding that champion swimmers need the support of champion coaches and champion teams. But remember that learning to swim in a pool doesn't prepare a swimmer for the rough seas. Informing a swimmer about the environment—the temperature, direction, speed, and flow of the water—helps him to adapt his technique and experience a new set of challenges, and to identify which skills will transfer and which will need to be developed or modified . . . and fast.

It will take time and money to develop assimilation as a core competence. More important, making your organization "assimilation-savvy" will require a mind-set change, whereby members of your organization don't view helping a new member succeed as a random act of kindness but rather begin to accept it as their responsibility. They must understand that they need to make themselves available and accessible to senior newcomers. In assimilation-savvy organizations people do not wait until they are approached by a new leader; they take the initiative themselves. In order to change the culture, it is critical that supporting the assimilation process be an important part of the values and norms reinforced throughout the organization.

Assimilation-savvy organizations provide multiple resources for support during an assimilation journey. One of the most important ones is the *HR Touchstone*. New leaders often need an external assimilation coach who can provide an outsider's view. The qualities to look for in hiring as assimilation coach are discussed in Chapter Four. On the other hand, the HR Touchstone can provide an "insider's" view of the organization. The HR Touchstone is a senior HR professional who is part of the business and can therefore provide the new leader with a unique perspective that combines intimate knowledge of the business with a view of the organization as a whole. The HR Touchstone should be available for coaching throughout the assimilation process, for the dual purpose of providing a comparatively objective assessment of team dynamics and interpersonal dynamics in general, and an organization-wide perspective on other issues.

Depending on a company's internal organization, the role of HR Touchstone may also be carried out by a member of senior management who is not a member of HR. But no matter who plays the role, the HR Touchstone is a key player in the assimilation process because there are many things that he, side by side with the hiring manager, can do at each stage to increase a new leader's likelihood of success. The reality is that the hiring manager may not have time to devote much attention to the details of the assimilation process. This leaves a perfect opportunity for the HR Touchstone to partner with the hiring manager to provide the new leader with the necessary support. Together, they can help new executives adopt a proactive approach to the assimilation process by making everyone involved consciously aware of the newness of the situation and of all the associated implications. The HR Touchstone can coach the new leaders and help them understand that past rules may not apply, thereby diminishing the effects of "negative transfer" and increasing the speed at which they achieve an appropriate depth of organizational understanding.

Assimilation-savvy organizations will be able to help new leaders become acclimated and productive more quickly as they adjust to their new roles. They will enjoy greater leadership stability, more cohesive teams, and greater alignment with strategic goals across the organization. Even if the patterns of senior executive turnover and short tenure cannot be stemmed, organizations that know how to assimilate their new leaders will be able to get more out of their senior-level hires during the time they are there.

Notes

1. Cited in P. Cappelli, "A Market-Driven Approach to Retaining Talent." *Harvard Business Review*, 78 (2000): 104.

2. Of these senior executives, 38 percent had been promoted internally, while 64 percent were external hires. D. Ciampa and M. Watkins. *Right from the Start*. Boston: Harvard Business School Press, 1999, p. 3.

3. P. Sweeney. "Teaching New Hires to Feel at Home." *New York Times*. 14 February 1999.

4. Associated Press. "For Many Workers, A Season of Worry." *New York Times*, 24 December 2000, B8.

5. M. Lubatkin, D. Schweiger, and Y. Weber. "Top Management Turnover in Related M&A's: An Additional Test of the Theory of Relative Standing." *Journal of Management* 25 (1999): 55–73.

6. Ibid., p. 51.

7. Nextera Enterprises, Inc. "Employee Turnover Depresses Earnings, Stock Price by 38%, Nextera Research Study Shows." Press release at www.sibson.com.

8. D. Braddock and N. H. Gibbs. "Occupational Employment Projections to 2008." *Monthly Labor Review*, Bureau of Labor Statistics, November 1999.

9. Nextera. "Employee Turnover."

10. S. Jordan-Evans. *Love 'Em or Lose 'Em: Getting Good People to Stay*. San Francisco: Berrett-Koehler, 1999.

11. Corporate Executive Board. *Employee Retention: New Tools for Managing Workforce Stability and Engagement*. Washington, D.C.: Corporate Leadership Council, 1998.

12. Kevin Dobbs. "Train Your Managers." *Training*, August 2000, pp. 62–66.

13. Claudia H. Deutsch. "Management: Companies Scramble to Fill the Shoes at the Top." *New York Times on the Web*, 1 November 2000, www.nytimes.com.

14. J. L. Heskett et al. "Putting the Service-Profit Chain to Work." *Harvard Business Review*, March/April 1994. The three-pronged relationship between service and profit is profit and growth, customer loyalty with customer satisfaction, and the value of goods and services delivered to customers and employee capability, satisfaction, loyalty, and productivity.

15. F. F. Reichheld. *The Loyalty Effect: The Hidden Force Behind Growth, Profits, and Lasting Value.* Boston: Harvard Business School Press, 1996, p. 96.
16. G. Hamel and C. K. Prahalad. *Competing for the Future.* Boston: Harvard Business School Press, 1994.

CHAPTER TWO

Reciprocal Impact: A New Assimilation Model

The purpose of this chapter is to provide you with a preview of the assimilation journey that every new leader takes and to familiarize you with the factors that influence the success of this journey. Regardless of how much experience and technical knowledge a new executive has, the discomfort associated with assimilation is rarely avoided. In fact, the more senior a new leader is, the higher the stakes and the more visible the failures. It is our hope that if you can anticipate the emotional and intellectual challenges new leaders are going to encounter, you can proactively prepare them and others in the organization.

As we have stated, the assimilation journey begins at the initial contact between a prospective new leader and an organization. Assimilation is a process of moving from being an organizational outsider to being an organizational insider. It is a process of moving from a state of expectation and potential to one of contribution and value-added input. If an organization's needs seem to align with what an individual has to offer, assimilation should be easy, right? Unfortunately, the reality is often just the reverse—assimilation, even for a seasoned executive, is a long and often uncomfortable road.

The model that follows reflects the experiences of the many executives and organizations we have worked with and observed.

THE RECIPROCAL IMPACT MODEL
OF ASSIMILATION

INPUT AND OUTPUT

The process of assimilation is similar to an input/output model. The new leader is an experienced player, with a history, skills, personal characteristics, and experience encountering unfamiliar situations. The organization has its own processes, procedures, history, and culture, which are fairly stabilized. This is the individual's and organization's fixed input, the "DNA" or raw material that both bring to the process.

When the organization provides a structured, supportive approach to assimilation, the *output* of the assimilation process is a fully contributing leader who is an influential presence in this new environment. This should result in the following output for the organization: leader retention, organizational commitment, productivity, and long-term value.

The chart shown in Exhibit 2-1 illustrates how an understanding of the assimilation process begins with an identification of the characteristics and experiences that the organization and individual bring to the table. It is only by understanding these "inputs" that the events of the transformation process of assimilation itself can be anticipated and dealt with proactively. Each key aspect of this model is presented in detail in the exhibit.

THE TRANSFORMATION PROCESS

Once the hiring decision is made, the organization and the individual bring their "raw material" or input into a transformation process, similar to a manufacturing process. In *Social Learning Theory*, Albert Bandura describes what goes on during this process in the following way: "Personal and environmental factors do not function as independent determinants, rather they determine each other."[1] The ease of a new leader's transition from outsider to fully assimilated insider depends on the combination of raw materials involved. This concept of each entity having an impact on the shape and attitude of the other is one of the key themes of assimilation. We refer to this as the *reciprocal impact* of assimilation. Both the individual and the organization are transformed by this process.

Exhibit 2-1. The assimilation process: Making an impact and becoming an insider.

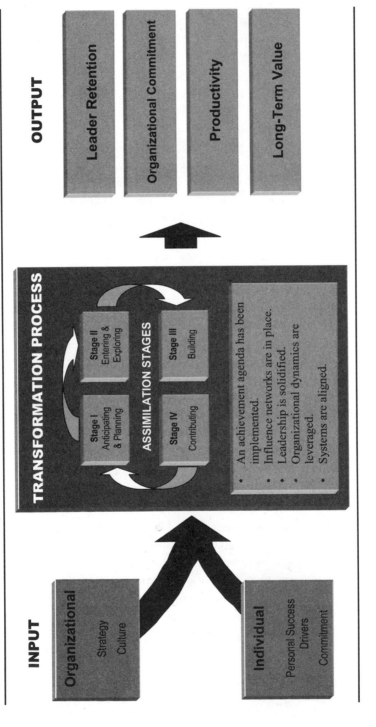

Specifically, the transformation process of assimilation moves the new leader toward the achievement of the following five assimilation goals:

Create an Achievement Legacy: The achievement legacy is the new leader's business agenda— the plan for how the new leader will create sustainable change within the new organization. Prior to the first day of work, this plan is in its preliminary form and is called an entry strategy. Once the new leader arrives on the job, the business plan is developed. Later, the plan is executed, and over time, feedback on the reactions to the plan is collected, modifications are made, and the changes are implemented.

Understand Organizational Dynamics: Understanding organizational dynamics and how to best work within these dynamics to accomplish the achievement legacy is a critical and often unstated goal of assimilation. This process begins with gathering information about the culture. Initial assessments are modified as the new leader becomes able to attribute meaning based on a clearer understanding of the organization. It is within this context that change must be made and, if possible, a new culture shaped.

Build Influence: Success within an organization often hinges on forming relationships with *key influencers* within the organization. These relationships provide the foundation upon which influence is built throughout the organization. This process begins with identifying the key people that surround the position. Once the new leader arrives on the job, relationships based on competence, commitment, and communication can be formed with the key influencers. Later, networks are built from these relationships and, over time, coalitions are developed that span the broader organization.

Assume Leadership: Successful assimilation depends on the new leader's ability to take command over a new team in a new environment. This presents an opportunity for the new leader to further develop an effective leadership style and to improve the overall functioning of the organization through improvements to the team. Once on the job the process of assuming leadership begins with assessing the team's skills and competencies while at the same time setting expectations and establishing norms. Later, once changes are made to the team, a self-empowered team is developed, leadership is solidified, and the new leader becomes an organizational player.

Align Systems: The systems that together make up an organization—the strategy, structure, people, processes, and metrics—must
be aligned with the achievement legacy. Prior to the first day of work,
the new leader can develop hypotheses about the current state of
these systems. Once on the job, the new leader tests these hypotheses. With further refinement of the business plan, the desired future state of these systems, along with the potential derailers and
dependencies, become apparent. These drive changes to the systems specific to the functional team as well as those that affect the
entire organization. Over time, organizationwide changes are made
to support and maintain the success of the achievement legacy.

This transformation process occurs in four distinct stages. Definitions of each of the four stages are discussed below and also shown in
Exhibit 2-2.

Exhibit 2-2. The four stages of the assimilation process.

The Four Stages of Assimilation's Transformation Process	
I. Anticipating and Planning (Chapter 4)	*The Anticipating and Planning Stage* begins on the date of hire and continues until the first day on the job. During this stage, new leaders plan an entry strategy and think about how they'll address the challenges of their new jobs. Obviously, the length of this stage varies greatly and depends upon the amount of time between acceptance of the job offer and the first day on the job.
II. Entering and Exploring (Chapter 5)	*The Entering and Exploring Stage* begins upon entering the organization. Here, new leaders inevitably find that things are different than they expected. They have to learn a new language, new ways of operating, and test all of their assumptions against new circumstances. They have to decide which relationships are the most important to build first and embark on a period of intensive information gathering. This stage can take up to nine months.
III. Building (Chapter 6)	In the *Building Stage*, new leaders begin building on the foundation of relationships and knowledge gained in the previous two stages. They build networks in order to take progressively more far-reaching and strategic actions. This stage can also take up to nine months, extending as far as the eighteenth month on the job.
IV. Contributing (Chapter 7)	By the *Contributing Stage*, new leaders are more comfortable in their roles, and they begin to build coalitions and amplify their influence across the organization. They become organizationwide resources and contributors. It can take up to three years from the first day on the job before the Contributing Stage is complete.

We have estimated time frames for each stage based on the timing of assimilation processes we have observed; however, they should be simply used as guidelines. The timing of how and when a leader moves from one stage to the next depends on his success in achieving the assimilation goals within each stage. The focus should be on building a platform that allows movement to the next step, not on the months or days since arrival.

Exhibit 2-3 lists the five overall goals of the assimilation process. Assimilation is considered successful when these goals have all been met by the end of Stage Four, the Contributing stage. At each stage of the process, the organization and individual work together to support the achievement of some or all of these goals. *Not all goals are addressed at each stage of the process.*

The themes listed under each goal shown in Exhibit 2-3 are designed to show how the individual builds toward the overarching goal from stage to stage. These activities *build on each other,* and as these goals are achieved, the strength of the individual–organizational bond increases. It is also important to note that as individuals progress, both the *depth* and *breadth* of their organizational understanding and involvement increase.

There are, however, certain external factors that either act as a catalyst or as a barrier to the process of building toward these goals. They will either shorten or lengthen the time spent within each stage. They are:

- *Size of the organization.* All other factors being equal, small organizations tend to embrace new leaders faster than larger organizations. In a small organization, each individual has a larger relative impact on the whole organization than in a large organization, thus heightening the effect of the reciprocal impact.

- *Average tenure in the organization.* Organizations whose employees have long tenures tend to take longer to recognize a new leader as truly part of the organization. This is especially true in organizations that grow their own leaders from within the organization.

- *Number of changes the new leader is making.* For first-time leaders, as well as those moving to a new country or new industry, assimilation will most likely take longer because they have

Exhibit 2-3. The challenges at each stage of the process.

Fully Performing Assimilated Leader

Achievements

Timing	Stage	Create Achievement Legacy	Understand Organizational Dynamics	Build Influence	Assume Leadership	Align Systems
Months 18	New Leader: Contributing	Modify strategy based on feedback	Shape the culture	Build coalitions	Utilize your resources effectively	Influence others to make changes that will support strategy
	Organization: Create Opportunities	Follow up on feedback	Formally integrate cultural changes	Create opportunities for organizationwide interaction	Provide developmental opportunities	Formally integrate changes to the system
Months 9–18	New Leader: Building	Execute business strategy	Attribute meaning within the context	Build networks	Make team changes	Identify potential dependencies and derailers to executing your strategy
	Organization: Support/Coach	Provide feedback mechanisms	Provide coaching	Create opportunities to build networks	Support personnel transitions	Establish parameters for change
Months 0–6	New Leader: Entering & Exploring	Develop a business strategy	Assess the culture	Build relationships	Set expectations; establish norms	Test hypothesis; learn about the organization as it will impact your achievement legacy
	Organization: Facilitate	Help get industry expertise	Facilitate cultural audit	Facilitate key relationships (act as a translator)	Facilitate assessment of team's skills and competencies	Act as a sounding board
Day One / Pre-hire	New Leader: Anticipating & Planning	Develop an entry strategy plan	Gather info about the culture	Determine with whom to build relationships	Self-assess leadership style	Develop hypothesis
	Organization: Preparing	Prepare a developmental plan	Advise new leader, provide information about culture	Prepare key stakeholders for new leader's arrival	Prepare team for the new leader's arrival	Provide access to systems information

more challenges to address than someone who is making an intraorganization move.

■ *Nature of the business problem you're asking the new leader to solve.* In turnaround situations, such as military or crisis intervention operations, assimilation is swift. Spending time to build relationships is generally unnecessary, as leaders are empowered by hierarchy and a universally accepted mandate.

WHY IS ASSIMILATION SO DIFFICULT?

The process of moving from being a new hire to becoming a successful, effective, and comfortable employee is a "journey" with two separate paths: emotional and intellectual. At any point in time, intellectual experience and emotional state can vary greatly. The emotional journey is often unpredictable, while the intellectual journey continues in a steady upward trajectory with little variation over time. It takes a long time for emotional comfort to catch up with intellectual achievements—more time than you might think. That is why assimilation is difficult, even for the most experienced executives. It's critical to remember that at each stage in the transformation process, new leaders experience both emotional and intellectual challenges. As depicted in Exhibit 2-4, these emotional and intellectual experiences differ greatly from each other at key points during the assimilation process.

Intellectually, new leaders experience continued and growing success as they learn more about how the organization operates. Most people understand the process of conquering the intellectual challenge or "learning curve" that comes with each new situation. At first everything is new and different, but most people accept the fact that they're going to have a lot to learn about the new organization and how it functions. This is the case regardless of how much subject matter expertise they possess. People accept that this process will take some time.

Inevitably, new leaders fall into "cultural potholes"—unexpected resistance and barriers that are a result of historical events and values. Cultural potholes are often emotionally charged disproportionate to the logic of the situation. These contribute to the emotional difficulty of the assimilation process. The best way to help the new leader navigate through these potholes is to recognize them and address them directly to support the new leader as he is managing the aftermath.

New leaders are typically unprepared for the wide range of emo-

Exhibit 2-4. The emotional and intellectual journey.

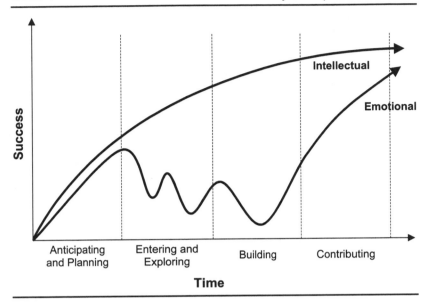

tional experiences that accompany this process. They experience highs and lows—multiple "dips" that actually follow a fairly predictable pattern—the first one typically occurs after about four weeks, followed by another after six months on the job. Almost without exception, new leaders experience another "big dip" shortly after they enter the Building stage (at roughly nine months). The dips are typically caused by people realizing that there's a huge gap between what they expected and what the reality is, leading them to question their suitability for the job. Many begin to question their effectiveness, and their feelings of being outsiders are reinforced. The organization can help the situation by raising awareness of the difficulties that most new leaders face during the assimilation process, allowing you and the others supporting the new leader to be more alert and tolerant, to provide support, and to avoid interpreting normal assimilation barriers as evidence of incompetence.

Senior executives, who have been successful in their careers and have strong professional identities, may have a difficult time acknowledging their feelings of disappointment and disorientation. They are used to being in control and having their competence recognized. The lack of "mooring" that emerges upon entry is unexpected and unsettling and is often compounded by a combination of several factors:

- They have less authority and discretion than expected.
- The scope and expectations of their role do not match what they were promised.
- Their team's capabilities are different than expected.
- Operating practices and procedures are counterintuitive.
- The loss of their own network is destabilizing.
- They are unsure of whom to trust.
- There is little or no reinforcement.
- They cannot begin to act as quickly as they had hoped.
- Their sense of self-efficacy is undermined because they have yet to establish a history of acting and achieving results in the new organization.

When faced with these emotions, new senior leaders tend to ignore or deny them. The stakes are high, and the fear of visible failure makes it very difficult to spend time reflecting on the other emotional reactions that are occurring. They might turn to former colleagues for advice, which delays acceptance of the new organization's norms. Many cope with this by burying themselves in work that may not be especially important—in other words, they work *harder*, but not necessarily *smarter*. To work smarter when this happens—to be able to prioritize work in the context of their learning process—new leaders must be allowed to acknowledge their emotional reactions for what they are. There's no way to *stop* the feelings, but awareness allows them to utilize their cognitive abilities and maintain focus and perspective.

AWARENESS AND DELIBERATENESS OF BEHAVIOR

A good way to think about the process of assimilation is to think of it according to a learning cycle, as depicted in Exhibit 2-5.

People typically begin by being unconscious of the fact that they are doing something incorrectly or that they need to behave differently. Upon entering a new organization, they quickly become conscious of the things they aren't doing well, or the behaviors they need to adopt in order to acculturate. The entry period is thus one of "conscious incompetence" followed, over time, by "conscious competence," in which people are able to perform as expected, but must constantly remind themselves

Exhibit 2-5. The learning cycle.

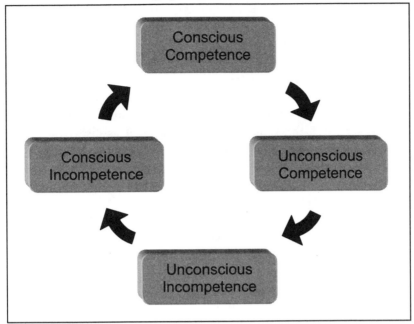

of what they need to do. This period of "hyperconsciousness" is particularly irritating for seasoned professionals, who are used to acting decisively. But the irritation doesn't last forever, and the payoff is enormous. After many months, the associated thoughts and behaviors become habitual, and the new leader becomes "unconsciously *competent*." But since people are always moving on to learn new things and are constantly expanding their knowledge, they are soon back in a position of unconscious incompetence. It is an ongoing cycle.

People only become conscious of the need to change when they make a mistake. Living systems try to reestablish balance, or stasis, at all costs: A new leader's entry creates a disruption that the system will seek to correct by constantly reminding her of the ways in which she doesn't fit in. When this happens, new leaders begin to feel frustrated—what they're being asked to do in place of their old behavior feels antiinstinctual to them. These behaviors may cause them to "GAG," or go against the grain. At the same time, they feel inclined to demonstrate their knowledge and have an early impact. A common mistake new executives make, during emotional "dips" or at any other time during the assimilation process, is to let their emotions—especially their frustration—rule their decision making. It is important to acknowledge and anticipate these feelings, in order to avoid their becoming a basis for action.

The new environment may require behaviors or modes of operating that exist in opposition to a new leader's preferred style. For example, an introverted executive who takes over a team that requires high involvement in decision making won't succeed if he keeps his thoughts and ideas to himself until they are thoroughly "hatched." People may find his silence disconcerting and may misread it as disregard for the feelings and ideas of others. In order to avoid this situation, the leader should make a conscious effort to share his thoughts and involve people in the process. Often this requires putting the team's needs and preferences ahead of his own. Until these kinds of behaviors become second nature, new leaders will constantly have to remind themselves to step outside of their preferred style when necessary.

When new leaders are called upon to take actions that are anti-instinctual to them, they must remember that the *right* decisions will *often* be anti-instinctual. At times, their decisions may not meet their personal needs or what they're most comfortable with, but *should* reflect what their team or the organization needs of them. These kinds of anti-instinctual decisions

- Necessitate the questioning of first impulses
- Require thinking and planning
- Can only be made if a new leader exerts self-control

In their prior jobs, new leaders encountered familiar prompts that allowed them to respond without much thinking. They're used to being able to put the more mundane day-to-day actions on automatic pilot—in other words, to act instinctually to meet their needs. There is often an impetus to force-fit new information, garnered from a new situation, into existing frames of reference. The result is that inappropriate inferences and conclusions may be drawn that, in turn, can lead to unanticipated consequences. This creates a cycle that is particularly unsettling for new leaders, because their sense of control is already somewhat minimized.

Furthermore, the impulse to act can be overwhelming—and sometimes completely wrong. During times of doubt or crisis, people have a strong impulse to take action for action's sake, just to feel comfort in the

POTHOLE: OLD MENTAL MODELS CAN BE AN INHIBITOR TO NEW LEARNING

The lessons of "negative transfer" defined in reference to Luchins's water jar experiment, are counterintuitive and go against the traditional definition of learning agility, the ability to apply past models and learning to new circumstances or challenges. Negative transfer, on the other hand, asserts that when people try to transfer learning and models from one situation to another, it can often inhibit learning because they apply past learning models to a new and nontransferable situation. This may explain why assimilation is easier for younger, more inexperienced leaders than it is for seasoned pros. The seasoned pros have a longer history of experience and success using certain models, which enhances their confidence that their way is the right way. The younger leaders may transfer fewer models and therefore be more open to learning new things in a new context.

fact that they are doing *something*, regardless of whether it's the right thing. Giving in to this impulse can have far-reaching implications—affecting a new executive's reputation, her team's reputation, and her ability to have impact in the organization.

Some people require more conscious effort to address and control their emotional reactions, but the reactions themselves are inevitable. People at different points in their career will experience changes differently. Junior people are less experienced and so bring fewer prejudices and formed opinions; as a result, they may experience fewer dramatic disappointments and frustrations than senior leaders. Senior executives come to a new organization as accomplished leaders in their field, bringing other frameworks that have worked for them, and worked well. New leaders usually have a strong sense of worth and are looking for challenge, impact, and a sense of purpose. Because their expectations about how things should be tend to be firmly ingrained, they encounter more pronounced frustration and find it more difficult to modify their outlook and behaviors when faced with situations that exist outside the frameworks with which they're already comfortable.

IS THERE A "RIGHT WAY" TO MANAGE THE ASSIMILATION PROCESS?

There are enabling traits that help new leaders enter new relationships and other unfamiliar situations more easily. Those who are better at managing the assimilation process are the ones who have been through other organizational changes and are more adaptable, more tuned into the cultural and emotional aspects of organizations. Successful new leaders have "ways of seeing" and "ways of doing" constantly at the ready. In our experience, those who assimilate most successfully demonstrate the following characteristics, which can be enhanced by awareness of their importance and by conscious application:

- *Honest self-assessment:* assessing how one's skills and experience are sufficient to meet the challenge and identifying skill gaps.

- *Utilizing their intuition:* understanding not to blindly act on intuition but knowing that there's something behind the "gut feel" one gets about unfamiliar circumstances. It's not that one has suddenly developed extrasensory perception, but that the current situation resembles something seen or felt in the past, which is triggering this response.

- *Systemic/holistic thinking:* determining how one's role fits into the structure of the overall organization and understanding the relationship between this role and the people or groups with which one will need to interact and work closely.

- *Learning adaptability:* drawing meaning from one's past experiences and utilizing these lessons creatively—and only as they apply—to master new challenges.

- *Interpersonal aptitude:* assessing the interpersonal dynamics and styles of both the team and one's superiors and leveraging how they impact each other and others throughout the organization.

- *Political savvy:* being sensitive to political realities and relationships.

- *Openness to feedback:* actively seeking feedback to determine whether one's performance meets expectations.

- *Emotional intelligence:* Emotional intelligence is defined by Daniel Goleman as potential for learning the practical skills in any profession based upon five elements: self-awareness, motivation, self-regulation, empathy, and adeptness in relationships.[2] Emotional intelligence has a high correlation with successful assimilation in that it allows one to accept and engage a wide range of emotions in oneself and others and use these emotions as clues to the dynamics within the organization and the various teams one is entering.

We are aware that not all people have all of these traits at their disposal at all times. Some new leaders may have had more opportunities to develop and apply them than others. But to be forewarned is to be forearmed. Therefore, we have laid out the assimilation process by highlighting some of the emotional and intellectual difficulties new leaders may encounter, along with specific, concrete tactics and approaches you can use to help them compensate for the skills they do not have and to enhance the ones they do.

As you read the rest of the book, it may occur to you that we are recommending tactics and techniques that any good executive or HR professional should know. The difference is that here we are dealing with *firsts.* As with any other firsts in life, these leave a long-lasting impression on everyone involved and therefore must be entered into with more attention and deliberate intent. Because a new leader has no history and no context with the new organization, every action carries a disproportionate weight. On the other hand, a new leader has an exciting opportunity to create the impression he believes will be the most effective. He has the opportunity to paint his image on a new canvas. It's your job to help him create the best image possible and build on and expand his past learning and experience.

Notes

1. Albert Bandura. *Social Learning Theory.* Upper Saddle River, N.J.: Prentice Hall, 1977, p. 9.
2. D. Goleman. *Emotional Intelligence.* New York: Bantam Books, 1997, pp. 43–44.

CHAPTER   THREE

Determining
Assimilation Potential

---

*I was in the process of interviewing for a job as the chief infor-
mation officer of a well-funded Internet supplier of discount
services. I liked the way the CEO and COO seemed to concep-
tualize the position. They saw me as doing more than running
the internal computing systems. I'd be a real strategic partner,
helping to build an infrastructure that supported the business
strategy, something I wasn't able to do in my current job. Before proceeding further I thought it would be a good idea to
explore how others saw this position and how they would describe the challenges. It would also be a good way to begin to
meet some of my peers and to learn a bit about the company's
culture. Several of the people I spoke with talked at length
about the possibilities. They shared their views of the current
systems—what was working and what needed to be revamped.
But two of the key players talked about how the CEO had
scaled back the system design work previously and mentioned
that it was difficult to focus on "managing the extrastructure,"
when the infrastructure was not functioning appropriately.
They said that the CEO didn't really believe that there was
anything terribly wrong with the infrastructure, in spite of
what they'd been reporting for the last year. They said the
changes the CEO approved weren't enough and that I should
assume that the bulk of my energy would be focused on fixing*

*basic internal systems because the CEO wouldn't make build-
ing more systemic long-term solutions a priority right now.
For example, it was difficult to get something as simple as HR
updates or salary adjustments done in a timely fashion.*

—Chris

What should Chris have done? Here are three options.

a. Request a follow-up meeting with the CEO to clarify his view
of current challenges and the timeline required to address both
short-term problems, and longer-term strategic priorities.

b. Assess his own strengths in this context, and decide whether
this was something he could handle.

c. Realize that people have their own perspectives, and that each
person was using this as an opportunity to set the agenda more
to their liking.

During the interview process, new leaders have a hard time evaluating all of the information they're receiving. Without having been ex-
posed to the organization for a significant period of time, they're not
sure whom they can trust, or how to ask the kinds of questions that will
elicit the most thorough responses. Each of the three options, exercised
by itself, would have been insufficient. To fully address the issues raised
by the situation, Chris should have exercised all three. He should have
spoken with the CEO, assessed his strengths, and tried to be aware of
each individuals' biases. Faced with contradictory information, it's always a good idea for prospective new leaders to ask follow-up questions
of their potential boss or others interviewing them. For instance, Chris's
colleagues who said there was no problem with the intranet may have
understood Chris's question to have been about the intranet's infrastructure, not user experiences. On the other hand, it's also quite possible that
they were each trying to influence Chris's perspective on things, according to their own hidden agendas. In any case, this scenario should provide Chris with an opportunity to reflect on the skills necessary not only
to manage the technical aspects of the job, but to deal with the kind of
conflicting philosophies that are apparently part of this culture.

THE ORGANIZATION'S PRE-HIRE GOALS

More than any other, the actions the organization takes, or fails to take,
during the interview and assessment period can make or break a new

leader's future assimilation. No hiring decisions have been made at this point, and the organization and the potential new hire are still separate entities. Yet keep in mind that at the moment you interface with them, potential senior hires develop plans and impressions about their ability to successfully assimilate into the organization. The probability of successful assimilation *can* be determined prior to hire.

This is the period of time in which you and the new leader are assessing and evaluating the "DNA" or "input" that each of you would bring to the transformation process and determine whether you're a suitable match. Remember that the input is fixed. The things that you and he discover about each other at this point aren't likely to change. If you each don't conduct your mutual due diligence in a patient and thorough manner to paint realistic pictures, even the most structured, effective assimilation efforts will be fundamentally flawed and extremely difficult to build upon. It would be like marrying somebody after the first date, just because you both liked the same movie.

The organization should provide all potential candidates with as much accurate information about the position and the organization so that they can make the best decisions possible for themselves, and for the organization. Your responsibility is to facilitate the new leader's decision making as well as make an informed decision about whether she will be *able* to join the organization. Thus, you have two primary goals at this point:

- Describe the position to include challenges and possible derailers.
- Assess the individual.

The specific actions required to meet these goals are illustrated in Exhibit 3-1.

PRE-HIRE GOAL: DESCRIBE THE POSITION TO INCLUDE CHALLENGES AND POSSIBLE DERAILERS

ACTION: WORK COLLABORATIVELY TO DESIGN THE JOB SPECIFICATION

Your decision to extend a job offer should be approached the same way that you would approach any other important business decision. All fac-

Exhibit 3-1. Organizational pre-hire goals and actions.

Organizational Pre-Hire Goals
Describe the Position
Work collaboratively to design the job specification.
Present a clear and balanced view of the position.
Assess the Individual
Assess for commitment predisposition.
Assess for reinforcing and extending fit.
Assess for actual achievements, not potential.
Identify the candidate's "career anchors."
Avoid hiring "best available."
Intervention: Use common criteria to obtain input from all stakeholders.
New Leader's Pre-Hire Goals and Actions
Assess Yourself
Determine multiple criteria.
Assess the Organization
Make "demands" for access to information as needed.
Determine the strategic position of the organization.
Determine where the organization is in its life cycle.
Determine whether the structure supports the strategy.
Assess the Position
Strive for clarity about the job description.
Assess the Culture
Observe how you are treated during the recruiting process.
Develop a comprehensive view of the culture.
Make an Educated Decision
Manage your cognitive dissonance.
Weigh the challenges the job presents.

tors should be considered, all options weighed, and all risks assessed. While most job descriptions are comprised of a set of tasks, activities, and key competencies, they rarely specify the real work to be done. One of our clients explained the result of not having a clear job specification this way:

> *There's still a disagreement to this day about what the job is about. My peer group is not clear about it as well. We spent the last year both with my superiors and my peer group to get clarity on what the position is. In one case this job is seen as a*

*line position but others see it as a coordinating position that I
never would have taken.*

You can reduce subsequent confusion by developing clear job specifications from the start. Job specifications, if they are written properly,
should:

- Provide a clear picture of the value of the position.
- Facilitate communication about performance expectations.
- Make selection decisions more realistic.
- Focus and facilitate communication among members of the in-
  terview team.

Executive jobs are dynamic and should change according to
changes in the business environment. We recommend that positions be
conceptualized in terms of the problems to be solved. For example, at
one point in time, the chief auditor's key task might be to merge the
regional audit functions into one coherent unit. This requires that the
person hired have experience in organizational restructuring, determining standards, as well as the ability to assess talent. Several years later
the problem to be solved might be ensuring that the line managers view
control as one of their responsibilities. The next auditor would need
experience in such areas as the creation of user-friendly systems and
managing organizational change. Position descriptions reflect points in
time, and the job will be different in eighteen months, with different
problems to be solved and different obstacles to be overcome.

Once the problems to be solved are identified, the competence of
the existing team should be assessed and its skill gaps identified. This
will provide input into the expected contributions of the role. These
should be framed in terms of results and focused on those contributions
that will distinguish this position from others. It is important for HR to
take the lead in ensuring that job specifications are rewritten to reflect
current needs. Meeting with the hiring manager and facilitating them
through this process guarantees a win for the organization and for the
new hire. The hiring manager is often too busy to give this the focused
attention it deserves. This is when expectations will be set.

ACTION: PRESENT A CLEAR AND BALANCED VIEW OF THE POSITION

Forewarn people about anticipated problems. Disclose all information
relevant to the job—highlight strengths and opportunities as well as

potential challenges inherent in the position. The interviewer should frame the anticipated problems and obstacles that need to be solved in a proactive way. That way, the candidate can pinpoint her questions and get more specific, detailed information that will allow for more informed decisions. Honesty during the interviewing process will minimize the "reality shock" that people experience when they assume new roles and find that the reality differs from their expectations.

A senior position is broader than the tasks that comprise it. It is important that you give the candidate a sense of the job context—the factors outside the actual position that will directly affect whoever fills the role. Job context can include the history of the department, circumstances in another department whose output directly feeds into the role as input, and resource availability. Common feedback from new executives once they are settled into their roles is that while the decision to take the job was right, they were not prepared for some of the complexities of the job. You can minimize some lack of preparedness by taking a holistic view of the new position and laying out the job context for the candidate.

The following is a story from an employee of a newly hired executive vice president at a regional bank. During the interview process the EVP neglected to obtain basic information, such as the skill level and technology history of the workforce:

> *My boss came in a couple of years ago—a really technologically savvy woman. It was her job to totally revamp the information systems of the business. Everybody had to be online and conducting business electronically in a matter of months. The problem was, no one but the VPs had a computer. We spent millions getting everyone set up with a computer and all the hardware and software they needed. Mind you, this was a place where, before my boss came on, not everyone had Internet access or even a computer at their desk. The problem was that there wasn't much training to go along with this massive technology rollout. People couldn't use the systems—some of them didn't even know how to navigate on the Internet. We weren't starting from square one but square negative one! Nobody had told her just how far we had to come before the organization would be ready for this.*

In 1998, we interviewed 10 percent of the top 300 leaders at a global financial services organization and found that many of them had not developed a clear understanding of their job during the recruiting process. Respondents from all parts of the company talked about their experience with the interview process. Even given such senior positions and the candidates' extensive experience, 25 percent of these top executives stated that they did not understand the job before they were interviewed. As you can see in Exhibit 3-2, this number dropped only slightly to 18 percent throughout the interview process.

When we asked people we interviewed whether their job had been made clear to them, they stated:

- *Part of the job was not made clear until I had already quit my other job. Had I known what was going on I would have done more due diligence and may not have joined the company.*

- *The position was clear to me but it was different from what the reality is. The job I interviewed for empowered me and offered me a supportive infrastructure, but these things don't exist with the job I have. Much of this has to do with the transformation my business is going through and my boss resigning shortly after I came here.*

- *I had an idea what the position was but it was not clearly defined.*

- *I asked questions about the future that my boss couldn't answer. When I asked him about how committed the chairman was, he*

Exhibit 3-2. Clarification of position.

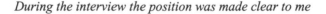

During the interview the position was made clear to me

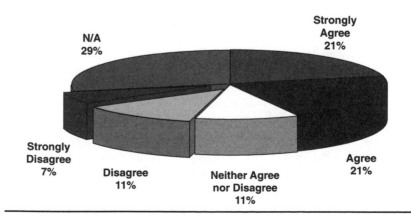

N/A
29%

Strongly
Agree
21%

Strongly
Disagree
7%

Disagree
11%

Neither Agree
nor Disagree
11%

Agree
21%

replied, "I don't know how committed the chairman is, but you do a position paper and we'll find out together."

- Many issues could have been addressed easily in writing or with a verbal presentation. It would be useful to see organizational charts, audits, articles from external consultants, or related data to help define the position and the expectations for success.

- The job and its responsibilities were not clearly identified. I think you have to start with the job objectives and specifications, and include the direct reports as well as the upward reporting relationships.

We asked people we interviewed whether, once on the job, they felt that the actual job matched the description that had been given to them. As Exhibit 3-3 shows, many responded negatively. Some of their statements were:

- This is an unfair question because here you never get the job that was described to you.

- The job is very different from the one I took because it's in a new area and I've gotten a new boss.

Exhibit 3-3. Match of actual job versus description.

Over 20% said the job they took wasn't the job that was described to them:

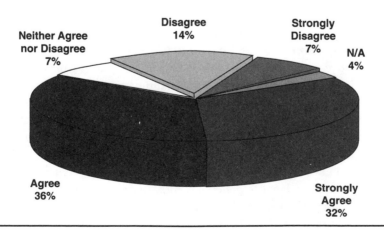

Neither Agree nor Disagree 7%

Disagree 14%

Strongly Disagree 7%

N/A 4%

Agree 36%

Strongly Agree 32%

■ *During the needs' assessment process, the HR person should inter-view the proposed boss so they understand the job dynamics. There are a lot of nuances and complexities that aren't conveyed in the job description.*

POTHOLE: OVERRELIANCE ON SEARCH FIRMS FOR ASSESSMENT AND INFORMATION

The search firm handling a position has a vested interest in the new leader's acceptance of the job, not necessarily in his long-term success and assimilation. Consider due diligence your responsibility and conduct your own reference checks.

PRE-HIRE GOAL: ASSESS THE INDIVIDUAL

ACTION: ASSESS FOR COMMITMENT PREDISPOSITION

We have found that, beyond commitment to a *particular* organization, the most successful new leaders demonstrate what is best thought of as a *predisposition to commitment*. People with higher levels of "commitment predisposition" will be more likely to weather the inevitable hard times that will accompany the assimilation period. Richard Mowday defines commitment propensity as "the sum total of specific personal character-istics and experiences that individuals bring to the organization, such that a stable attachment to the organization is more likely to develop."[1] In his definition, commitment propensity is one variable that predicts later organizational commitment. I/O psychologists have suggested, on the basis of research conducted on twins, that attitudes toward work (and the outcomes or satisfactions we want from it) may be inherited. Some research indicates that "between 30 percent and 40 percent of job satis-faction may be related to genetic factors."[2] Commitment predisposition is a composite of several different inherent traits that together are corre-lated with the ability to stick it out through difficult times. Commitment predisposition is a combination of "metacommitment," attribution style, problem definition style, and sense of identity.

Metacommitment

Metacommitment is an individual difference variable that is defined by Scott Stanley as the degree to which people understand that commitment means making choices and giving some things up. Stanley, a marital researcher at the University of Denver who is renowned for his work on commitment, believes that this concept can be applied to nonmarital relationships and can specifically be applied to an individual's level of commitment to his job. Accepting a job and committing to that job requires making a choice to give up other choices, just as entering marriage and committing to that marriage does.

People vary a great deal in the degree to which they accept the notion that exploring some options more fully often requires giving up other options. Their ability to protect their choice from the attractive alternatives that do not disappear—such as additional appealing job offers that come after the first day on the new job—impacts people's ability to follow through on choices they make. When times are tough, those people with commitment predisposition recommit to their choices every day.

Attribution Style

Another aspect of commitment propensity is what Elliott Aronson calls "the self-serving bias." He defines this as "a tendency for individuals to make dispositional attributions for their successes and situational attributions for their failures."[3] In other words, people who have a self-serving bias tend to attribute success to their own doing, while they blame others for their failures. When people don't recognize the part they've played in their own failure, the result is often that little learning about how to modify behavior occurs because "it is always someone else's fault." However, if people believe that they have control over both successes and failures, they are more likely to stay and work through challenging situations.

Problem Definition Style

A third component of commitment predisposition is how a person defines a problem. Understanding how a person sets parameters for problems generally can identify how that person might define problems in the future. How a problem is defined is the boundary within which the problem is solved. Often, people who do not possess such cognitive flexibility are unable to "switch gears," resulting in an inability to see things through to completion if unforeseen problems materialize. Thorough planning can offset this inflexibility, but only to a degree.

Sense of Identity

A final aspect of commitment predisposition is whether or not a person's identity incorporates a long-term vision. Often, if a person feels strongly about something and the job taps into that passion, that person will be more inclined to commit to the job because she recognizes that the job is a vehicle for achieving her vision. For those people who truly have that commitment, whose personal identity is very wrapped up in the work that they do rather than the organization they work for, pay and other levers that are usually used to motivate people become less important.

Commitment propensity has been hypothesized to positively predict subsequent organizational commitment. Organizational commitment is defined in terms of strength of an individual's identification with and involvement in a particular organization. Such commitment can be characterized by a strong belief in and acceptance of the organization's goals and values, a willingness to exert considerable effort on behalf of the organization, and a definite desire to maintain organizational membership.[4] Lyman Porter's seminal study on commitment found that commitment to the organization was clearly the most important variable that differentiated between stayers and leavers.[5] Porter's findings demonstrate that the attitudes held by an individual predict the potential for subsequent turnover.

This research strongly indicates that those people who display stick-to-it-iveness can be distinguished from those who tend to drop out during hard times. Actual organizational commitment cannot exist prior to organizational entry and, therefore, cannot be meaningfully measured prior to entry. However, some of these unique, inherent characteristics can be measured in advance of day one, which can provide information that, if viewed as an indication of how a person might react to certain circumstances, can reduce some of the risk involved in hiring a new executive. Taken together, these factors answer the all-important question—Is this a person who will stay the course?

The following story illustrates the differences between people who have shown commitment predisposition and those who have not. When we interviewed a senior executive about this topic, he told a story about his two daughters:

> *My younger daughter Sarah works for a mutual fund company that has a very proactive human resources division. The HR people meet with her about once every four months or so to go over how her performance has been in the position she holds, the possible openings available to her higher in the organization, the training they want her to complete, etc. The company appears to be open to communication and clearly, in her case, has gone out of its way to reward her for her work and to encourage her to aspire to higher positions. She, in turn, really likes the company, believes in what it is doing, what its top executives say, and can see herself in a top administrative position in the relatively near future. The company has been extravagant in its rewards to employees, rapid salary increases, good benefits, and very nice bonuses on a quarterly basis. Sarah has moved up faster than anyone else who came in at the same time and level. She says she feels like a cult member when she thinks about the company. At the same time, she knows she can be employed by any number of other mutual fund companies, and has received headhunter inquiries.*
>
> *My older daughter Jill works for the State Department of Law Enforcement in Welfare Fraud Investigations. Her environment is truly staid and parsimonious compared to her sister's. However, Jill is very proud to be with the agency and is content to climb the ladder at the state's leisure. She has become even more enthused by her organization, because it is law enforcement and Jill believes that they are first rate in what they do. So, she volunteers for committee assignments that she could have ducked; she avidly reads the in-house publications and calls our attention to things she believes we would find interesting.*
>
> *Jill's work group is one in which she has had a long history, not all of it pleasant and happy. Amongst other hardships, she has filed and won a sexual harassment case against her supervisor. Like her younger sister, she likes doing a job well and takes pride in handling tough cases that lead to legal actions. But unlike Sarah's experience, Jill is in an organization*

*with relatively little HR support, a relatively static structure
without much upward mobility potential, somewhat ambiguous
performance standards and evaluation procedures. Despite the
bureaucratic structure of the agency, she is really upbeat about
its mission, its people, and her future in it.*

In the first example, Sarah is portrayed as a competent, intelligent,
and motivated young woman. She seems committed to her job until such
time that an even better offer comes along. This leaves her future within
the organization in the hands of fate—whether she stays or goes depends
largely on circumstances. The older daughter, Jill, on the other hand,
was certainly disheartened and frustrated by the challenges that were
emerging—having commitment predisposition doesn't necessitate having an unrealistically optimistic outlook. But instead of giving up and
placing blame when the opportunity arose, Jill buckled down and did
the best job possible under the circumstances. Quitting really wasn't an
option for her because her job is more than a job to her—it contributes
to her sense of self and her vision of herself and taps into a deep-seated
passion for what she is doing.

The executive interviewed, Jill and Sarah's father, noted that based
on Jill's behavior over many years, her commitment to this particular
organization is not surprising. He believes that Jill has an *inherent propensity* toward commitment that her sister Sarah lacks. He has observed
consistent behavior over time that has led him to this conclusion. Research supports this father's observations in that it suggests that independent of the specific work context some people may be more predisposed
than others to hang in through the inevitable rough times.

Organizations can use the following questions as guidelines for
assessing individuals for commitment propensity:

QUESTIONS YOU CAN USE TO ASSESS METACOMMITMENT

- Do they believe that they will have to give up some things in
  life in order to have other things that they want more?
- Can they describe what options they will be giving up?[6]

QUESTIONS YOU CAN USE TO ASSESS ATTRIBUTION STYLE

- How do they describe their role in past events? Did things happen to them, or did they take action to affect the events?

- Do they see conflict as something to probe and learn from, or something to avoid?

QUESTIONS YOU CAN USE TO ASSESS FOR PROBLEM DEFINITION STYLE

- Do their past experiences show a pattern of seeing things through to completion?
- Do their past experiences demonstrate their ability to continue to engage and produce during unpleasant times?
- What indications do you have that they believe in the principle that one should finish what one starts?

QUESTIONS YOU CAN USE TO ASSESS FOR SENSE OF IDENTITY

- Do they describe their career in terms of patterns or in terms of jobs?
- Do they have values or beliefs that indicate they are able to commit to some things larger than themselves?

ACTION: ASSESS FOR REINFORCING AND EXTENDING FIT

Why is fit such an important issue? Simply put, people tend to get along best with others who think and act like they do. People like others who are similar, whether the similarity is in the area of opinions, personality traits, or background. When we meet new people and are searching for clues about how to understand them, we initially evaluate them based on our shared similarities. But fit is not just about similarities. There are two key points about fit relative to assimilation—that fit isn't everything, and that the relative importance of different *kinds* of fit varies according to your organization's current needs. Someone who mirrors the current culture, values, and goals may fit in just fine as a direct replacement, but may therefore be less likely to contribute new ideas to emerging change efforts. It is important for a new leader to share the *core* values of an organization, and maybe even have alignment with its preferred work style. But fit is not simply a matter of similarity.

The ideal candidate should have sufficient strengths to both balance organizational weaknesses and to propel the organization into the

POTHOLE: GROUP THINK

" Group think," which Irving Janis defines as the tendency for groups to come to false agreement for the sake of maintaining similarity, is as large a risk as extreme polarization.[7] Someone who fits too well into the current status quo would be unable to offer fresh perspectives or champion alternative positions to move the business in a new direction.

future. In fact, organizations hire senior managers for a number of reasons, other than skills and abilities:

- To fill a position
- To gain a missing skill or competency
- To bring in new ideas—"new blood"
- To implement strategic change

Gary Powell distinguishes "reinforcing fit" from "extending fit."[8] He argues that reinforcing fit, or hiring people who can contribute to an organization's "cohesiveness," does not prevent an organization from simultaneously trying to *extend* fit, or hire people with diverse experience and ideas who can be instrumental in implementing change and expanding the organization's identity. In fact, according to Powell, the most successful organizations will be those that recognize the need to hire for both kinds of fit.

In order for assimilation to occur, the new leader and the organization should share enough similarities to build common ground. At the same time, there should be adequate space for each to offer unique contributions and add value to the other. So, if the purpose of the hire is to push the organization in a new direction, finding the *proper* fit (not too close, not too far away) is critical.

On the other hand, if the person hired is too different from the rest of the organization, there is a risk that the new person would not be able to find common ground with others in the current organization. The person will most likely not be accepted, which will mean that moving from the current state toward a desired future state would be very difficult. Many organizations hire senior executives to make change but have given little thought to how they will support them. This is a little like planting a flower in the desert and expecting it to grow, thrive, and even propagate.

ACTION: ASSESS FOR ACTUAL ACHIEVEMENTS, NOT POTENTIAL

At this point in an executive's career, assessment should be based on achievement, not potential. You can determine achievements by using an achievement interview. The purpose of an achievement interview is to allow candidates to tell their own stories about the results they've achieved and, more important, *how* they've achieved them. With senior hires, the organization is not looking for potential but for a demonstrated track record and self-knowledge about what has worked and what hasn't. Whoever is conducting the assessment should ask about specific situations and probe for tangible results. Ask if they have encountered a situation like the one described and how it was addressed. Try to avoid hypothetical questions such as, "What would you do if. . . ?"

As candidates tell their stories, the following questions can be used to probe for more information about *how* they achieved results and whether they have learned from past mistakes.

- How did you approach the situation?
- Why did you do it that way?
- What other options did you consider?
- What have you learned from this experience?
- How have you applied what you've learned from this experience to other challenges?
- What might you have done differently?

ACTION: IDENTIFY THE CANDIDATE'S "CAREER ANCHORS"

The concept of "career anchors" is not a new one. It was developed following a longitudinal study of Sloan School alumni. The study's author, Edgar Schein, noted the difficulty people have in identifying their own career patterns: "The person being interviewed usually did not see the pattern spontaneously, but would readily see it once it was pointed out."[9]

New leaders have pointed out that during the interview process, too much emphasis was placed on the most recent job, and not enough attention was paid to the career themes or career anchors that inform the future direction of the individual. According to one executive:

> *There was an enormous amount of focus on the job I was leaving (where I had spent twelve to thirteen months) and inadequate focus on my whole career span. That constrained the interview because it became "let's see how your current skill set fits with the job you are going to take." I think the interviewers should look back at least three jobs (or five years) and I don't think that happens automatically.*

For many people, finding a career where they can feel comfortable may involve a series of false starts, and a series of self-confrontations. There are numerous ways to examine someone's past jobs. It's important that you push the candidate to examine his past jobs honestly, to identify areas where he had the most success, the causes of his transitions, and the factors that motivated him. You want to evaluate this particular position in terms of its desirability for the particular individual and its consistency with his *career* journey. One way to begin is to look back at a candidate's career, and think about the career anchors or themes that can be identified and the aspects of each job that align with each of these anchors. Examples of possible career anchors are:

- Managerial
- Technical/functional
- Security and stability
- Creativity
- Autonomy and independence[10]

You may want to ask the candidate questions to gain further insight into his thinking, such as, "Are these anchors in fact the things that satisfied you about your previous jobs? If so, what about the job you are seeking will allow you to continue doing these things?" Furthermore, you should be asking yourself whether the organization is expecting the candidate to possess skills or competencies that he may not have developed and may not want to.

After you've worked through three or four of the candidate's most important jobs, a clear pattern should emerge. A few of these anchors will have a number of things listed next to them. You might be surprised by the similarities you've found.

Roger provides an example of someone whose career has had a strong theme line that might be overlooked at first glance due to the diversity of the jobs he's held.

> *I began my career in the '60s, working in the slums of NYC, organizing community food programs. I returned to school to get an advanced degree in psychology. My next job was at a local community college focusing on at risk populations— people in prison, school dropouts, and women who had been out of the workforce. Eventually, I got a degree in sociology, and for the next several years I was happy, teaching at several universities. When I was about 35, though, my career took a marked turn, and I accepted a job at a major corporation and focused on workplace effectiveness and organizational transformations. I took a substantial pay cut, but that's what I thought I had to do if I wanted the experience that would take my career to the next level. I'm now a senior executive in a small firm. What do these jobs have in common? They each focus on individual self-help, systemic interventions, and change. Each job had an entrepreneurial bias, and security was clearly not my dominant motivator. I'm in my mid-fifties now, and I've just been offered a job heading up the strategic planning function for one of the Fortune 100s, at a salary that would have been unheard of several years ago. I'm not sure yet whether I should accept.*

While each of Roger's jobs may look radically different from each other at first glance, upon closer inspection the commonalities and successes of his career become clearer. If you were to assess Roger for a position, you would want to assess him in terms of his career theme line. He found satisfaction implementing change, implementing systemic interventions, and helping others to help themselves. With this awareness, making decisions about his suitability for a position based on whether it will allow him to continue engaging in similar activities, within what may be a very different context becomes easier.

ACTION: AVOID HIRING "BEST AVAILABLE"

The organization should assess the individual for assimilation potential in order to find the best person for the job. It is important to avoid hiring the "best available" for a key executive position, although in the face of tremendous pressure to fill a role this can be a tempting option. Here is an executive's description of a situation where the attempt to fill the vacuum with the "best available" resulted in a loss for the entire firm:

> *Jonathan was the CEO of a major news provider. He was a high-powered, fast-paced man who expected the entire organization to operate at his pace. One of his top three strategic points for the remainder of the year was to create an Organizational Development and Training Department as quickly as possible in order to maintain a competitive edge. Fran, my boss and the global head of HR, was tasked with staffing this position. This was one of Fran's first big assignments. Six months passed, the position was still vacant, and Fran was beginning to get nervous. Six months on Jonathan's calendar may as well have been six years, all Jonathan knew was that the position had been vacant for too long and he began to place blame.*
>
> *The pressure to hire someone and get this department started hit Fran quite hard. Our team watched the buildup of tension between Jonathan and Fran and knew that the situation would not end well. Fran met Rose, who had some OD and training experience but also had never held any job for more than two years, highly unusual for someone of her generation. Even though the twenty-year veteran internal recruiter expressed strong objections to Rose, insisting that something was just "not right," Fran turned a blind eye to the spotty resume and to the recruiter's gut reaction. In spite of all the data she had against the hire, Fran felt backed into a corner and justified to herself that Rose was the best available. She extended Rose an offer, which she promptly accepted.*
>
> *Within Rose's first three months on the job, her perfor-*

mance was so bad that business leaders from around the orga-
nization began to refuse her entry into their business units—
even some of the very people who pushed for OD and training
support early on. People from all levels of the organization
began complaining about Rose to whoever would listen. As if
the barrage of negative feedback was not evidence enough of a
mishire, within six months her entire team quit, including me.
After I left, I heard that Fran was under more pressure than
ever to deliver and now there were no resources and many
skeptics as to her and Rose's competence. The situation was far
worse than it would have been if Fran had waited for the best
candidate for the job rather than moving forward with the best
available.

INTERVENTION: USE COMMON CRITERIA TO OBTAIN INPUT FROM ALL STAKEHOLDERS

Encourage the stakeholders of the candidate to take the time to meet with her. Underscore the importance of the members' participation in the due diligence process and their ability to collaborate with the new leader in order to meet their goals. Point out specifically how the potential hire can help them achieve their goals. Using a peer roundtable is a good way to ensure that the candidate's skills and abilities are considered from a variety of perspectives.

We have found that when peers are involved in the selection process, they have more "skin in the game" once a hire is made and will more actively help the new leader assimilate. Peer roundtables reduce the mystery about the new person coming on board. Participants in this process will know a great deal about the candidate and can become linking pins to the rest of the organization, reducing speculation and misinformed gossip about the new entrant, as well as unnecessary resistance to the process. In addition, exposure to a number of interviewers' perspectives can provide the candidate with a more realistic view of the organization. When these interviewers are the new leader's peers, this process helps to ensure a more integrated executive team.

Peer roundtables allow a process in which several different people interview and evaluate the same candidate according to previously determined common criteria and standards. To ensure that the organiza-

POTHOLE: TOO MUCH FOCUS ON CONSENSUS

It's difficult to ascertain what the motives are behind participants' resistance to particular candidates. For example, is it because the change the candidate represents is threatening to the person, even though it would be good for the organization? If the process is too focused on building consensus at all costs, there is a risk that the "least objectionable" candidate, rather than the most qualified, will be hired.

tion obtains a well-rounded view of the individual, after the interviews are completed, the interviewers meet to share their assessments.

Here is how peer roundtables work:

- *Develop common standards and criteria.* It is important that those doing the interview determine in advance the base-level competencies they are looking for, and how they will be evaluated. A high rating given by one interviewer must have a similar meaning to all. It helps to have a rating scale based upon an evaluation of where a candidate stands in relation to the optimal competency for the position. For instance, for a given competency, you might determine the qualities that differentiate baseline, from expert or role model/thought leader levels. For most leadership positions, you probably want people who demonstrate competencies at the role model/thought leader level. Having these clearly defined criteria will help the members of the roundtable to contextualize their evaluations and ensure that they're "speaking the same language."

- *Use a structured interview.* It's important to determine areas to assess in advance. We recommend using a structured interview process that uses a standardized set of core questions (we have included some questions in an upcoming section). This ensures that there is consistency in the data collected, with each interviewee being asked the same questions. Roundtable participants can then compare and contrast the candidates. Using a standardized set of core questions has the added benefit of allowing the interviewer to be free of the burden associated with thinking up the next question, allowing him or her to focus more closely on the responses to the questions.

- **Plan the interviewing sequence and content.** Determine in advance who will ask which questions. A common complaint from interviewees is "I kept having the same interview over and over again." You want each interviewer to pursue in-depth questioning about different areas. The task of the roundtable will be to identify common themes that emerged throughout the process and to compare these candidates, who will all have been asked the same questions, to the ideal candidate spec and to each other.

- **Following the interviews, lead open, candid discussions with all interviewers.** The group discussion is a way to surface data that may have been overlooked. It also allows managers to understand performance requirements in the context of the larger unit and organizational objectives. This discussion also helps to align everyone around common goals and builds commitment to the new candidate. In the roundtable process, a number of opinions are expressed about the candidate's strengths and weaknesses. In order to facilitate the entry of new leaders into the organization, as well as their coming up to speed in their jobs, it's important to identify areas for developmental improvement. If all key stakeholders were not part of this roundtable, it might be appropriate to ask them for their assessment of the candidate as input into the decision and/or the developmental plan.

Of course, while the organization is assessing the individual, the new leader is also assessing the organization. See Appendix A, The New Leader's Handbook, to understand the factors that the new leader will be taking into account during the interview process.

Notes

1. R. T. Mowday and L. W. Porter. "The Measurement of Organizational Commitment." *Journal of Vocational Behavior*, 14 (1979): 226.
2. D. Schultz and S. E. Schultz. *Psychology and Work Today: An Introduction to Industrial and Organizational Psychology*, 7th ed. Upper Saddle River, N.J.: Prentice Hall, 1998, p. 250.

3. Elliott Aronson. *The Social Animal*, 8th ed. New York: Worth, 1999, p. 173.
4. Mowday and Porter. "Organizational Commitment."
5. Lyman W. Porter et al. "Organizational Commitment, Job Satisfaction and Turnover among Psychiatric Technicians." *Journal of Applied Psychology* 59.5 (1974): 603–609.
6. S. M. Stanley, e-mail interview, 5 October 2000.
7. Irving L. Janis and L. Mann. *Decision Making: A Psychological Analysis of Conflict, Choice, and Commitment.* New York: The Free Press, 1977.
8. Gary N. Powell. "Reinforcing and Extending Today's Organizations: The Simultaneous Pursuit of Person-Organization Fit and Diversity." *Organizational Dynamics* 26 (Winter 1998): 50–61.
9. Edgar Schein. *Career Dynamics: Matching Individual and Organizational Needs.* Reading, Mass.: Addison-Wesley, 1978, p. 127.
10. Ibid., Chapter 10.

Part Two

THE

ASSIMILATION PROCESS

Stage One: Anticipating and Planning

Worlds Apart

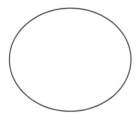

New Leader   **Organization**

There was about a month between my hire date and my start date. I already knew a lot about the company, and didn't want to treat this time like a vacation. David, my boss, had been pretty forthcoming—we'd already had three meetings where we talked about the team's problems and what I would be expected to do in the first year to make some progress in these areas. But I didn't want just David's opinion—I wanted the views of people who had been in the organization and the views of customers to confirm or disconfirm David's views. In any case, I reasoned that doing this research would definitely flesh out what David had said and trigger some new questions.

*I knew a few people who had worked for the company in
the last five years and who were willing to talk about their
experiences, how the leadership team functioned, and what service standards had been like. The Internet was also a useful
resource; I got information about what customers were saying
about the company's products, and which wholesalers might be
approached as potential new customers. Even with the understanding that this information was imperfect and subject to
interpretation, I got a lot out of this research and revised several of my key plans. Armed with some pretty good suggestions
about what we could start implementing during my first couple
of months on the job, I called David and told him about my
plans. I was excited, but he was slow to respond and finally
just said, "Interesting. Let me get back to you on that." I was
really disappointed by his response.*

—Paul, head of distribution for a major retail firm

What should Paul have done?

a. Paul should have waited to pursue these plans after his start
   date.

b. Paul should have discussed these ideas with several new peers
   on the leadership team, to get their feedback before presenting
   them to David.

c. Paul should have realized he might have moved too quickly,
   and should have discussed David's reaction with him.

It was natural for Paul to feel excited about the possibilities of the
new job, and David's apparent lack of interest made Paul feel stifled.
Paul obviously wanted someone to hear these ideas and provide feedback—the question is how to go about this without stepping on anyone's
toes. Presumably, in hiring Paul, the organization was seeking to bring
in someone with the skills to confront the team's challenges. So why did
David seem less than enthusiastic about Paul's ideas? It could have been
something simple—maybe David was having a bad day, or just didn't
have time to talk. But it didn't seem that way to Paul. By backing off
completely, choosing Option a, Paul would have wasted the valuable
time afforded by the post-hire period for additional knowledge gathering
and thinking about how to approach the challenges of the job. Discuss-

ing the ideas with members of the leadership team, Option b, could have created a number of new problems. On the one hand, the leadership team might begin to view Paul as responsive and action-oriented and would probably appreciate Paul's deference to their judgment. However, David would have felt undermined if Paul did this without his approval. This would not have been the best way for Paul and David to begin their relationship.

If Paul stepped back and thought about the possible causes of David's reaction, Option c—talking to David and honestly soliciting his reaction—would have emerged as the wisest choice. As new leaders enter an organization it is important that they test their assumptions before acting. It's possible that in some instances they might be inadvertently overstepping their mandate—and it's better to learn this while they're planning, rather than later as they begin implementing.

Even the best intentions can lead to trouble if new leaders aren't careful. Paul seemed to have done all the right things—gathering information from a number of sources, laying the groundwork for participation, and beginning to learn about the organization. New leaders begin to speculate about the ways in which they can demonstrate impact and the relationships they need to form with their teams and superiors. The natural impulse is to focus on the *possibilities* of this new situation, rather than on things that might get in the way and must be addressed prior to acting.

THE NEW LEADER'S EXPERIENCE

In Stage One, "Anticipating and Planning," new leaders continue the process of familiarizing themselves with the organization. At this point the new hire has committed to his new position but has not yet started the job. His first steps are to gather more information about the organization and his new position from whatever sources he can. His enthusiasm at this stage, represented by the upward swing of the emotional curve on the graph shown in Exhibit 4-1, should be deliberately tempered by an awareness that there are challenges ahead that he has yet to fully define. *Your* role at this point is to help him develop that awareness. As he learns more, his intellectual experiences follow an upward trajectory. This stage is one of "unconscious incompetence"—new leaders don't yet know what they don't know. Help them take advantage of

Exhibit 4-1. The emotional and intellectual journey: Stage One.

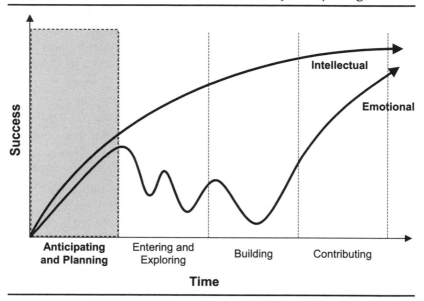

the momentum of this upward curve to take a forward-thinking approach and enter a proactive "planning mode."

The New Leader's Handbook in Appendix A is addressed specifically to the new leaders and is focused on those things only the new leaders can do. They include personally assessing their intellectual content-specific knowledge gaps; hiring an industry specialist; assessing their leadership skills; determining what needs to be modified in this environment; and most important, developing a command philosophy. We recommend that you duplicate this material and provide it to your new leader.

Once a new leader has accepted a job offer, he has made a public commitment, and it's no longer a decision to be made but a reality. He hasn't spent a day on the job yet, but it's *his* job now, and there is a great opportunity to help him begin planning for how he's going to enter and have an impact on the organization. Complications can arise while the new leader is disengaging from his prior employer.

Advancing to a new level of responsibility ratchets up the degree of difficulty in assimilating by at least one notch, as shown in Exhibit 4-2. These changes are complicated when a new leader is moving into a new position that represents a promotion or a broadening of responsibility. It's not just a matter of taking another job requiring different skills.

Exhibit 4-2. Changing jobs: Multiple degrees of difficulty.

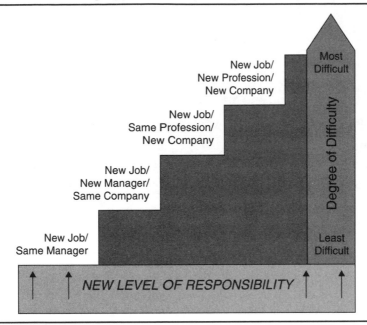

For example, when someone moves from managing a function to managing a business, he transitions from needing in-depth knowledge of a specific function to needing to learn enough about a variety of functions to make trade-off decisions, and to integrate diverse plans and programs into one coherent business plan. As a leader's span of control is enlarged, he considers longer time spans, decisions are bigger, and uncertainties and risks are greater. His mind-set changes from a functional perspective ("Can we do it?") to a profit perspective ("Will it make us money?") to a strategic perspective ("Should we do it?"). Moving to a new company and a new industry simultaneously significantly compounds the difficulty.

THE ORGANIZATION'S EXPERIENCE: PREPARING FOR THE RECIPROCAL IMPACT

During the period between acceptance of the offer and the first day on the job, your role is to prepare both the new leader and the organization for the new leader's arrival. This can be done in two ways: by arranging

> ## POTHOLE: TOO MUCH WEIGHT
> ## ON THE INDIVIDUAL
>
> To accelerate the speed of change, organizations hire those people who represent what the organization wishes to become, with little attention to the support mechanisms necessary to achieve that change. As new leaders gather information and plan, they should keep an eye out for what they'll need when they enter. Be very clear about what the organization is willing to provide to support their success.

support for the new leader and by contributing to the development of an entry strategy.

It is especially important to emphasize to the new leader that he has a great deal of latitude to determine his own fate by constructing an entry strategy that will meet *his* strategic needs. An entry strategy has four components:

- Acquisition of knowledge about the industry and business
- Honest delineation of development needs
- Identification of key influence relationships
- Specification of preliminary priorities and approaches

The activities you undertake during this period also help the new leader to begin to reach his achievement goals, as shown in Exhibit 4-3.

Finally, remember that the assimilation process represents a series of "firsts." It's important that the new leader sets the right tone in his initial interactions with people, so that when he enters the organization, it will be easier to establish networks and build credibility. You can prepare the new leader to anticipate how to best respond to the needs and demands of the organization by encouraging him to engage in *visualization*, a technique top athletes use in order to prepare themselves psychologically for "the big event." In *Hope Is Not a Method*, Gordon R. Sullivan shares these thoughts about how visualization can prepare someone for the future: "As I wrestled with the challenges of the post–

Exhibit 4-3. Stage One: Key goals supported.

Stages \ Goals	Create Achievement Legacy	Understand Organizational Dynamics	Build Influence	Assume Leadership	Align Systems
Stage IV: Contributing	Follow up on feedback	Formally integrate cultural changes	Create opportunities for organizationwide interaction	Provide developmental opportunities	Formally integrate changes to the system
Stage III Building	Provide feedback mechanisms	Provide coaching	Create opportunities to build networks	Support personnel transitions	Establish parameters for change
Stage II: Entering and Exploring	Help get industry experience	Facilitate cultural audit	Facilitate key relationships (act as a translator)	Facilitate assessment of team's skills and competencies	Act as a sounding board
Stage I: Anticipating and Planning	**Prepare a developmental plan**	**Advise new leader; provide information about culture**	**Prepare key stakeholders for new leader's arrival**	**Prepare team for new leader's arrival**	**Provide access to systems information**

cold war world, I tried to mentally position myself in the future and, in my mind's eye, look back. It is a technique used by distance runners and other athletes—they 'see' themselves at the finish line, and then 'look back' to pull themselves along. Seeing themselves at the finish line, in the future gives them the intense concentration needed to win."[1] Like that of a top athlete, a new leader's visualization process must encompass more than the end-state. It should include the methods that will propel him forward. Many of the activities we recommend in this chapter are designed to help you facilitate the new leader's visualization of the organization that he will find upon entry.

ARRANGE SUPPORT FOR THE NEW LEADER

You can also help select the people for the support roles that will help the new leader navigate through the assimilation process. It is at this time that the organization can appoint a mentor and advise in the selection of an assimilation coach to begin working with the new leader.

HIRE AN ASSIMILATION COACH

You may have hired the new leader on the basis of his knowledge, skills, and experience, but to be truly effective in his new role, the new leader has to know how to deploy this arsenal within a new context that will have its own unique demands. This is *especially* true if he is moving into a new industry. At this time, before the new leader is officially on board, it can be particularly useful to hire an external assimilation coach.

Assimilation coaches are external consultants who have expertise in helping leaders manage the *specific personal and professional issues* that arise during the assimilation process. Typically, they have witnessed the process in a number of organizations, at a number of levels, and can bring that experience to bear when advising new leaders on actions and helping them to contextualize their experience. An assimilation coach should be able to provide a valuable external perspective on the dynamics of the organization and, more important, provide objective feedback to the individual about her interactions with her team. An assimilation coach often assists in performing organizational and cultural assessments, facilitating a series of entering meetings and providing support and an objective sounding board. A relationship with an assimilation coach can last as long as eighteen months, acting as a bridge between the individual and others in the organization as necessary and ensuring that the individual receives the timely feedback needed to succeed.

One assimilation coach we spoke with shared her approach to dealing with a client who is facing assimilation issues.

My approach might be to find out a lot more about what is expected of the person on the job, such as what behavior and performance are they expecting and what are they getting and what is the cause of the gap. I might then triangulate that with the people who will be rating the new leader's performance and the people who will be working with him. Following these conversations, I would conduct a new manager assimilation program, which is an effective way to accelerate the getting to know you stage. This can be accomplished either by interviewing the people in the team first and then reporting it back or by conducting the same type of exercise in a group setting. The outcome is a platform that is then used to create a springboard for the manager and the team to identify the issues and to develop a business agenda that will cover the first six months. It also provides an opportunity to begin working on behavior routines with the individual. In some cases, the person may have been a great Mr. Inside but the new job maybe requires a lot more outside presence, either in handling investors and analysts or in dealing with public bodies that the person never had to deal with before. In that case, the goal would be to identify the issues involved.

Sometimes it boils down to an issue of confidence. The person may know the numbers but he may just not have been put in a situation where people are trained to attack. It is very different to move from having to prepare the numbers for your boss to being the one who is out there defending the numbers. With experience people get better, and as you get better you get a better handle on the data. But in the process you can be helped by some training and coaching on how to handle a hostile media and not get defensive, for example.

Many leaders are using external coaches today, not only for their specific expertise, but because their managers often lack the time to provide this coaching on a consistent basis. In the *Wall Street Journal* on

September 5, 2000, Eleena DeLisser reported that even entrepreneurs are beginning to take advantage of executive coaches due to their "anxiety and lack of self-confidence . . . in the face of rapid changes in technology."[2] In other words, even those leading new business ventures—as innovative and brave as they may be—can benefit from outside help and coaching during times of intense change. As you know by now, the assimilation process is one of those times.

Some organizations provide new senior players with an assimilation coach. While the organization should provide advice and recommend the best coach given the new leader's needs and style, to ensure the best possible match it's important that the ultimate choice of an assimilation coach be left to the new leader. We recommend that either the new leader pick her own or that HR provide her with a slate of two or three from which she can choose. Chemistry is as important as competence. If the assimilation coach isn't familiar with your organization it is important for you to brief him. When selecting an assimilation coach, consider his knowledge of organization dynamics and design as well as his experience with helping people at an executive level negotiate a change process. Assimilation coaches can be very instrumental in situations in which a new leader is moving to a more senior job. They provide assistance to someone who may have all the technical skills but not the seasoning required to function at that new level—to "get senior quickly." Often the task of coming to grips with what the job might be is large, and the time frame in which to gain that understanding is short.

APPOINT PEOPLE WITHIN THE ORGANIZATION TO SUPPORT THE LEADER

In preparation for a new leader's arrival, we recommend that in addition to an external assimilation coach, you select a designated Touchstone and a mentor. Each of these functions provides a distinct, important role throughout the initial stages of the assimilation process.

Touchstone

As noted in the Introduction, we suggest the designation of a "Touchstone" to partner with the new leader through the process of assimilation. This professional may come from corporate HR or from the HR organization supporting the new leader's line of business. As with most HR activities, the "touchstone" role requires HR to both advocate for the individual and ensure that the objectives of the organization are being met. Throughout the process the HR touchstone initiates a series of interventions to:

- Help the new leader assess himself and the organizational environment.
- Coach the new leader as well as his boss.
- Facilitate relationships between the new leader and his boss, peers, reports and other stakeholders.
- Develop and implement an assimilation strategy.

Mentor

A mentor is key in providing an immediate networking opportunity as well as providing internal, experience-based assistance. By providing new leaders with a mentor, organizations can connect them with more established leaders who are held accountable, to varying degrees, for their successful assimilation. Ideally, the mentor should be a senior player who has been with the organization for a relatively long period of time and can provide an "inside view" of the organization and the leader's place in it. A mentor should be an experienced senior professional who understands the organization and the leadership teams, has a strong investment in the leader's success, is sensitive to the entry process, and is recognized as a leader and skilled manager. Possible competition between a new leader and his boss is one reason why some organizations choose to provide the new leader with a mentor who is outside his direct line in the hierarchy (skip-level mentor). A skip-level mentor can be a good way for the new leader to network across organizational boundaries and receive guidance with minimal competition.

CONTRIBUTE TO THE DEVELOPMENT OF AN ENTRY STRATEGY

No person in the organization is going to be fully conscious of all of the things a new leader needs to know in order to do her job. You and your colleagues already live in this organization; its operations, assumptions, common understandings, and informal operating procedures are probably second nature to you and you rarely give them a second thought. Before starting the new job, new leaders are deprived of familiar information or networks, and this deprivation makes them extremely trust-ready—inclined and strongly desiring to trust. They should be encouraged to look at this information critically—to read between the lines and ask questions to verify or disconfirm the inferences they draw. Think of this stage as helping the new leader acquire pieces of a puzzle. If the new leader is representing the future of the organization, rather than the current state, communicate her strengths and how they will help the organization achieve its goals. In addition to providing direct support to the new leader through meetings and information sharing, you can open lines of communication between the members of her team, as well as with the departing leader, thereby helping to pave the way for entry. This strategy is outlined in Exhibit 4-4.

ACQUISITION OF KNOWLEDGE AND SUBJECT MATTER EXPERTISE ABOUT THE INDUSTRY AND THE BUSINESS

Legitimize Access to Information and Key People

Once the new leader is officially part of the organization, it's appropriate to provide support for her gathering a broader range of information about the business. Things that were off limits during the interview process because of confidentiality and proprietary concerns should now be available for her benefit. Bear in mind that new leaders might not know which documents to ask for—a new leader doesn't

Exhibit 4-4. The entry strategy: An overview.

Components of an Entry Strategy	What the Organization Can Do	What the New Leader Can Do
1) Acquisition of knowledge and subject matter expertise about the industry and the business	Legitimize access to information	Conduct an assessment of knowledge gaps Hire an industry specialist
2) Honest delineation of developmental needs	Provide feedback about personal development and design a plan	Identify personal developmental gaps
3) Identification of key influence relationships	Prepare key stakeholders for new leader's arrival Prepare team for new leader's arrival	Understand the key stakeholder relationships
4) Specification of preliminary priorities and approaches	Identify competencies of team Gain outgoing leader's support	Identify an appropriate management style Develop a command philosophy Gather information from the outgoing leader

know about strategic meetings that have happened in the past, and so can't ask for those proceedings. It's not just documentation that new leaders need; they also need the stories, history, and internal customs that make the organization what it is, the things only a member of the organization could know.

The new leader's boss should think about which documents the new leader needs and ensure that they are provided. Once the Entering and Exploring stage begins, there won't be a lot of extra time for background reading. The HR touchstone can recommend people the new leader can meet with to talk about the organization's history and the informal kinds of information that come only with membership. The new leader's boss may show him performance evaluations and P&L sheets, but you should take it upon yourself to make sure that the new leader has access to things like:

- Quarterly and annual reports
- Consultant feedback reports
- Past performance reviews of members of his team
- Proceedings or notes from key offsites and strategic meetings
- Strategy documents
- Biographies of the organization's key—but not public—players, if available (example: those executives two or three levels down from the CEO)
- Recent presentations made by key players

The new leader may need some help figuring out what his stakeholders need. To conduct a stakeholder analysis, the new leader may need more detailed information that only the people themselves can provide. Unfortunately, not everyone will be willing to set aside time to talk to him. The HR Touchstone, or the leader's boss, should make it clear that his acquisition of this information is a priority; helping him now will mean less confusion later. Some of the information a new leader receives may contradict his previous assumptions or force him to amend his view of the organization and the situation he's entering. The most important thing to stress to the new leader is that this increased depth of knowledge from the widened access you're providing doesn't negate the *information* he received during the interview process. However, it may cause him to modify some of his *conclusions*.

HONEST DELINEATION OF DEVELOPMENT NEEDS

Provide Feedback and Design a Development Plan

During the hiring process, it will have become clear that the new leader has flat sides in certain areas. It may be the case that members of the team are sufficiently skilled in the areas of her weakness to provide high-level support until she comes up to speed. This not only helps her compensate while maintaining smooth operation of the business, but it provides the team members in question with useful experience in utilizing their skills in a more strategic way.

If a leader's team cannot compensate for her weaknesses, or if the skills desired *must* reside in the leader, you can begin to mitigate the risk of marginal performance by fashioning a development plan for her *at this stage*. Defining development gaps in advance accelerates the pace at which the new leader will achieve the appropriate level of competence after entering the organization.

Most leaders feel that they do not receive effective feedback about their hiring process. The top 300 leaders of a large multi-national financial services company were asked to respond to the statement in Exhibit 4-5.

A quarter of the respondents did not receive any feedback at all. Here is what some of the respondents said in response to the statement in Exhibit 4-5:

- *I got some indirect feedback from HR, but no one identified any gaps on my ability to fill the job.*
- *Nothing was said about my shortcomings.*
- *I received feedback but it was in the form of informal discussions. For example, someone may have said to me, "Pay attention to administrative issues."*
- *There were no gaps identified but it's hard to discuss my gaps when the job clarity is missing.*

The same respondents were asked whether or not a developmental plan was generated as follow-up to the hiring process, as shown in Exhibit 4-6.

Here is what they had to say about follow-up:

Exhibit 4-5. Feedback.

I received effective feedback about my fit and gaps for this job.

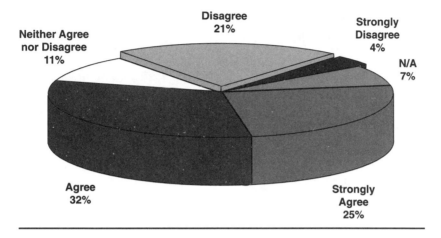

Exhibit 4-6. Follow-up.

A plan was made to help me fill the gaps.

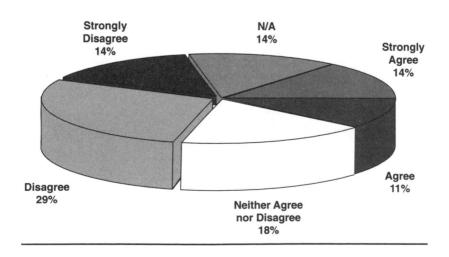

- *There was a lot more emphasis on fit than things I need to be cognitive of, like the organizational structure and related things.*

- *There was no follow-up done with any of the interviewers apart from "Here's why you were the best." I've developed a plan to address my gaps.*

- *I have things that need improvement, but none were identified and no plan was put into effect to fill the gaps.*

- *I hired my own consultant to help me with the assimilation process. I received no support coming in the door.*

- *I didn't receive any feedback, which is unfortunate because I believe it would have shortened my learning curve. This has been the longest learning curve I've ever had.*

Lack of relevant industry or functional experience makes the process of taking command more difficult. Gabarro writes, "Managers who failed . . . were more often industry outsiders whose prior functional expertise may not have been a good fit."[3] In cases where the new leader needs to develop more industry knowledge, you have a number of options. Executive-level courses at the leading business schools offer intensive instruction that minimizes time away from the job while providing thorough training in specialized topic areas. As a follow-up to this training, or as an alternative, you can provide opportunities for the new leader to meet with or be coached by others who have demonstrated expertise in the leader's "weak" areas. This can come in the form of periodic meetings in which the new leader receives advice on actions to take and improvements to make, or in mentoring relationships of greater duration, as in the case of assimilation coaches. We often recommend that a new leader hire an industry specialist to conduct personal tutorials. This is often an alien concept for new leaders. They may have hired consultants for their prior organizations but rarely for themselves. One senior executive hired one of the most prominent organizational strategy consultants to spend a day with him. As he reported, "Boy did I look smart when I met with my new boss."

IDENTIFICATION OF KEY INFLUENCE RELATIONSHIPS

Understand Key Stakeholder Relationships

At this stage it is important to ensure that the new leader understands key stakeholder relationships. Work with the new leader to begin to map each key process in which his team is involved. This will help him to understand:

- How he and his team fit into the overall structure of the organization
- What he needs from others
- What others need from him

Exhibit 4-7 depicts the basic organizational relationships of a CFO.

Making a chart like this for the new leader's role will help you organize the process of recording various stakeholders' needs for review as you work together to plan the entry strategy.

As the new leader begins to develop a complete picture of how he supports others and how they support him, help him to develop hypotheses about the problems that must be solved and begin to prioritize stakeholder needs:

Exhibit 4-7. Example: Stakeholder relationships.

- Whose needs are more important from a practical perspective?

- Whom must he please before he can begin implementing any of his changes?

- Whose support will he need the most?

Prepare Key Stakeholders for the New Leader's Arrival

We have observed that when a new leader joins a team whose members felt strong loyalty toward the former leader, the risk of team turnover is especially great. People may feel pulled in different directions—should they remain loyal to what the old leader started, or to what the new leader is beginning? A new leader's peers and subordinates may feel as if it is not in their best interest to help or provide information. They may adopt the attitude that, if she is so competent, she *shouldn't* need any help. Your job is to help the new leader anticipate and plan how to address these kinds of barriers—the sooner you start, the less disruptive the barriers will be when she arrives.

As the new leader begins to build influence within the organization, she needs a clear sense of what people think about her mandate, how her team operates, and the problems that need to be solved. Views of her team and its function differ depending on the nature and position of the roles within the organization. In the next chapter, we provide some guidance on conducting the assessment itself, but as you help the new leader plan her entry, begin thinking about the kinds of information she'll need and the best sources of that information.

> To announce my arrival, my boss sent a memo out to the business heads throughout the organization, as well as all of their direct reports. I saw this after it had already gone out, and I felt great after reading it. It was this triumphant, glowing letter—he made me out to be almost superhuman in how he described what I was there to accomplish, and why I was the best person to do the job. He outlined all of my key goals and underscored how confident he was in my abilities.
>
> Well, it turns out I shouldn't have been so thrilled. On my second day, I walked into my office to discover over forty voice mails and seventy e-mails. Granted, some of them were just to say "Welcome," but most of the time "welcome" was

followed by "while I'm at it, maybe you could help me with . . . ." It was brutal—how could I possibly satisfy all of these people? If I even tried, I'd go crazy and not be able to help anyone fully. If I didn't, they'd feel like that announcement memo was a piece of false advertising.

—Senior Vice President, IT

In addition to conducting a formal meeting with the new leader's team, it is helpful to distribute a formal communication throughout the organization. However, in order to avoid the example in the previous story, the memo should include only a *realistic* summary of what she has been hired to do. Don't advertise goals that are tentative, have not been confirmed, or are tied to especially volatile circumstances. This only fosters the development of unrealistic expectations about her and can lead to unfair assessments of performance. The purpose of this memo is to inform the organization of the new leader's arrival and provide relevant information about her, including:

- Brief biography
- Business experience
- Rationale for the hire
- Role within the organization
- The standards to which she will be held

As it is important to be realistic in the communication of the new leader's arrival, it is also important to be prompt. The following story illustrates the importance of communicating the leader's arrival as soon as possible. Colleen recently took a job as a senior executive in a consulting firm, and as she tells it, not having the arrival communicated early can present a real barrier to planning.

The organization I just joined sets up your entry process like this. You have a thirty-day period in which to get an understanding of what's going on, what the current state is. You also build a plan during this time. Then at the end of the thirty days, you present your ninety-day and hundred-eighty-day plans. They encourage us to go around and network with other very senior people to get a wide view of what our vision and mission are, and how we can help each other. But here's the problem: It's mid-October, and my "official" start date is in November. They can't officially announce my arrival until then because they have to wait and announce my boss first and he can't move his whole family up to New York before the beginning of November. So I am in an awkward position. I am getting paid as though I were already in my new job and so I feel an obligation to go into the office. But because my arrival hasn't been communicated I have to be careful about keeping my presence to a minimum. The most frustrating part for me is that I have so much to do to prepare for my new job and I can't even use this time as an effective "interim" planning period because I cannot contact certain people for fear of possibly disrupting a potentially sensitive situation.

Prepare the Leader's Team for His Arrival

Prior to entry, you can do a number of things to prepare the new leader's team. It's best to use a formal team meeting for the purpose of preparing the team and getting its feedback. The length of the meeting can vary, depending on the nature of the transition; for example, if there is a great deal of emotion involved, such as when a highly admired leader has left, the meeting should last significantly longer, and one-on-one sessions should be offered as follow-up. The purpose of the preparation meeting is to:

- Explain the rationale for the hire. What were the criteria upon which the organization based this hire, and what value is the new leader expected to bring? This is especially important when existing team members were passed over for the job. They should be coached individually. If someone else in the organization has been passed over for the job, the new leader's boss needs to be very clear about why and explain this first to the person, or people, who were passed over for the job, and then later to the team. This will help to absorb any protest the team members might have regarding the decision. Having clear rationales helps to prevent people from personalizing a decision and reflexively resisting a new leader on the basis of hostility they feel toward the organization for making what they perceive to be a bad or unfair choice. It helps to show people the job spec and competency model for the job, in order to provide a framework for discussing the rationale.

- Surface issues and concerns that team members have about the transition process or the new leader himself.

- Publicly support the new leader and enlist the support of the team. Regardless of the reasons for the departure of the former leader, the new leader's boss must begin enlisting the support of the team before he starts. People need time for reflection; it's not enough to inform people of an impending change and expect them to do whatever is necessary in order to adjust. This is true for the new leader as well as for the team. HR can coach surviving team members about how to manage the change prior to his arrival. Be available for ongoing coaching.

- Communicate the outcomes of this meeting to the new leader, to help him in the development of an entry strategy.

SPECIFICATION OF PRELIMINARY PRIORITIES AND APPROACHES

Leadership is a series of deliberate acts. As the new leader enters unfamiliar terrain, feeling her way somewhat blindly, she must manage yet another polarity: consciously managing the pace of her activity as those who report to her will be looking for immediate guidance and clarity about her goals and who she is. At this stage, it is important that you prepare the new leader to position herself *as* a leader. Most of what you can do falls under the category of planning designed to make the leadership transition smoother. Once she's begun the job, she won't have the time to think about her overall leadership philosophy. Focusing on this now will help her send a consistent message from Day One about who she is, what she can do, and what she expects from others. Preparing the organization for the new leader's arrival, smoothing the leadership transition, is one of the most critical ways you can help ensure successful assimilation.

Identify the Competencies of the Surrounding Team

It is critical to begin to identify the competencies of her direct reports now that the new leader has greater access to them and to information about their past performances. If the new leader has a change mandate, this will also help her determine how best to leverage current skills against proposed future changes and where there are gaps in the team profile, as compared with the ideal profile required to achieve the new leader's strategies.

If you find that the new leader's team lacks some key competencies, you may need to think about working with the new leader to make some hires. One new leader who did not have help conducting such an assessment before beginning the job explains the implications in the following way:

> *One potential success factor that I did not explore was the competencies of the members of my team. I was told something about them but I did not have any real sense for their capabilities. I am uncertain how I would have ascertained this, but in retrospect I can clearly see how this has impacted adversely on my ability to achieve my goals.*

There is probably much retrospective data that you can provide to the new leader at this point. Provide him with past performance appraisals, resumes, results of talent review processes, 360-degree summaries, and various other developmental assessments. We suggest that after you and he have had a chance to review these data, you initiate a focused discussion about your findings. The combination of data and a rich discussion will present him with a baseline to assess the competence of his team once he arrives on site. You should emphasize to him that the information you provide should be viewed as tentative until he makes his own judgments.

Gain the Outgoing Leader's Support

Obviously, there are a number of possible reasons for a leader's departure, some more difficult to manage than others. Let the new leader know why the previous leader has left—and probe beyond the official reasons. It may be true that he left to "pursue other opportunities," but if he was helped along in his decision to leave—that is, pushed out the door—the new leader needs to know. The circumstances surrounding the previous leader's departure can exacerbate the problem of resentment and resistance from the team. Share with the new hire what the previous leader's reputation was. Not only might this give her an idea of the shoes she will be expected to fill, but it will give her a sense of the attitudes in her division that she'll be inheriting. If the previous leader was well liked, the new leader is going to have to deal with her team's—and perhaps her colleagues'—resentment of the organization itself, which may be directed at her.

Regardless of the specifics surrounding the leader's departure, the organization should make a concerted effort to ensure that the outgoing leader doesn't "poison the well" for the new leader who is about to arrive. In the worst case, the outgoing leader goes to great lengths to solicit the sympathy of others in the organization, especially his reports. In the best case, the outgoing leader coaches his team on how to bring the new leader up to speed. The organization's role in handling this transition is to:

- Intervene early to neutralize any negative broadcasting that might make the new leader's arrival more difficult than it needs to be.

- Work with the outgoing leader to formulate a face-saving rationale for his departure, which helps to eradicate the need for him to spread discontent

- Help the outgoing leader identify those activities that the team can do to ease the new leader's entry. These might include:
  - Preparing summaries of current projects and their progress
  - Updating all reports—P&L, receivables, accounts payable, budget, etc.
  - Preparing individual responsibility reports detailing current project responsibilities, as well as ongoing responsibilities

The recruiting process has excited you about this new leader and excited her about the job. You both made a deliberate decision with full awareness of the challenges you will need to address. The preparations that you make during this post-hire stage should help to mitigate some of these difficulties. By the end of this stage, she should be as mentally and emotionally prepared as possible. With your guidance, she will have built knowledge and subject matter expertise, assessed her developmental needs, and identified the bases of her influence relationships. The next chapter focuses on the unique challenges that the new leader will face during the Entering and Exploring stage—challenges that she may not have anticipated and that you must help her to successfully engage in in order to implement her entry strategy.

Notes

1. G. R. Sullivan and M. V. Harper. *Hope Is Not a Method: What Business Leaders Can Learn from America's Army*. New York: Broadway Books, 1996, p. 78.
2. E. De Lisser. "More Entrepreneurs Take Help of Executive Coaches." *The Wall Street Journal*, 5 September 2000.
3. J. J. Gabarro. *The Dynamics of Taking Charge*. Boston: Harvard Business School Press, 1987, p. 62.

Stage Two: Entering and Exploring

Establishing Connections

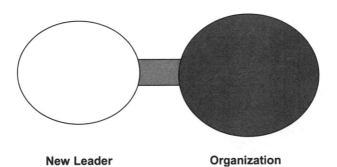

New Leader   **Organization**

During my first week as head of sales for [a global banking concern], I got invited to lunch by one of my new colleagues, Tyler, someone I'd met with several times before. I liked and respected Tyler a lot. At lunch, he told me all about how the place "really works," which seemed strange to me because we'd already had a conversation about this during our interviews together. Tyler went over the history of the business and the department, most of which he'd already mentioned to me, at one time or another.

This time, though, he spent half an hour talking about the relationships among the other people on my sales team and throughout the senior leadership team. I was surprised by some of the stuff he told me. For one thing, my two top performers apparently couldn't stand each other. If at all possible, the best thing to do was to let them work on separate projects, he said. Apparently, the previous boss had taken this approach, and it worked out well because when the two were competitive, they accomplished more.

—Claire

What should Claire have done?

a. Claire had seen this kind of behavior before and knew better than to pay attention to what may be just gossip.

b. Claire considered this conversation as one data point and decided to assess the situation more thoroughly.

c. Claire was grateful to have been forewarned and modified several key plans.

As new leaders formally enter an organization, they need to obtain information from as many sources as possible. Dismissing information as mere gossip without further exploration means neglecting an important data point—not necessarily that the information is correct, but that this is what people *think*. On the other hand, by jumping to action with only the information Tyler provided, Claire would have been acting too quickly on limited information. Before acting, she would want to take into account that Tyler might have his own personal agenda—and she doesn't know enough about Tyler at this time to make that determination. Information is always shaped according to the interpretive lens of the person providing it. Because Claire doesn't know Tyler well enough to define his lens, the best thing Claire could have done would have been to keep Tyler's comments in mind: "Beware of strangers bearing gifts but do not reject them." She could then test the veracity of Tyler's comments by speaking with other people about their view, without actually sharing with them the reasons she was asking the questions. The degree of congruence among these various people would give Claire a sense of what to watch out for.

THE NEW LEADER'S EXPERIENCE

Now that the new leader has started in his new position, the expectations and plans he developed in the previous phase are being tested by the realities of the organization. At this stage, new leaders often feel overwhelmed by the number of things to which they must attend. There are certain emotional experiences in the beginning of a new leader's tenure that are common for both internal and external hires, seasoned veterans and first-time leaders. No matter how much experience one has, no matter how successful the track record, one cannot avoid the unease that accompanies having to do things for the *first* time. These early days will set the tone for all future relationships. Very few actions have been taken at this time. Interpersonal dynamics and human emotion contribute greatly to most of the difficulties the new leader experiences. Entering and Exploring is characterized by the new leader's initial reactions to the unique combination of people and relationships resident within the organization he is entering.

It's crucial that he balance his learning about the organization and its dynamics with the impressions he is making on others. He has to work to understand the new position, new colleagues, and the operating style of the new organization simultaneously. New leaders may know how to acquire new information, but they're often unclear about how to build new relationships, reevaluate prior assumptions, and manage the emotional reactions inherent in a change of this magnitude.

At this point, he is both an observer and the subject of observation. This position is a difficult one to negotiate and often requires anti-instinctual behavior—he will often have to act in a way that differs from his first inclination, which requires acute awareness of natural predispositions and an understanding of how these may be perceived. Everything he does is watched and evaluated. The new leader's team is as unknown to him as he is to them. They will be determining whether his level of competence is up to par, and what kind of leader he will be. They will be assessing him to determine whether or not they want to be led by him, and whether he is a person they want to support. The new leader should choose his actions based on the impact he would like to have, instead of on the degrees of comfort he feels.

The new leader was hired because of certain skills and experiences that will add value to your organization. There is no way that a new leader can predict how his past experience will apply. New leaders are used to being the expert at their previous job and suddenly at the new place, none of what they know or did before seems to be valued or even considered. Instead, when they walk in a new door, it is as if they have gone back to zero and have to prove themselves all over again. Sometimes even if others have a sense of what the new leader can bring to the table, the previous experience may be deemed to be irrelevant in this context and hence undervalued. Organizations tend to take the stance that the new person has to prove her worth, rather than extending her the benefit of the doubt.

During the Entering and Exploring stage, which can take as long as nine months to complete, the organization comes into greater focus. Once this happens, the new manager is usually hit with the reality of the divergence between the organization anticipated during the enthusiasm of the planning stage and the reality encountered on the first day. Many people experience strong feelings of discomfort and disorientation in reaction to the stark contrast between what was expected and what really is. This is compounded by the number of changes. For new executives entering into a new job, in a new organization, within a new industry, there are at least three major changes happening at the same time. Add a potential relocation and the new leader is probably on overload. This jolt of awareness between expectations and reality often comes into full consciousness at around the fourth or fifth week and may be experienced as a bit of an emotional letdown.

Typically, many aspects of the new job are different than expected, including the amount of authority and discretion, the team's capabilities, the operating practices and procedures, the scope of the job, and expectations regarding the role. After the initial flurry of activity has subsided, new leaders have time to reflect on their actual situations. It is our experience that after four to six months the "real" job begins to emerge. As one senior executive explained, "The job I accepted was right, but the job I came to was wrong." Another said, "I came to this division to run a strategic unit, but when I came on board that was a low priority. I was asked to focus on the new acquisitions business." The emotional impact of this can't be overstated—it is depicted as the second, larger emotional dip in Exhibit 5-1.

The process of moving from being a new hire to becoming a successful, reflective, comfortable leader involves two separate paths: intellectual and emotional. They operate very differently. At any point in time the intellectual experience, or cognitive learning about the new company or job, is very different from the emotional experience, or what

Exhibit 5-1. The emotional and intellectual journey: Stage Two.

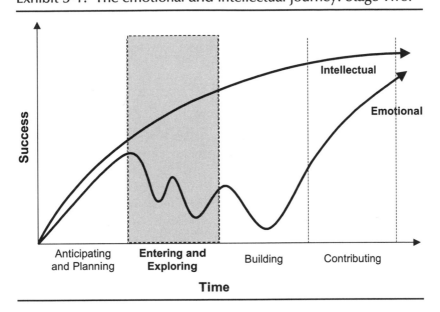

the new leader is actually feeling. Raising these issues and legitimizing the feelings can be a great source of comfort and relief to the new leader.

The new leader should use the emotional dips experienced during this stage as opportunities to reassess commitment to the decision to join the organization. She will most likely be periodically checking her "hedonic abacus"—the internal mechanism that is subconsciously used to calculate whether the pain of a situation is outweighed by the gain. If the discomfort of the current experience outweighs the gain, refer her back to the initial decision-making criteria she used to make her employment choice. She should use this as a baseline and check it against the realities of the job. If she accepted this job because it met a range of needs, then if one or two aspects of the "real" job do not conform to her expectations, the situation can be managed. If she took the job primarily for one reason, for example, because she wanted a particular experience that she is unlikely to get, then it is important that you discuss these unmet expectations with her. If appropriate, encourage her to speak with her boss as soon as possible. Thinking through these and other issues in advance will prepare you to respond to situations in a more deliberate, and therefore more constructive, way. If you share with her the knowledge that what she is experiencing happens to most new hires—that everyone hits these emotional dips—you can provide much-needed confirmation at this time.

THE ORGANIZATION'S EXPERIENCE

The entrance of the new leader brings with it expectations and pressures to fill the organization's requirements. The organization clearly had a need that the new hire seemed to fill. There may have been pressure on you and others to make this hire—perhaps it was a position that had remained unfilled for a long time. Hopes are running high—people want this new person to fill the gap, to be the "silver bullet" that will solve the organization's problems. Yet, the organization as a whole may have an adverse reaction to the new ideas and knowledge that the new leader brings to the table. People are likely to see many of these new ideas as anomalous, no matter how relevant they are to the challenges your organization is facing.

The new leader's team experiences the most disruption during a new leader's entry. During the leaderless time prior to entry, informal leaders can arise from within the ranks of the team, creating a power dynamic that may inhibit assimilation once a new leader arrives. Furthermore, teams often have an expectation that a new leader will immediately provide direction and solutions. Invariably, they are disappointed when he, in spite of his qualifications, may want to pace himself as he becomes familiar himself with the organization.

New leaders in global positions, which require heavy travel, have to balance the perception among the people in the home office and those in the satellite offices. They will have to try to achieve a balance between focusing too much on the global offices at the expense of the home office and remaining at home at the expense of making connections and forming relationships with their global counterparts. You can help them by coaching them through their travel strategies and raising their awareness of the need for balance.

THE RECIPROCAL IMPACT

This stage begins with the first day of work. For the first time, the new leader is operating within the organizational context. It is at this stage that a new leader needs the most support because all the factors involved in becoming established—in a new position, in a new organization, and perhaps, in a new industry—are particularly challenging, given that he does not yet know whom to trust and how to gain access to information.

The organizational support systems, the internal support roles, and the assimilation coach that were selected during the first stage, Anticipation and Planning, will be critical in helping him navigate through Stage Two. This support network provides needed guidance, legitimizes feelings of discomfort, raises awareness to the difficulties of assimilation, and provides a structured approach to solving some of the problems inherent in taking over a new position.

We focus specifically on what you—whether as the HR Touchstone, as another member of senior management, or as the assimilation coach—can do to support the new leader. But part of your role is to create an assimilation-savvy organization. Far too often we hear people discuss the revolving door through which their senior hires go. Rarely do we see evidence of the introspection that should follow. Your role is to hold a mirror to your organization and ensure that an evaluation of the causes of the revolving door is conducted, that those organizational barriers to newcomers are at least acknowledged, and that steps are taken to reduce them. Just as a new leader needs an entry strategy, the hiring manager needs a transition strategy: how he plans to transition the power and control to his new hire, how he plans to support him, and how he will measure his progress.

We are aware that the number of things to think about and actions to take provided in this chapter may add to the leader's feeling of being overwhelmed. We have given you a lot to attend to. While we believe that each of these activities has merit, you should customize your approach to fit the specific needs of the entry process you're currently managing. Exhibit 5-2 depicts the assimilation goals that you and the new leader should focus on together at this stage. The assimilation goals that are the primary focus of Stage Two are shaded in dark gray.

THE ORGANIZATION'S INTERVENTION STRATEGY

During the Entering and Exploring stage, there are seven key interventions that the organization can perform to accelerate the assimilation process:

- Entry management checklist
- Basic orientation information
- Organizational assessment

Exhibit 5-2. Stage Two: Key goals supported.

Goals / Stages	Create Achievement Legacy	Understand Organizational Dynamics	Build Influence	Assume Leadership	Align Systems
Stage IV: Contributing	Follow up on feedback	Formally integrate cultural changes	Create opportunities for organizationwide interaction	Provide developmental opportunities	Formally integrate changes to the system
Stage III Building	Provide feedback mechanisms	Provide coaching	Create opportunities to build networks	Support personnel transitions	Establish parameters for change
Stage II: Entering and Exploring	**Help get industry experience**	**Facilitate cultural audit**	**Facilitate key relationships (act as a translator)**	**Facilitate assessment of team's skills and competencies**	**Act as a sounding board**
Stage I: Anticipating and Planning	Prepare a developmental plan	Advise new leader; provide information about culture	Prepare key stakeholders for new leader's arrival	Prepare team for new leader's arrival	Provide access to systems information

- Cultural audit
- Stakeholder analysis
- Skills and competence assessment
- New leader assimilation meeting

These interventions are discussed in detail below.

INTERVENTION: ENTRY MANAGEMENT CHECKLIST

One way that a leading Fortune 100 uses to keep track of the entry management activities is through the use of an entry management checklist. You will notice that this checklist requires that the new leader meet immediately with his manager or boss to clarify his role and to begin to delineate the nature of their relationship. The focus of the discussion should include how success is to be measured, how decisions are made, how the boss prefers to be communicated with, and his perception of the current hot issues. It should also include team, subordinate, peer, and client discussions. Encourage the new leader to be proactive in shaping all these relationships, but encourage him to be especially attentive to the relationship with his boss. An example of an entry management checklist is illustrated in Exhibit 5-3.

INTERVENTION: BASIC ORIENTATION INFORMATION

In addition to providing support for the new leader in building relationships and assessing the organization, the organization should provide basic "getting started" information that one would find in a more traditional orientation program. Packaging this information in modular, customized, computer-based information kits can be especially valuable and efficient for new hires, ensuring both relevance and ease of access. Organizations can improve productivity and reduce stress for new executives by providing convenient access to comprehensive information about how to get things done at the new company and work location. A portion of the kit might cover companywide information, such as policies, procedures, work processes, and resources. Additional modules can be custom-assembled to suit the new executive's needs with information about his new division, and information about relocation, housing, schools, and

Exhibit 5-3. Entry management checklist.

Goal
- *To establish the new leader in the new position*
- *To clarify the roles and relationships between the new leader and his or her manager(s), peers and colleagues, team and subordinates, and clients*

Process
- *Planning meeting and discussion*
- *Manager/peer/team interviews*
- *Facilitated group meetings/conferences/off-sites/follow-up, sustaining interventions*

Tasks with Manager(s): Clarify and understand role/relationship with manager(s)

Goals
- —What are the performance expectations and deliverables for you and your team? .... ☐
- —How is performance going to be measured/success evaluated? .... ☐

Priorities
- —What are the key business issues that you need to focus on? What are the priorities? .... ☐

Decisions process
- —What is the decision framework? How much operational freedom/autonomy is there? .... ☐
- —What types of decisions require approval, consulting, or advising, and/or are subject to veto? .... ☐
  - ■ People .... ☐
  - ■ Expenses .... ☐
  - ■ Business functions .... ☐
- —Who else is significantly involved in any decision making? On what basis? .... ☐

Communications
- —What is the frequency and type of preferred communications? .... ☐
  - ■ Regular meetings .... ☐
  - ■ Written, v-mail reports .... ☐
  - ■ Event-based communications .... ☐

Current "hot issues"
- —What are the current "hot issues"? What do you need to watch out for? .... ☐
  - ■ Relationships among team members .... ☐
  - ■ Client histories and experiences with the company .... ☐
  - ■ Operating and performance problems .... ☐

Tasks with Team/Subordinates
  Current activities
    —Who are the current members of the team you directly
    supervise? What are their roles, and what are they currently
    working on? .... ☐
    —What are their priorities? How are the priorities being set?
    Are their priorities consistent with your understanding/with
    the direction you've been given? .... ☐
    —Is the work appropriately organized and coordinated within
    the group? Between groups? .... ☐
  Capabilities
    —What is your evaluation/assessment of the quality, con-
    sistency, and timeliness of the work product? .... ☐
    —Do you think the team has the skills and capabilities to
    perform the work that is expected? .... ☐
    —Where are the gaps? Can training improve capabilities? ..... ☐
  Interpersonal style
    —What is your understanding/assessment of the "manage-
    ability" of the team members? .... ☐
    —What is the best way to work with this team and these
    individuals? .... ☐
      ■ Are they independent, or will they easily take
      direction? .... ☐
      ■ Can they be "told" what to do, or do they need to be
      persuaded? .... ☐
      ■ Do they respond well to feedback and coaching? .... ☐
      ■ Are they emotionally well balanced? Are they "high
      maintenance"? .... ☐
Tasks with Peers/Colleagues
    —Who are the other professionals within the company/
    business unit who: .... ☐
      ■ Have influence/impact over the quality of the work
      being done? .... ☐
      ■ Have authority over some aspect of the work product
      (e.g. legal, compliance)? .... ☐
    —What are the working relationships within the peer-
    management team (the other professionals who work for
    the same manager as you)? What issues exist? .... ☐
Tasks with Clients
    —Who are the current clients? Prospects? Targets? .... ☐

Exhibit 5-3. (Continued).

—How well has the group/team been doing at meeting client
expectations? .... ☐
  ■ Are the client expectations consistent with the work
    being done by the team? .... ☐
—What are the client's relationship styles? (e.g., passive—
  demanding; consistent—episodic; polite—contentious/
  difficult, etc. .... ☐

geographic locations he might be scheduled to visit on his initial fact-finding trips (information about the city, restaurants near the office, and so on).[1]

INTERVENTION: ORGANIZATIONAL ASSESSMENT

The entrance of a new leader is a good time for her to take a structured approach to observing and understanding the organization in terms of its component parts and their mutual interdependencies. Analyzing the organization's strategy, structure, people, processes, and rewards/metrics will allow her to:

- Develop and test hypotheses about how the various parts of the organization function.
- Determine possible barriers to her ability to successfully do the job she was hired to do.
- Identify those aspects of the organization that may need to change.

You, as a member of the organization, can collaborate with the new leader in conducting this assessment. You could also utilize the assimilation coach if you feel he has the relevant competencies. An organizational assessment is often a good precursor to the new leader assimilation meeting and provides a springboard for building a common strategic agenda.

INTERVENTION: CULTURAL AUDIT

The new leader is joining multiple teams, each of which will have differing and often conflicting norms around decision making, conflict resolution, participation, and communication. Taking a close look at the way things are done within the organization can help a new leader on multiple levels. The organizational assessment describes the bones of the organization; the cultural audit describes how things flow within the body.

INTERVENTION: STAKEHOLDER ANALYSIS

This is the time to implement the stakeholder analysis that you helped the new leader prepare for during the Anticipating and Planning stage. During that stage, you also helped to pave the way for the new leader by legitimizing the process itself and preparing the stakeholders for the new leader's queries.

J. P. Kotter found that one of the key determinants of success within an organization is the quality of relationships the leader is able to cultivate.[2] In the best of all worlds, the new leader should build relationships with everyone in the organization. Unfortunately, there is not enough time, and it may put the leader at risk of potentially neglecting the most important relationships. During this stage, you can help the new leader by identifying the key internal stakeholders that will have the most impact on his success. A stakeholder is any group or individual who can affect or is affected by the achievement of a business unit's purpose.

INTERVENTION: SKILLS AND COMPETENCE ASSESSMENT

The resources—the skills, competencies, and knowledge—in the existing team should be identified. This will provide a sense of the high performers and identify the most glaring skill gaps. Specifically, it is important to identify who on the team is able and willing to help the new leader achieve his goals. The risks and opportunities should be noted. The emphasis of the assessment should be a future-focused perspective of the team as a whole in the context of the new leader's initial view of what the team must accomplish in order for him to be successful.

INTERVENTION: NEW LEADER ASSIMILATION MEETING

The primary purpose of holding a new leader assimilation meeting is to create an environment in which the new leader and the team members can air their thoughts and begin to build relationships. The process increases the speed of assimilation and maximizes the probability of success in the assignment. It is designed to:

- Clarify working styles, role definition, and expectations.
- Reduce apprehension of what the future holds for both the leader and direct reports.
- Introduce a positive climate of two-way communication.
- Provide a foundation for growth as a high-performing team.

These activities support the new leader's attainment of assimilation.

In the remainder of this chapter we discuss the assimilation goals of Stage Two, as summarized in Exhibit 5-4.

ASSIMILATION GOAL: CREATE AN ACHIEVEMENT LEGACY

SUPPORT/COACHING: SET PRIORITIES

A new leader is joining multiple teams—functional teams, executive teams, cross-functional teams, and project teams—each of which is destabilized by this change. Unforeseeable "extra" demands will take up a lot of time. They will affect how new leaders allocate time, as well as the pace at which they act. These are two major challenges throughout this stage. For those taking on a leadership position for the first time, these challenges might be particularly difficult.

A new leader must set priorities and make decisions about how he spends his time. These decisions should be driven by what is needed in order to accomplish the business and interpersonal agendas. In an attempt to prioritize and determine how to allocate their limited time, most new leaders choose their business agenda over their enabling agenda. During the Entering and Exploring stage it's crucial to find a balance between beginning to develop a business strategy and building a foundation for later action. Leaders who choose their business agenda as their primary focus often cite that decision as their biggest regret when they look back at their first ninety days. They wish they'd taken

Exhibit 5-4. Assimilation goals: Entering and exploring.

Assimilation Goals	Organizational Role
Create an Achievement Legacy	
Set priorities.	Support/Coaching
Focus on "small win" activities.	Support/Coaching
Conduct an organizational assessment.	**Intervention**
Understand Organizational Dynamics	
Be aware of the dynamics of first impressions.	Support/Coaching
Be aware of paradigm conflicts.	Raising Awareness
Be aware of unique cultural cues.	Raising Awareness
Conduct a cultural audit and identify cultural dynamics organizationwide.	**Intervention**
Build Influence	
Utilize power and influence.	Support/Coaching
Establish trust.	Support/Coaching
Build a collaborative relationship with the boss.	Facilitation
Plan for the "dips."	Support/Coaching
Build relationships with peers.	Facilitation
Conduct a stakeholder analysis.	**Intervention**
Assume Leadership	
Act "as if."	Support/Coaching
Help the new leader to clarify roles and expectations within the team.	Facilitation
Manage resistance to change.	Raising Awareness
Assess the team for skills and competencies.	**Intervention**
Help new leaders hire "their own people."	Raising Awareness
Schedule a new leader assimilation meeting.	**Intervention**

more time during this stage to plan and learn about the organization and its people.

One executive we interviewed felt that she was not as successful in executing her strategy as she would have been had she developed more relationships from the start. Recently she reflected on what she might have done differently in order to feel more a part of the organization or to be more effective:

> *I would have spent more time up front, really learning the organization, the business that we are in and spending more*

time with the senior players. I jumped into the work too soon and then I did not have quite the same opportunity. I didn't have the time to travel the organization and really learn what it is that we do. I always thought I'd have time later, but I never did.

If the new leader is not careful, the different demands placed on him throughout this stage can easily become overwhelming. One executive who recently joined a new organization found himself overwhelmed by the various demands people across the organization placed on him:

Here I am, three months into this job, and I haven't been able to spend any real time on a single one of the goals I'm expected to achieve in my first year. I get over thirty phone calls a day from people requesting my assistance or input. It takes me two hours just to answer my e-mail—and I'm not writing lengthy tomes to people. Two or three sentences, that's it. I've been sucked into more meetings than I can count where I walked out wondering why in hell I'd been asked to come. The bottom line is that everybody wants something, and they all want it now.

POTHOLE

One study at a leading brokerage found that people who remained with their previous employers for more than five years had more difficulties with setting priorities than people who remained with their employers less than five years.

One part of a new leader's job that takes up much more time than one might expect is talking to people, explaining new ideas, and helping to ease resistance to proposed changes or even just to the addition of a new person into the organization. This especially holds true in organizations that are unaccustomed to change. Remind the new leader that talking to people is critical to being able to accomplish any "real work," and encourage him to legitimize this action and include it as a priority when he is allocating his time. As one new senior executive explained,

"It was literally 50 percent of my job just to manage all the relationships. That required a lot of talking to this one and talking to that one."

There is a natural tendency at this stage for new leaders to say yes to everyone's demands on their time, borne out of a desire to affiliate and build relationships. If the new leader busies himself with numerous tactical items, there are several implications. One is that at the end of the day, he may have created nothing of value and have had little impact on the organization in any of the areas he had planned. Another downside is that people will come to view him as he behaves in these early days. So, even if someone asks something of him and he replies, "Well, this really isn't part of my job," but complies with the request anyway, that person will observe his actions and will expect that he will continue to behave that way in the future. This will be a difficult reputation to break, and he may have to continue to deliver the same services (that he didn't want to be involved with in the first place) for a long time to come.

The way that one senior executive chose to spend his time when he started as the head of HR and a member of the executive team at a major international bank is a good example of someone whose choices about spending time and priorities were driven by his strategy and were very controversial.

> *I had assumed responsibility for a global HR function at a major international bank. My team was comprised of several hundred people. The function had been without leadership for almost a year, and the people were hungry for direction. It was almost six months before I had any significant contact with the HR community, and over a year before we had an "offsite" meeting. By that time I had built the relationships I needed with the CEO and his executive team to ensure that we would have the necessary support at the top of the house to implement the changes I believed I was hired to make. I believed that any HR initiative I undertook had to be grounded in the needs of the business. Everyone says that, but do people really do it? So I spent those first few months meeting with all the business heads worldwide, and building relationships with them. My "team" wasn't happy. They felt neglected and negated. I heard the rumors that people thought I was a power player, dealing for myself, but I didn't care because I got the mandate I needed and within two years we had transformed the function.*

Faced with a number of decisions at every step of the journey, reactions to challenging situations can cloud a new leader's judgment. These decisions have a direct impact on the performance of the teams he belongs to and leads. Every choice must be carefully considered. You can help the new leader set priorities by encouraging him to ask himself:

- What are my choices?

- What are the advantages and disadvantages of choosing one direction over another?

- Who will be satisfied by these choices? Are these the right people to satisfy at this point in time?

- Why do I want to make this decision? Am I being influenced by a negative emotion like apprehension or uncertainty, or is there a clear business reason to move in this direction?

SUPPORT/COACHING: FOCUS ON "SMALL WIN" ACTIVITIES

It's common for people at the beginning of a new job to experience an overpowering impulse to *act*. It often doesn't matter *what* they do, only that they do *something* in order to feel active and thus relieve their frustration and feelings of helplessness. However, this is one of the polarities experienced during assimilation that is difficult to manage. On one hand, if a new leader acts before he is ready, he risks losing credibility because he has not established organizational readiness and there is a good chance that he will make mistakes. On the other hand, if he waits too long, people may question his effectiveness as a leader. How can a new leader take action that will build credibility? The answer lies in focusing on small wins. We view small wins in a strategic context, as small but meaningful aspects of a longer-term plan. The concept of small wins has been in the change lexicon for a long time, usually in terms of breaking a project or a problem into its component parts and addressing it in manageable pieces.

The benefits of focusing on small wins are that it allows the new leader to:

- *Experiment with the system.* "Uncover resources, information, allies, and sources of resistance."[3]

- *Test the boundaries of an organization's capacity for change.* Focus on being a good learner, and not trying to make the organization fit preexisting paradigms. Test things out, try to learn from them, and modify the approach in the future.

- *Reduce the anxiety of those with whom there is a lot of interaction.* Small changes are not reacted to with the same intensity as are larger ones. A good example is the proverbial boiled frog—you can boil a frog without any resistance if the heat is turned up very gradually.

One small but highly influential way to act is through the use of pilot tests or lead initiatives. The point of this phased implementation is to encourage new leaders not to launch large-scale changes without first testing how these may be received by the organization. For example, if a new head of manufacturing wants to reorganize the department by instituting self-managed work teams, he should first create a model in one location or region that allows him to anticipate barriers and make modifications prior to implementing the changes on a companywide basis. Another example would be a new sales executive who wants to put in new measures for assessing performance. But since measures often have unintended consequences—for example, increased sales calls that have no real potential for increasing organizational profitability— she may want to first pilot test the program in one or two small territories.

Using pilots as a first step allows new leaders time to test assumptions and to modify their actions according to the feedback they receive. It's important to encourage the new leader not to launch large-scale changes without testing organizational receptivity. Failing to test receptivity and capacity for change can seriously undermine a new leader's credibility and likelihood of success. The more drastic the proposed change is, the greater the anxiety of people in the organization will be. Without taking steps to gauge the likelihood of this reaction, a new leader cannot prepare to neutralize it in advance or respond to it properly. When this happens, new leaders can appear rash and out of touch with what others in the organization think and feel. On the other hand, a phased implementation provides others in the organization with evidence of success that relates to *their* culture and issues. This creates a platform for the new leader to make more comprehensive changes later.

Operating in this way allows a new leader to diagnose the organization, to *begin* to build credibility, test assumptions, and, most important, visibly take action. You should help the new leader tailor his plans to the culture of the organization. For example, you should inform the new leader of the organization's appetite for risk so that he can take it into account in his planning.

INTERVENTION: CONDUCT AN ORGANIZATIONAL ASSESSMENT

There are many models and frameworks that can be used to analyze an organization's component parts and their mutual interdependencies. Regardless of which one is used, you are going to want to help the new leader take a structured approach to observing and understanding your organization. This will help her develop and test hypotheses about how the various parts of the organization function, determine the possible impact on her ability to successfully do the job she was hired to do, and identify those aspects of the organization that may need to change. We propose examining the organization in terms of the points outlined in Jay Galbraith's star model, as shown in Exhibit 5-5.

You can use the following questions, related to each of the five points on the star in Exhibit 5-5, to conduct your own organizational assessment.

Exhibit 5-5. Conducting an organizational assessment.

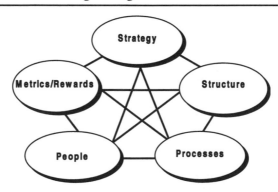

Jay Galbraith, *Designing Organizations*. Copyright ©1995 Jay R. Galbraith. Reprinted by permission of Jossey-Bass, Inc., a subsidiary of John Wiley & Sons, Inc.

STRATEGY

- What is our business mission?

- What are we becoming as a company—can we describe a "from" and a "to"?

- Do we have a business mission that is sufficiently distinguished from the missions of other companies in our industry?

- How have competitors tried to differentiate themselves in our industry?

- How could we increase the differentiation in some of these dimensions?

- Could we offer customers something closer to a total solution to their needs by expanding our definition of product scope?

- Could we increase our share of wallet as well as our share of market by expanding our scope?

- Would a different definition of scope allow us to capture more of the life cycle profits associated with our product or service?

STRUCTURE

- How is your organization currently structured? What are the strengths and weaknesses?

- What problems do you encounter in the current organizational structure?

- What are the key interfaces in the current structure, and how does work flow across them?

- In an ideal world, how would work flow through the organization?

- Is there work that you would locate out of this unit or share with other divisions?

- Are there any parameters or "givens" to which your structure must conform?

METRICS/REWARDS

- How do reward structures, compensation, and/or performance management need to be adjusted?

- Do employees have the technology support they need to do their jobs? If not, what is needed?

PROCESSES

- What are the key business processes of this division? How have they changed recently? Which activities do you think belong together?

- What are some of the important decisions that you make? Do you feel your decision-making authority is appropriate to your level of responsibility? If not, what changes would you want to see?

- What are the work processes or decisions that need to be integrated across the different organizational units?

- Have you thought of any processes that would move resources closer to your customers?

PEOPLE

- Tell me about the work of people in this unit. What are their tasks? What skills do they require? What is a typical workday like for them?

- What do you see as the key decision-making roles in your organization?

- Tell me about your direct reports. How are they performing versus your strategy?

- What key decisions should involve more than one unit?

- How are these interfaces currently structured? What works well? What doesn't work well?

- What do you see as the priorities for training and development?[4]

Because you know the organization, help the new leader compare the current state to the end-state goals she has visualized for each milestone:

- What activities will need to be completed in order to make this scenario a reality?

- Whom will you have to work with to accomplish each of these tasks?

- What will their roles be, and what will you expect from them?

ASSIMILATION GOAL: UNDERSTAND ORGANIZATIONAL DYNAMICS

In a new, unfamiliar environment, new leaders find it difficult to know when they're overreacting to dissonant information, circumstances, or even behavior. The problem is that they haven't been in the organization long enough to know just how serious these things are in the broader scheme. For example, what does a new leader assume when her boss doesn't say hello in the hallway when they pass each other in the morning? Does it mean that the boss is unhappy with her? Or does he think he's too important to waste time in idle chat? Or is it just that the culture doesn't value non-work-related affiliation? Listening to and understanding emotional reactions and using them as tools for understanding the environment is central to the process of adapting to situations where radically different behavioral assumptions exist.

SUPPORT/COACHING: BE AWARE OF THE DYNAMICS OF FIRST IMPRESSIONS

No matter how successful a new leader's track record, she cannot avoid the discomfort created by the series of firsts in this stage. Human beings are rarely so naïve as to be unaware of the fact that others are observing them very closely. Managing the information one gives to others is a strategic choice, one referred to as "impression management" by Erving Goffman. To paraphrase, people are aware that others are observing them and so they provide the kind of information that will create the impression they think it would be profitable to evoke.[5] The new leader needs to understand that she is not the only one managing impressions. Others are just as conscious of managing the new leader's impressions of them as the new leader is of managing their impressions of her.

A recent article in *Fast Company* about an account executive, Molly Buchholtz—two weeks into a new job in an advertising firm—explains just how stressful firsts and first impression management can be:

> *Though she believes she made the right decision [about disagreeing with her colleague], Buchholtz frets over the fallout: Did she come off as pushy? Did she break an unwritten rule? Did she insult someone whose support she'll need down the road? Buchholtz was a star performer at her previous gig but she feels tentative at her new one. She doesn't yet speak their language. Using it has been exhausting. "I spend a lot of time worrying about how I act and react in different situations," she says. "I feel like I'm under a microscope."[6]*

POTHOLE: THINKING THAT ASKING TOO MANY QUESTIONS IS A SIGN OF STUPIDITY

Many people assume that if they ask too many questions, others will think that they lack intelligence. In fact, those who ask questions usually appear *intelligent* to the people they're asking for information. In a classic study published in the *Journal of Personality and Social Psychology*, Lee Ross, Teresa Amabile, and Julia Steinmetz (1977) found that people observing study participants in a mock quiz show perceived those who were asking the questions as smarter than those who were responding. The assumption seems to be that if you *ask* the question, you are aware that there is an answer, regardless of whether the person asked can provide it.

RAISING AWARENESS: BE AWARE OF PARADIGM CONFLICTS

To begin providing a framework from which new leaders can interpret new information, values, and ways of operating, organizations need to help them become aware of the difficulties that often arise due to the conflict between old and new paradigms. In addition to the discomfort created from feeling as though they're living under a microscope—the result of the weight of firsts—new leaders also carry the weight of previous paradigms. Edgar Schein, of MIT's Sloan School of Management, argues that to make this change "one must undergo a learning process that is functionally equivalent to what the POWs underwent in the communist prison camps."[7] Entering a new situation with few familiar prompts or trusted relationships intact forces new leaders to question their basic assumptions. This is in itself anxiety provoking and might cause them to mistrust themselves. A natural reaction is to dismiss new views as irrelevant or walk away from the situation.

Every discipline, society, or organization has a shared body of knowledge and set of assumptions that help them determine what data are relevant and how to organize these data. But the framework used to judge these data doesn't allow for critical judgments of the framework itself. Those pieces of data that do not fit the values or assumptions inherent in this framework are considered anomalous and discounted.

In other words, while paradigms perform a useful function for groups, by organizing thought and thus facilitating communication, they also screen out disconfirming information, or force it into sometimes artificial or inappropriate constructs. As a new leader develops a business strategy, or achievement legacy, he should be aware that he may be relying on old paradigms to define and interpret the reality of a new situation. The story from Greek mythology of the "Procrustian bed" illustrates this problem well. The Procrustian bed was a fixed size. Those who slept in it were "force-fit" to the bed's dimensions—if they were taller than the bed was long, their legs were cut off, and if they were shorter, their bodies were stretched to fit the bed's length.

The new leader is in a similarly difficult position—he's being asked simultaneously to learn and also, by virtue of the new knowledge and experience he brings, to *change* the dimensions of the organization's paradigms. For security, new leaders are likely to anchor new knowledge in the information they already have. But if a new leader forces his observations to conform to a frame of reference that doesn't describe the reality of your organization, he runs the risk of distorting valuable intelligence information (cutting it off), or making more of it than he should (stretching it). Overemphasizing similarities between old and new paradigms only blinds a new leader to real differences of which he needs to be aware.

For these reasons, it's especially important to help the leader recognize that two, potentially conflicting, frames of reference are in place as she begins to evaluate new information. It's valid for her to recognize the value of the cumulative knowledge and experience gained over her career to this point. At the same time, it's critical that she be reminded that her ideas about what works and what doesn't are based on her previous organization and may or may not hold true in your organization. In order to assimilate successfully, new leaders must exist in a state of readiness to reframe assumptions, learn new concepts, and develop new attitudes and behaviors. It is a very different frame of mind from being prepared for adaptive learning, which only requires new ways to apply old concepts or skills.

A new leader will be receiving data from multiple sources and is required to both observe and absorb what is happening around her. Data are available everywhere, from everyone and everything a new leader encounters, *including herself.* Help her understand that her emotions are good sources of data for generating hypotheses, although not good sources for decision making. When leaders pay attention to their own emotions they gain a deeper insight into a major motivation force and source of meaning. They need to pay attention to their thoughts ("I am feeling uncomfortable here—let me try to understand why"). At the same time, coach the new leader to consciously make efforts to check her assumptions and frames of reference before making conclusions based on the data she receives.

Data is not neutral. People selectively attend to data, add their own meanings, make assumptions, and draw conclusions. They then act on information that may not be a true reflection of reality. In new situations, it is best to base actions on observable data—those things that can be verified. For example, react to the specific behavior—"John didn't return my call" as opposed to "John doesn't want me here or is withholding information."

One senior executive did not step back to frame his interpretations of his team's behavior:

> I was hired to lead a team of very ambitious professionals. They were all in their mid-to-late thirties, all of them real "hotshots" in the company—and, really, in their field, as well. They worked hard, and they worked long hours—at least sixty-five to seventy hours a week, usually more. That's just the way it was. And I was comfortable with that; it's the way I always worked, and frankly I was probably hired because I understood the way these people think and respected the choices they'd made about how they wanted to balance, or not balance, work with the other things in their lives. My boss sort of casually recommended that I start looking for ways to get people to take some time away; he was afraid of burning people out. I understood them better than my boss, I thought, and they understood me. My boss just didn't fit in with that kind of extreme work ethic—I was new, and I fit in more than he did! I wasn't going to start treating them like children, insisting that they all go home at seven o'clock, take all of their vacation, and find nice people to date. If they didn't want that, it was up to them. As a result, we all got along great. My first two quarters there were outstanding—we hit and went beyond every target, and I give them the credit for that. People were getting burned out, though. Toward the end of the third quarter, I lost

a couple of top performers. I got called on the carpet, big time.
Looking back, I realize that they were looking to me to set the
limits, and I didn't do it because I was too busy relishing the
fact that this was a team of people "like me."

One aspect of taking a deliberate approach to managing impressions should be to consider all situations and changes, big or small, from various points of view. In order to move from individual perception to an understanding of the larger reality, it's helpful to take account of each of the following perspectives:

Internal (One's own reality—how does this affect me?)

Empathetic (As seen from the other person's perspective—how does the other person see it?)

Inside Observer (Someone within the organization who is not directly connected to the situation—what is the impact on the organization?)

Outside Observer (An outsider—how would this look to someone outside the company?)

RAISING AWARENESS: BE AWARE OF UNIQUE CULTURAL CUES

Erving Goffman talks about "culture pattern slips" as the special problems of intelligence agents. No one notices unique or idiosyncratic cultural behaviors until someone—like an intelligence agent—is trying to infiltrate the group by passing as a member. Then ways of doing things that had always been taken for granted stand out by virtue of the presence of someone who is inadvertently doing things differently, as when milk is put in a cup before the tea, or pie eaten from the apex not the side, or using your left hand.[8] When a new leader enters an organization, it will be with the frame of reference that he built up at his last place of employment. There, he knew what worked, and what didn't. He knew the language and the "work-arounds." He knew whom to call to get things done. As he enters an entirely new environment he will inevitably, unconsciously, do the same things that he has always done. Doing the very same things that were his ticket to success in his last job, he will rub people the wrong way. It takes time to learn "the way things are done around here."

This is a time when you can provide valuable information about the culture and political lay of the land. Moving into a new organization requires one to reframe assumptions, learn new concepts, and develop new attitudes and behaviors. People aren't really conscious of the informal rules that guide their behavior in an organization until somebody breaks one. You can support the new leader as he inevitably falls into cultural potholes and can coach him to learn from the experience. You can also alert him to the emotional reactions people have when he makes one of these missteps and let him know that however silly they might seem, traditions and cultural norms have significance for others.

Marion, who was hired as the head of operations for a product line in a financial services firm, tells a story about how asking questions and clarifying assumptions can avoid unnecessary misunderstandings and conflict:

> *Part of what I was asked to do was to cut costs. The CEO wanted me to reduce expenses for my office by 15 percent. This wasn't a short-term goal by any means, but I wanted to start getting a bead on where costs were higher than they should be. During my first week, I discovered that our clerical staff was being paid a huge amount of overtime. Some people were putting in over twenty hours in overtime per week. There weren't any major projects going on that would have required so much overtime. I thought something needed to be done, and quickly—this was adding up to tens of thousands of dollars per month, not so much that trimming it could totally solve my cost problem, but not a drop in the bucket, either. So I formally initiated a review of overtime for the past six months. I wanted the supervisors to account for why the overtime had to happen, and I started a new policy of requiring supervisors' bosses to sign off on employee overtime. This was just to get me the information I needed to determine where to make cuts.*
>
> *Well, I didn't count on getting the reaction I got. Nobody likes extra paperwork, but there were some very angry people all the way down the line. The supervisors felt completely undermined, because they had always been able to use their discretion when approving overtime, for the reason that they were closest to the action and knew what was needed. Their bosses*

already reviewed the overtime numbers every month and flagged anything that seemed strange. As it turns out, there were problems because the previous head of operations had insisted on a divisionwide shift to a new computer system—it was better, but there were problems importing old data into the new system, and it was taking a lot of extra time to work out these kinks.

Obviously, I had to tone down my approach. But I'd already wasted some credibility that was hard to get back. It just didn't occur to me that the supervisors would have been trusted with this vetting responsibility—they weren't at my last job. But here, people at that level were much more competent and had been promoted based on their broader management potential. There was a real investment in making careers for people from the bottom up that was a strong part of the culture. And even though I might have been justified in gathering the information I needed, I sure didn't go about it the right way. It didn't occur to me to look for answers in a different way, and I lost the trust of the supervisors for a long time.

As Marion's story illustrates, before discounting any new information or operating norm that seems illogical or counterproductive, the new leader should ask questions of his team, peers, boss, and others. He may ultimately determine that some things need to change. Encourage him to avoid making that judgment based *solely* on his past experience. The following is an example of a cultural norm about giving feedback in private, after a meeting is adjourned, as opposed to having a critical dialogue during a meeting. The story is told by an employee of a large entertainment conglomerate who found herself labeled "difficult" because she engaged in critical dialogue—which was the very behavioral style that made her successful in her previous job.

People were always looking for feedback, and part of it is an incredible need for consensus, and an incredible need not to be wrong and a wanting to be liked on top of making a difficult decision. The fact that people were always looking for feedback was interesting because I am of a mind-set that everyone goes through continuous learning. However, here it was taken to a whole new level—people would analyze every piece of every detail of everything, but only in private. For example, we were having a meeting and I was expected to present something or just give a dialogue about something. Say if someone presented in the meeting then literally ten minutes after the meeting ended people would call and say, "How did I do? Do you have any feedback for me? Should I have done this? How was it received, etc., etc." or "I got the impression that you were disagreeing with what so-and-so was saying and I didn't want to confront you in the meeting, so can we get together at lunch tomorrow and talk about it?"

I think that having critical dialogue is exciting, energizing, and expected. Here, however, it is seen as being confrontational in many cases. Or you are viewed as difficult. I think if you asked people to describe me they would have probably put me in that category. Which is interesting when you think of what makes you so successful at one organization and it actually makes you unsuccessful at another organization. I was not rewarded for being a critical thinker and adding value and making decisions because none of those behaviors were considered appropriate for the role I was in there. I won't say it wasn't a painful year of my life. I always felt I knew my strengths and weaknesses. But working there for a year made me question my confidence.

Intervention: Conduct a Cultural Audit and Identify Cultural Dynamics Organizationwide

Organizational dynamics are the key to how things really work within the organization. Observing and understanding them will provide the basis for building influence. Misunderstandings at this level are a primary cause for assimilation derailment. The HR Touchstone, mentor, and/or assimilation coach can support a new leader by sensitizing her to these dynamics and by teaching her how to observe, diagnose, and intervene appropriately. Most confusing to a new hire is the reality that the various teams they join may have differing and often conflicting norms around decision making, conflict resolution, participation, and communication. Taking a close look at the way that things are done within the organization can help her on multiple levels. These detailed observations will allow her to understand the challenges she faces. Each group—the executive team, peer groups, and the team—will have to be assessed. Some or all of the following questions can be used in the assessment:

1. *Identify how decisions are made:*
   - How are decisions made (minority, majority, or consensus)?
   - Are the resources of all team members shared and used?
   - Does anyone make a decision and carry it out without checking with the other group members?
   - Are decisions clearly stated and agreed upon?
   - Does the team test for agreement?
   - Who is responsible for which decisions?

2. *Identify communication patterns:*
   - Do members listen to each other?
   - Are members getting their ideas across?
   - Who talks to whom? How often? For how long?
   - Who talks after whom?
   - Who interrupts whom?
   - What styles of communication (e.g., hostile, probing, and friendly) do group members exhibit?

3. *Identify levels of trust and risk taking:*
   - Do members seem willing to propose ideas even if they seem foolish or extreme?
   - How are new ideas responded to?
   - Do other members build on new ideas?
   - Do members feel free to express their feelings?
   - Are there hidden agendas?
   - Do people ask how others feel about matters under discussion?
   - Are group members free to question ideas/comments by the group leader?
   - Does the atmosphere seem informal, comfortable, and relaxed?

4. *Identify how conflict is handled:*
   - Is difference of opinion encouraged?
   - Are disagreements suppressed or overridden by premature group actions?
   - Is conflict dealt with openly; are disagreements surfaced?

- Do disagreeing members express hostility or try to dominate the group?
- When there are basic disagreements that cannot be resolved, do these tend to block the group from moving forward?

5. *Identify participation patterns:*
   - Who initiates discussion?
   - Are there withdrawers or monopolizers? Who are they?
   - Are leadership roles rotated among the group members as appropriate for the topic under discussion?
   - Does someone dominate the group?
   - Are there power struggles as the group operates?
   - Do members seem involved and interested?
   - Is there a great deal of participation in discussion?
   - Do some members seem to be "outside" the group?
   - Are there power differentials in the group?
   - The group makes full use of its resources.

New leaders should watch for the following warning signs that indicate a lack of team cohesion:

- Dismissive attitudes
- Inflexibility about one's own ideas
- Lack of interest in others' ideas
- Unwillingness to speak up
- Interjecting personal or extraneous issues into the discussion

Once this assessment is completed, meet with the new leader to determine specific actions he can take to shape the behaviors of his own team and manage the ones in which he is a participant.

ASSIMILATION GOAL: BUILD INFLUENCE

The new leader has a number of stakeholders outside his immediate team. In the previous stage, you have encouraged the new leader to engage in the process of identifying who he is and what his needs will be. It is impossible to distinguish the formation of relationships from the amassing of organizational influence. As a result of building relationships with the key stakeholders, the new leader will create opportunities to increase his credibility, build his power base, and lead to additional opportunities for him to demonstrate impact and utility to stakeholders. If he does not focus on building relationships, he may not have the support he needs to develop and implement his Achievement Legacy.

SUPPORT/COACHING: UTILIZE POWER AND INFLUENCE

In order to begin having an impact, and to set the stage for future success, the new leader should understand the dynamics of how power and influence build on each other. *Power* and *influence* have variable definitions, depending on the context in which they are applied. Power is a latent resource, like money in the bank. Money is nothing more or less than green paper until the moment you spend it. Power provides you with the potential to impact the actions of others. Power must be unleashed by other processes, and the use of power is influence. It involves using interpersonal and social skills to get another person or group to accept ideas and plans. *When* and *how* new leaders choose to use power determines how much influence they will have. Increased awareness of levers of power and their ability to strategically apply these levers to create influence opportunities allows one to *intervene* purposely, thereby increasing one's credibility and impact as a professional. Increased credibility and a record of successful impact leads to increased power and influence. It is a virtuous circle, as illustrated in Exhibit 5-6.

If actions are managed properly, this process is, in effect, an upward spiral of expanding influence—influence that can be leveraged on behalf of the new leader, his team, and in support of changes for the betterment of the entire organization.

Upon entry, a senior player has some sources of power, namely expert and positional power. He will have positional power simply by virtue of the position he's in—but even this cannot be acted upon until competence has been demonstrated, and until trust and credibility have been established. At this stage, you can work with the new executive to help him assess the power he has, and to determine how he can develop and leverage it to build his influence and credibility. As Exhibit 5-7 shows, any leader has multiple sources from which he can develop bases of power.

Exhibit 5-6. The virtuous circle of organizational influence.

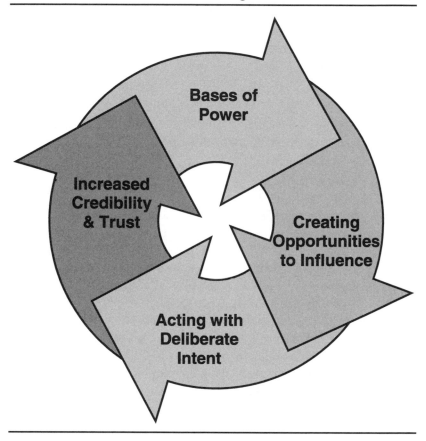

Influence can be built informally through affiliation, as illustrated by the following example:

> *The other night as I was leaving a late meeting, I spotted George, a colleague of mine from the Technology Corporation where I now work, putting on his jacket to walk outside. I called out to him to ask him if he was walking to Grand Central Station (I knew that he took the train home from there and so knew that the answer would be yes) and asked if I could walk with him. The truth is that after a long day, the last thing I wanted to do was make small talk with someone I didn't*

Exhibit 5-7. Sources of power.[9]

	Power	Description
1.	Expert Knowledge	Your specialized expertise gained through training or experience; the fact that you know more than someone else about a particular topic
2.	Information	Your ability to gather and share information you know will be relevant to others; "staying ahead of the game" by finding out what is going on in other areas
3.	Tradition	Your knowledge of the company and the company's traditions; knowing how "things usually work around here"
4.	Leadership	Your ability to charm, inspire, and persuade others through the force of your personality
5.	Reputation	Your reputation for past work and accomplishments
6.	Professional Credibility	Your standing in the profession including credentials, recognition by professional associations, talks you've given, or articles you've written
7.	Political Access	Your informal networks and relationships within the company; the people you know and can call upon
8.	Staff/Team Support	The capability, credibility, and success of the staff that report to you
9.	Consequence	Your ability to reward and punish and create consequences for others; your ability and willingness to set and enforce standards
10.	Position	Your control over valuable resources (budget, time, staff, technology, etc.) as a result of your position in the organization

know. Although George was a nice enough guy, I just really didn't want to bother.

Why did I ask him to walk to Grand Central then? Because I knew that it was a pivotal moment. I will need to work pretty closely with George in order to be successful and so I thought this was a good opportunity to get to know him in an informal way. Informal networking, if done properly, can be so time-consuming. If I really wanted to be successful I would *be out to dinner and drinks every night, constantly schmoozing and creating relationships. I'm not that corporate-savvy and I don't want to eat that much so I thought a nice walk to Grand Central was at least a good start.*

SUPPORT/COACHING: ESTABLISH TRUST

Trust forms the foundation upon which all new leaders build. Organizations depend on trust to function—their internal interdependencies are strong and are built on this "self-evident" truth. Trust is built over time and can't be willed. When organizations were more hierarchical the hierarchies provided a clearly defined structure—the boss is the most important person to get along with and the highly structured environment clearly dictates what has to be done and with whom. Today, however, much more of the work in organizations relies on relationships. Therefore, trust has become the glue that holds decentralized, often fragmented, organizations together.

Clients often ask us to conduct trust-building sessions. As in everything we discuss, the right building blocks must be in place early on, but it often takes years until trust is fully developed. It is easy to destroy trust by not speaking honestly, or by overpromising. The aftertaste of a perceived betrayal lasts a long time. Every action a new leader takes will be scrutinized and judged. One new executive explained how building trust is a delicate and deliberate act:

> *I'm new, and my colleague doesn't know me, so if I start stomping around in his vineyard, he's never going to trust me. I give him input on the things he's asked me about, and I've given him a lot of good ideas that he's implemented. This is the only way I'm going to get the guy's trust and be able to have some impact. If he can see that I'm competent and that I know a lot and am here to help him, not hurt him, I think he'll eventually open up to some feedback about the service standards.*

Trust is not a unitary concept. In *Trust and Betrayal in the Workplace*, D. S. and M. L. Reina describe three types of trust—contractual, communication, and competence—that the new leader must simultaneously understand and develop in order to be fully effective.[10]

Contractual Trust: *Will You Do What You Say You Will Do?*

Contractual trust is about managing expectations, delegating appropriately, and keeping agreements. The key to contractual trust is being clear with others about what is expected of them. This can be done face-to-face on a daily basis and in a public way at an assimilation offsite. It is critical that if a stake is put in the ground and specific statements are made about what will be accomplished, these things actually get accomplished. Therefore, it is better to underpromise and overdeliver than overpromise and underdeliver. The tendency when someone is new and anxious to please is to do the latter.

Communication Trust: *Do You Say What You Mean?*

Communication trust is the willingness to share information, tell the truth, admit mistakes, maintain confidentiality, and give and receive constructive feedback and speak with good purpose. This is about authenticity and reliability. These determinations are often made early on and form impressions that are difficult to overcome.

Competence Trust: *Are You Capable Enough to Do What You Are Expected to Do?*

Competence trust refers to the ability to do what is needed and to have high internal standards. Given that the organization tends to view a new person as someone who has yet to prove himself, and given that in the beginning of a new position, work standards have not yet been shared and calibrated, a new leader will be under a great deal of pressure to "perform." He has to prove his competence, even if he has proven it ten times over in his previous jobs. In a new context, everybody goes back to zero.

FACILITATION: BUILD A COLLABORATIVE RELATIONSHIP WITH THE BOSS

Perhaps the most important stakeholder is the new leader's manager, because in order to assimilate effectively, new leaders need the support of their bosses. Some executives, even those who are proactive in every other aspect of work life, are more reactive in shaping the relationship with their boss. They assume that given his position, the boss should take the lead. This assumption has derailed many potentially good relationships. In the beginning of any working relationship, and the boss-subordinate relationship is no exception, before people know each other, each is dependent on the other to externalize views on decision making, expectations, and values to build mutual understanding. The new leader should be encouraged to initiate communication whenever possible. If she fails to involve her boss, she may be inadvertently sending the message that she doesn't respect his input, and the boss, observing that the new leader thinks she can go it alone, may question her judgment.

One aspect of business that hasn't changed is that the boss is still a "hub" in a wheel of influence in an organization. Although in-person meetings are best because they afford an opportunity to read nonverbal signals that e-mails or the telephone lack, in today's environment, this isn't always possible. Even if the communication is an e-mail, the contact gives the boss a chance to correct and advise on potentially damaging missteps, and it also builds his trust and confidence in the new leader's abilities.

Although communicating frequently and deliberately may be uncomfortable at first, it is often the fastest way of finding commonalities and, perhaps more important, differences that will have to be worked through.[11] If you see this dynamic is not taking place in the relationship between the new leader and the boss, try to determine the reason they may not have the degree of contact they should. Some of the possible reasons are listed below:

- The boss has many other priorities and has breathed a sigh of relief now that the new leader is on board.
- The boss is not outgoing and feels uncomfortable reaching out.
- The boss is giving the new leader his space to find his own way.
- The boss just hasn't thought about it.

For those who truly have nothing in common with their boss, it may be difficult to build trust. However, there must be some level of congruence in styles and approaches because the new leader accepted the position. You can begin by looking for similarities and common interests—personal and professional—which can serve as a basis from which to negotiate differences. This is the time for the new leader to begin to build bridges where there are gaps in fit and to leverage the areas where she and her boss converge. A good fit in certain areas, such as style, will make the bridge building easier. New leaders who have been hired to complement their bosses—which is a plus from an organizational view—will need extra help with the negotiation and effort required to manage the differences.

A common example of this concept of complementary fit is the relationship between a CEO and a COO. In general, a CEO is a strategic thinker, while a typical COO should have a more detailed, operational focus. They will often want to approach things differently because they don't see things the same way. Yet this is a clear example where the whole is more powerful than the individual parts. It is important to surface areas of complementarity and conflict to be better positioned to manage it constructively. Don't wait until there are problems to consider the importance of this relationship and therefore the relative attention you and the new leader should pay to it. If you wait it might be too late to make repairs.

There are also common circumstances in which conflict is most likely to occur. These circumstances will require more facilitation. Such circumstances include, but are not limited to, competition between the new leader and his boss, differing expectations about degree of autonomy, or having two bosses. You can help the new leader build a collaborative relationship with the boss by acting as a translator between the two of them.

Competition between the New Leader and His Manager

Managers want a new leader to be good, but they don't want to be upstaged by him. There are things the new leader can do to make linkages with and demonstrate respect for his boss. The boss should be engaged differentially, depending on his level of knowledge and interest in the new leader's job. The new leader can try to involve him in things—ask his opinions on matters, even if he thinks he is clear about what he has to do. This will engage the boss and will also help to surface the differences in assumptions and frameworks. Remind the new leader that part of his job is to make his boss look good, just like part of your job is to make the new leader look good. Encourage the new leader to share credit with his boss whenever possible. For your part, facilitating the understanding between the new leader and his manager and intervening if necessary is critical.

You can support the new leader in assessing the appropriate nature and frequency of contact between himself and his manager. You want to help him strike the balance between going overboard in an attempt to demonstrate that he has command over the job and leaving the boss wondering what he is doing. This is particularly important during this stage because the new leader is an unknown quantity without a track record to fall back on.

In cases where the new leader is filling the boss's previous position and he is now taking over "her people," or even if it just lies within the boss's area of functional expertise, it is more than likely that the boss "knows too much." She will tend to want to be more involved in the new leader's job than necessary. Along with involvement come opinions and, at times, interference. This could create barriers to the assimilation and to the ability of both the boss and the new leader to transition and assimilate into their respective new roles. What can you do? Encourage the new leader to proactively provide his boss with all the details and logic behind any decisions and recommendations.

On the flip side, the new leader's boss may be managing from the "30,000 feet" perspective, with little knowledge or interest in the nuances of her direct reports' position; or she may be managing virtually from a remote city or country. They may have very little face-to-face time at all. Because you know the new leader and his boss, you can help provide the linkage to understanding. For example, if you know that the boss is not interested in the details and will get bored and irritated with overcommunication, encourage the new leader to communicate only the "big picture" and key points, providing backup only when requested.

Differing Expectations about Degree of Autonomy

At this early stage, there is a danger for miscommunication and misunderstanding between the new leader and his boss because they haven't worked with each other long enough to have established trust or truly hammered out a common management philosophy. Therefore, the beginning of the working relationship between the new leader and boss will often be characterized by high control and frequent contact. This may be a difficult adjustment for a new leader who has just come from a job in which these relationships were already well established, and he didn't have to give his boss a chance to vet every decision he made.

Encourage the new leader to refrain from passing judgment about the boss and the nature of their relationship based on these initial interactions. As the new leader becomes more assimilated into the organization and as the trust grows, the level of control should shift. As this happens, the new leader's manager should become more comfortable transitioning power and authority to him. If tight control and an incompatible management style continue after they have had an opportunity to establish trust in each other, you should begin to think strategically about how you can help them to work together. Perhaps the boss needs to examine his assumptions and revisit his own transition plan.

Having Two Bosses

Given the large number of mergers and acquisitions in today's economy as well as the prevalence of matrix reporting structures, it is not uncommon for an executive to enter into a situation in which she has to report to two bosses. This is particularly challenging for a new leader, who will have to learn two different people's management styles and how to reconcile them without having the guidance of trusted associates to turn to. An assimilation coach shared her observations:

> *I've seen some great practices in handling the assimilation of leaders after a merger or acquisition. In one recent example, the decision was to let the acquired company keep its name and, as a result, the executives from that company maintained their identity. Within twelve hours of the announcement, most senior executives in the acquiring organization reached out to their counterparts in the business being acquired. They set up a copresentation for a town hall meeting. They shared the stage. The truth is that ultimately, they won't both be there, but whoever will be there needs to have been visible and in that role at this time. Everyone goes in with 100 percent of their authority intact. With integration teams, there is a role for everyone who has a leadership role. Everyone needs to be genuinely involved. You get the best of both organizations. So, how do people deal with having two coleaders—one whom they know, the other whom they don't? They have to get to know and please both, even though they may be doing some different things. It's just like if you had two managers in a matrix environment.*

One executive, who is the HR Touchstone for many new leaders within a large organization, explained some of the challenges of having coheads:

> *Tim and Jeffrey were assigned as coheads of a major business unit of a global investment bank. This wasn't a postmerger situation in which one of the leaders was destined to be pushed*

out eventually, but quite the opposite. They were hired for their complementary skill sets. Each had over twenty years of experience in the business and a well-developed set of core business competencies. Although the pairing made good business sense, the challenge was to get the two men working as a coherent unit. They had to learn to trust one another and operate independently but responsibly and predictably. In the beginning, there was a real risk of either Tim or Jeffrey being approached independently for decisions. It became clear very quickly that this resulted in miscommunications between Tim and Jeffrey as well as some duplicative effort. To combat this, they instituted a rule that all decisions must be passed by each of them for approval. It became the team's responsibility to ensure that both Tim and Jeffrey were equally informed.

HR played a pivotal role in developing the relationship between these two coleaders. In addition to facilitating face-to-face meetings between them, the HR Touchstone instituted a weekly three-hour meeting that the two leaders would have by themselves. It took place every Friday morning and they were only supposed to be interrupted in the case of an emergency. This practice was designed to last only the first ninety days of their tenure as coleaders, with the assumption that, by then, they would have been able to develop more informal ways of communicating. Tim and Jeffrey found that given the high-paced environment, it was useful to have a dedicated three hours every week to discuss the competitive marketplace as well as any issues they needed to address within the unit.

Support/Coaching: Plan for the "Dips"

A new leader's boss is not usually involved in the day-to-day operations of the new leader's business. For this reason, there aren't always opportunities to clarify expectations, and a lot gets assumed that should be made explicit from the very beginning. You've probably spent some time with the hiring manager while revising the new leader's job spec. Now is a good time to act as a facilitator between the new leader and her boss, using the job spec as the common framework. Schedule a time for the new leader and her boss to return to that job spec and talk about the expectations that are clearly spelled out and those that only exist "between the lines."

Prior to the meeting, help the boss prepare to make these expectations clear and raise his awareness that new leaders do experience emotional dips, regardless of industry, experience, or business. Using the job spec as a starting point, this meeting should be a time in which the new leader can obtain specific feedback about performance and to "check in" regarding any assimilation-specific issues that have arisen. The first of these meetings should happen during the first week, followed by a minimum of two more—one after thirty days, and another after six months, to correspond with the periods during which she is likely to be experiencing an emotional "dip." This seems so obvious yet is rarely done.

> *When working with a senior executive who was floundering in what appeared to be a no-win situation, I asked the head of HR what she or the boss were doing to provide support. Her reply was, "We let nature take its course around here." This wouldn't be so tragic if a billion-dollar business hadn't been put at risk and if, in fact, it wasn't easier for the senior executive to find another job than for this company to replace him.*

Help the new leader develop specific questions that will give her an accurate sense of what she is doing well and not well. Asking open-ended questions or general questions will generate broad answers. For example, having her ask the boss "How am I doing?" is not sufficient. Only by asking specific questions will she get a clear idea of what problems or concerns keep the boss awake at night and also how her performance is being assessed.

FACILITATION: BUILD RELATIONSHIPS WITH PEERS

A new leader may choose to focus on developing relationships with his peer group first, believing—often correctly—that the judgment of his peers will have more impact on his success than that of his direct reports. Building good relationships with peers on the executive team from the beginning will ensure the support he will need when he begins to make suggestions for changes. They are also a source of information. This will be particularly difficult for a new member because most other members have worked together for a long time. Forging good relationships on the executive team will also help the new leader get what he needs for his home team.

> *I started with a specific job to do—to bring the marketing function to the next level. For the first time in the bank's long, prestigious history, marketing was going to be fully represented on the executive team. I had a lot on my wish list and really wanted to obtain the proper resourcing and funding that marketing would need to be able to propel the bank forward. As a new person in a new position, I had a lot to learn and many people to meet. I had to make a choice and after much thought I decided that it would benefit my department in the long run if I spent a majority of my time greasing my wheels with the executive team. That way, I would have more power and influence when it came to getting what marketing needed. The result was that I spent a disproportionate amount of time playing the political game, meeting all the higher ups and really getting to know them. That meant that I didn't get to spend as much time with my own team members. The result was that much of what I recommended got approved, but in the process, I alienated and offended many members of my staff.*

As you can tell from this story, there is a price to pay no matter how a new leader allocates time. There are difficult tradeoffs. When teams find their expectations unmet, they often become resentful and feel that nothing has improved. The new leader must determine the balance that is right for him, the organization, and the current business situation.

INTERVENTION: CONDUCT A STAKEHOLDER ANALYSIS

The organizational assessment, cultural audit, and stakeholder analysis could be conducted simultaneously, but new leaders often find it easier to "chunk" it down. Earlier, you worked with the new leader to identify key relationships. At this time, you can add value by helping the new leader conduct a stakeholder analysis. You may want to include external stakeholders such as:

- Customers

- Regulatory bodies

- Suppliers

- Government (local and national)

- Strategic alliances

- Competitors

A stakeholder analysis should serve as a guide to determine who has the biggest impact on the new leader's ability to succeed. This will help him determine priorities and begin to separate the critical relationships from the rest. For new leaders to begin building their stakeholder relationships, it is helpful if they get a broad view of what these relationships *should* look like over time. Help the new leader to visualize how the relationship with each stakeholder should be in six months from now, a year from now, eighteen months from now, and two years from now.

The stakeholder analysis will give the new leader a better idea of which relationships should be cultivated. Encourage the new leader to obtain information on current perceived effectiveness with each stakeholder. This can help identify the best way to get things done with each stakeholder and will allow the new leader to begin to map a strategy for addressing the needs of each stakeholder. It will also form the basis for building networks and eventually coalitions.

ASSIMILATION GOAL: ASSUME LEADERSHIP

The fact that a new leader knows few people and knows little about the organization and yet is a leader of a team to whom people will turn for answers, is a paradox that creates problems during assimilation. She is trying to shape and have an impact on the environment around her while trying to learn and understand it.

SUPPORT/COACHING: ACT "AS IF"

You can help the new leader overcome the Impostor Syndrome and the organization's response to him by coaching him to act "as if"—to act based on how he wants people to perceive him. "Troops want a leader

POTHOLE: *IMPOSTOR SYNDROME*

When beginning something new and finding himself surrounded by capable and competent people, the new leader may perceive himself as an undeserving impostor who will sooner or later be "unmasked." Others may seem to have a wealth of experience and to be working in such insightful and innovative ways. This feeling, labeled "The Impostor Syndrome" by Brookfield,[12] is common—even among people with many years of experience and deep skill sets. In unfamiliar situations, even the most seasoned professionals sometimes view themselves as who they were in the past.

who exudes self-assurance. In a battle at sea, sailors want to look up at the bridge and see 'the old man' calmly overseeing the battle—not struggling nervously into his life jacket!"[13] In order to be able to successfully lead a group of any size, a leader must display confidence. If he acts "as if" he believes in his own success and that the team should have confidence in him, it will go a surprisingly long way in making that come true. Even if he feels more like an impostor than a leader, it is important to his success and the team's success that he act as if he were feeling confident. Eventually he will grow into the role and the confidence will no longer be an act. But until that time, this is a crucial first step in the process of assuming leadership. This tactic will be especially important for first-time leaders.

FACILITATION: HELP THE NEW LEADER TO CLARIFY ROLES AND EXPECTATIONS WITHIN THE TEAM

A big source of confusion as the new leader assimilates is lack of role clarity. Who does what? What are the gray areas? What is the work flow? What needs to be changed? This undertaking is especially challenging if the new leader is developing a new area—one that didn't exist before.

It's important that the new leader communicate norms and expectations. Until he and his team calibrate norms and expectations, they may be operating under very different assumptions. People approach work very differently and every new leader has to make explicit his approach and expectations. Remind the new leader that the team will expect him to model his expectations for the team. For example, different leaders have different expectations about work hours.

One executive shared a story with us about differing perceptions about work ethic.

> *In the London office, there was a sign-out notebook for people who stayed past 7 PM, and the head of the investment bank would look at it, and he would think people who were consistently signing out after 7 PM were great guys because he interpreted that as really working hard. But the head of the financial institutions would look at the same book and say that's trouble because people who work after 7 PM are the people who can't get their work done within a day. The head of financial institutions was an efficient thinker and was more strategic than transactional. He expected that his organization would be organized to do the work required within the time allotted while the head of the investment bank was more transactional.*

A result of the organizational assessment should be a description of how current roles are defined, and you certainly can supply job descriptions. It is often useful for the new leader to meet with each team member or functional unit (if the numbers are too large) and ask them to describe what they are responsible for, where they think they are placed in the value chain, and, most important, their perception of the gray areas. This often reveals dissonant information and provides a basis for clarification.

RAISING AWARENESS: MANAGE RESISTANCE TO CHANGE

People are naturally wary of that which is new. Envy or resentment of a new leader's status or the degree to which her arrival has been celebrated can create an unwillingness to provide assistance. Therefore, new leaders can expect to encounter many sources of resistance. There are two such sources we have observed most frequently, which if not ad-

POTHOLE: THE PREDECESSOR— FRIEND OR FOE?

In the period between hire and entry, or should the predecessor still be present when the new leader arrives, it is important that you determine whether the predecessor is friend or foe and what his relationship with the new leader's team has been like. There might be animosities or loyalties—between the predecessor and members of the new leader's various teams—of which you and the new leader should be aware.

dressed and managed, can potentially derail any positive assimilation efforts:

People Who Were Passed Over

Gauge the mood and receptivity of the leader's new team. Pay special attention to those from within the organization who were considered for this job—regardless of how seriously they were considered. You can bet that these people will harbor some resentment about the new leader's selection—and you can't be sure about its degree or whether it will manifest itself in a way you can detect. There may also be a situation in which someone was expected to get the job and didn't, and the team identifies with the person who was passed over or dismissed. They may see the hiring of the new leader as an indirect message that they are inadequate. People may also lack an understanding of the rationale behind the hiring decision and they may draw inaccurate conclusions about why she got the job over someone else from within the organization (even when the new leader comes from *within* the organization). Help make the new leader aware of these and other related issues and the extra distance they and she may need to travel to build a relationship. Ideally, prior to her joining the new organization, you or the hiring manager will have addressed the issues of standards and criteria as you prepared the team for her arrival.

A Former Leader Who Remains in the Organization

Sometimes a new leader is hired to replace someone who will still be in a leadership position when he arrives. This can happen because you believe that having overlap between leaders' tenures will allow the new executive to acclimate to the environment and learn about its operations more quickly. Or, it might be a longer-term situation, such as when the appointment is part of a succession planning process in which the new leader will be reporting to the existing leader for a year or more before taking the helm himself. In any case, make sure the situation is clear to the new leader: Do you want a duplicate leader, or do you want someone who can eventually take the team in a new direction? Remember, people on the team may feel pulled—they may fear being perceived as disloyal to one or the other. It is often uncomfortable to be friendly to both authority figures.

Reinforce that the new leader should not to take this personally and should focus on the issues involved, not on the people. Don't underestimate how strong personal bonds can be. Coach the new leader to assure people that he doesn't expect them to give up their prior relationships. This is the time to begin building trust; don't let his silence feed people's fears and paranoia.

Robert, a charismatic leader who had been in his position for several years, overlapped with his replacement. He describes his exit this way:

I was a classic example of someone who liked doing the work more than managing others. I didn't really like my boss. I was a bit burned out. But the decision to leave was mine. I had been there for ten years. I had strong feelings of affection for many of the remaining staff and I believed the feelings were reciprocated. I had more or less picked my successor. She had been with me for three and a half years, and prior to joining my team she had been rather underrated. Some of that had to do with her appearance, and some of that was a realistic assessment of where she was developmentally. The department had an established reputation and at this point the role was more of a maintenance function. I had promoted her frequently, testing and coaching her simultaneously, and she clearly wanted the position.

My boss and I decided that it was best for me to stay for several months after we announced my departure and she assumed full authority. We knew it might be a bit awkward, and so I scheduled a meeting with her and we discussed our relative roles. She hugged me and thanked me for all my sup-

port over the years. And that was the last civil conversation we ever had. From then on, coming to work was like walking into Coventry. The rule of silence prevailed. She made the team feel that it was no longer appropriate to talk to me about anything. If they wanted to be perceived as loyal to her, it meant that I had to be metaphorically "murdered." People I had known for years would not be seen talking to me. They would call me at home but not at work. New people joined her organization, people I could have helped, but they weren't even introduced to me. I could have fought back and made her job more difficult, but I did want to leave and, more important, I would have made it much more difficult for the survivors.

INTERVENTION: ASSESS THE TEAM FOR SKILLS AND COMPETENCIES

The new leader has inherited a functional team. This team will determine, at least in part, how successful he is in his new job. Obviously, the new leader can't achieve his agenda alone and needs to know what support he can count on from his team. This is not a matter of building relationships. And it's not about liking team members as individuals. It's about beginning to identify the resources—the skills, competencies, and knowledge—that he has on hand to help him achieve his goals. He should identify those people and those functions whose support he needs to be successful. This is a particularly complex paradox to balance at the entry stage because there is an urge to affiliate, but the new leader must also be prepared to make tough decisions about people down the road. If relationships with team members are built on the basis of affiliation rather than on the basis of competence or ideas, then when it comes time to make difficult personnel decisions, the new leader runs the risk of being tagged a hypocrite, and people may no longer trust him. One situation that occurred in one of our client organizations is a good example of why it is important to avoid building personal friendships with your team.

A new senior leader came in who affiliated with all of the people on his team. They went out drinking together at the pub and the new leader had the ability to make everyone feel as though he was their friend. After some time, the new leader had to make some difficult personnel decisions and had to cut some of the very same people he had gone out drinking with night after night. The people who were let go, along with the people left behind, felt extremely personally betrayed by the leader's actions. I spoke with them and heard the same message from many different people, "I thought he was interested in me; we were out drinking together. Now he is firing me, which is sending me and my teammates the message that I am inadequate." While this was not at all the leader's intention, because he affiliated with his teammates on such a personal level, when he had to let people go, everyone took it personally.

One of the long-lasting fallouts of that episode was that people decided they could not trust him to communicate honestly.

You can help the new leader to assess the skills and competencies resident within the current team, both to get a sense of the high performers and to identify the most glaring skill gaps. Work with the new leader to reexamine the job spec or success criteria that she and her boss developed, or her initial plan. She should have clearly defined goals for the near, medium, and long term. You can then work with her to identify who on the team is at the level or quality that they should be to achieve these goals. Ask her the question, "If no changes are made within the first six months, where are the risks and opportunities?"

When assessing the team, the emphasis should be on gaining a future-focused perspective of the team as a whole. Given their knowledge of the organization's strategy, their initial view of what they want to accomplish, and their assumptions about what skills, knowledge, and abilities will need to be resident within their department, new leaders should ask the following questions:

- How does the current team profile fit with the strategy?
- What would your ideal team look like?
- Are there entire skill sets that are missing?
- Is the breadth and depth of the skill sets on the team commensurate with what will be needed to implement the strategy?
- Can people be retooled?
- Could they work in tandem with a consultant to effect a transfer of skills?

- Can you shift people around?

- How does the team need to be rebalanced?

- How interdependent is your team on other teams?

- How hierarchical is your organization?

- How familiar are you with the function you now head?

Equipped with this information, the new leader can begin to provide developmental planning, appropriate training, and give a "heads up" to those who aren't making the grade. The answers to these questions can also inform the leader as to how to put the right people in place, thereby ensuring performance. Last, the information will begin to clarify the team's recruitment needs.

Raising Awareness: Help New Leaders Hire "Their Own People"

The new leader often has to achieve an important balance between leveraging the strengths that exist on the team and bringing in new people and new skills. One response to the uncertainties that result from being in a new organization is to hire people from past experiences to replace the existing team members. There are some people who always bring their own credit person, their own operations person, or others they have worked with before. But to execute a strategy, a new leader needs people who have the right competencies *and* who possess organizational memory. More times than not, these two bases of knowledge do not reside in the same group of people. You should coach the new leader to be honest about assessing what exists, while respecting the history of the team and the organization. It is particularly important that the new leader take a structured, data-driven approach to making these decisions. This will have a great impact on the team's morale and will affect the team's perception of the leader's fairness and honesty.

You should also coach the new leader to understand that although working with people with whom he has worked before and already trusts will bring him a certain level of comfort, these past relationships tend to overshadow the newer relationships he should be building with the team. It may isolate him from the realities of the new organization and may inhibit the development of the working relationships necessary to effect change and learn about the organization. In any organization there is a developmental pipeline, people who have been identified as being able to grow into certain jobs. When a new leader brings a consortium of new team members, good people may leave if they see that a position to which they had aspired has been filled with a new person. The overall organization suffers as a result of reducing the talent depth.

A "survivor" in the packaged goods industry described the following situation:

> *When Harry came and then started bringing Company X people in with him—not necessarily personal friends but people who knew the system that they came from—what happened was that they had their private jokes and they talked about the organization like it was alien to them. During meetings they would all band together and talk about this organization that they have all joined like it is something that is external to them. I was in a meeting where I was the only non–Company X person and they were talking about my (our) organization. And I was thinking, oh, this feels very uncomfortable. And yet if you join an organization you should really think of it as "This is my organization now, what is the best that I can do?"*

Keep in mind that the new leader has to assess the new team at the same time that she is building relationships with them. This will be particularly challenging if she is developing the roles and responsibilities for the first time (starting a new department, or creating a blended department after a merger), if she is leading a virtual team, or if the former leader offered new jobs to some of the best team members. These are all challenging situations for a new leader because she may be forced to fill positions before fully understanding the needs of the team and the organization.

INTERVENTION: SCHEDULE A NEW LEADER ASSIMILATION MEETING

One of the most important steps you can take to facilitate the assimilation process is to schedule a new leader assimilation meeting. This assimilation technique was developed by the U.S. Army and was designed to help senior officers take command quickly and effectively. The army found that the process cut the learning curve in half, while increasing the acceptance of and cooperation with the new officer. Citigroup, Ford Motor Company, Exxon, GE, and Allied Signal are a few of the corporations that have utilized this process to help establish a sound foundation for future working relationships. They were among the first companies to formally acknowledge that, especially within the first few months, new leaders need to spend time with their direct reports and to learn, listen, and communicate. New leaders need opportunities to ask the kinds of questions that will engage people in open and honest conversations about the issues and challenges facing their teams. The new leader assimilation meeting accelerates the development of *contractual trust*.

One assimilation coach described the benefits of a facilitated meeting as follows:

> *The organization had a structured assimilation process along with coaching and so they held a new leader assimilation meeting with the new leader and a couple of layers down. She spent the evening before the meeting getting coached and receiving feedback about the concerns of her team, including their concerns that she was a workaholic—she worked all the time. Her team didn't want to see their lives being wrecked by her extraordinarily high expectations: working all the time, leaving e-mails in the middle of the night. She went over all the questions that she would be asked so that she could give some thought to how she was going to address the concerns. In the new leader assimilation meeting she was very direct about it: "I don't expect others to work the way I do, and I've struggled to find balance in my life." She made herself pretty vulnerable. And they really liked it and they really liked her. And it turned out not to be a problem because it was all out on the table.*

There are many different ways to conduct a new leader assimilation meeting. No matter how you approach it, the important thing is to create an environment in which the new leader and the team members can air their thoughts and begin to build relationships. The process increases the speed of assimilation and maximizes the probability of success in the assignment. It is designed to:

- Introduce the new leader to the group and allow him to present his vision for the team.

- Allow team members to discuss what they want to know about the new leader and what they want him to know about the team.

- Clarify expectations and provide an opportunity for the new leader and the team to get to know each other better.

- Allow the new leader to reaffirm what he wants the group to know about him and provide additional important information not yet touched upon.

We recommend that a new leader assimilation offsite meeting not be any shorter than one day, and we suggest longer meetings because people bond better when working together toward a mutual goal. For this reason, we recommend that the meetings be designed around the actual work of the business—in which the new leader and team clarify work style expectations, examine goals, and discuss how they are going to work together to achieve those goals. The meeting should be designed so that a structured dialogue occurs between the new leader and her staff. If an organizational assessment has not been conducted, the facilitator and the direct reports first meet alone and generate questions about their new leader as well as descriptions of their perceptions of how they function as a team and the challenges they feel the leader may face. The leader then reacts to their information and responds to their questions, as well as provides information on vision, direction, expectations, and work history and experience. Many new leaders find it useful to participate in multiple assimilation meetings involving the various groups that they lead or of which they are an integral part.

For example, a major, multinational tobacco company provides every new leader with a full-day assimilation program about expectations. It also holds a monthly communication meeting. A multinational bank holds a two-day new manager assimilation program, where interviews are conducted with the people on the team first and reported back either prior to or during the meeting. Exhibit 5-8 is a sample design for such a two-day new leader assimilation meeting.

During the first day of the meeting, a two-hour stakeholder analysis is conducted, where the people on the team identify the critical stakeholders of the business, both internal and external, and present their analysis of what those stakeholders require of the new leader, how well the team is currently delivering, and what they need to improve on. This acquaints the leader with the milieu he is walking into. Following

Exhibit 5-8. Two-day new leader assimilation: Sample design.

The following sample is based on a program delivered for a senior executive of a large multi-national financial institution.

Monday, Day 1		Tuesday, Day 2	
8:30	**Welcome and Introduction** Purpose: *To share the purpose of the meeting and to provide a context for the activities of the next day and a half*	8:00	**Review of Day 1 Agreements** Purpose: *To review results of Day 1 activities and surface additional issues*
9:00	**Feedback Report or Direct Report Input Session** Purpose: *For direct reports to generate candid input on concerns and questions they have about the new manager, their own characteristics, and their view of the problems the new leader faces*	8:30	**Setting Long-Term Goals** Purpose: *To identify and prioritize goals for the next 18–24 months*
		10:00	**Matching Initiatives to Goals** Purpose: *To align key priorities with existing initiatives*
11:00	**Manager Response Session: In-Depth Questions and Answers** Purpose: *For the new leader to honestly answer questions, conveying her initial expectations, and begin to build a team*	10:15	**Evaluating Initiatives against Goals** Purpose: *To provide an opportunity to review decisions reached, make changes as needed, and determine the success factors for the short term*
12:00	**Lunch**	12:15	**Lunch**
1:00	**Half-Day New Leader Assimilation**	1:15	**Increasing the Contribution** Purpose: *To examine identified priorities and initiatives from the perspectives of time and cost; to have participants negotiate cross-functional agreements on priorities and cost savings*
2:00	**The Business Context: Q&A** Purpose: *To provide a context for future action planning and decision making*		
4:00	**"How We Fit Together": Presentations** Purpose: *To allow participants to learn about each area of the business, from presenters in each area*	2:30	**Defining Immediate Action Steps** Purpose: *To obtain feedback and reach agreement; to determine the process owners for key short-term priorities*
5:30	**"How We Fit Together": Group Discussions** Purpose: *To have participants identify opportunities for leveraged action planning and decision making*	4:15	**Linking with Other Parts of the Business** Purpose: *To identify and agree on how to leverage relationships with each other and with other parts of the business*
		5:00	**Communicating Back** Purpose: *To identify the key messages to communicate in the workplace, the methodology, and the timing*
6:30	**End Day 1**	5:30	**End Day 2**

the stakeholder analysis, there is an assimilation component that lasts from four to six hours. This is used as an accelerated "getting to know you" session.

The interviews conducted during the organizational assessment are used to create a springboard for the new leader and for the team to identify the issues and to provide the basis for the development of a business agenda. The executive may be asked about his marching orders, what he came here to do, giving him the opportunity to present his view of the future. The team can then ask clarifying questions and determine collaboratively how they will achieve this agenda, how they will identify barriers, and how they will solve problems. Although it is an interactive process, the new leader should always be realistic and identify for the team any nonnegotiable issue.

The second day might be used as a strategic-planning session, with the intention of helping the team gel around an action plan for the work of the team and the positioning of the team within the company. This time might also be used for the team to share with the leader things she will need to know. Together they might contract on what they will need to do relative to each other and relative to how she will manage the team. The second day also helps the team to come together and determine their goals and aspirations, to identify what they have working in their favor and what is working against them, and to define what needs to be accomplished in the coming six to nine months. This is often a time where members present current initiatives, which are then aligned with the revised priorities to determine whether any need to be dropped or modified and whether others need to be added.

IS THE NEW LEADER READY TO MOVE INTO BUILDING?

The following questions will help you assess whether the new leader is ready to move to the next stage in the assimilation process. You can ask these questions during coaching sessions, or use them as a handout.

1. You started today and your boss meets with you just after you finish orientation. She gives you a list of people to meet with and regular meetings you should attend. You start making ar-

rangements to meet with people and to your surprise find that everyone is available and accommodating. What is happening?

2. After several weeks on the job, you notice an obvious opportunity to save time and money with a new way of preparing the work. You don't really understand why no one has noticed this before. You present your idea to your colleagues and boss, and they say, "Interesting." What happened? What do you do?

3. You are feeling really great about the client proposal you've just finished and presented, when you discover that your recommendation is completely contrary to the normal operating process for the business. What happened?

4. You notice that the area you are responsible for would benefit from working with a consultant that you know from your prior job. You call the consultant and arrange for him to come in and start work. After the work is completed, you discover that you need the approval from the division controller to pay the invoice. What happened? What should you have done?

Notes

1. Lesley Sanders, Custom Communities, Inc. New York.
2. J. P. Kotter. *The General Managers.* New York: The Free Press, 1982, p. 67.
3. K. E. Weick. "Small Wins: Redefining the Scale of Social Problems." *American Psychologist* 39 (1984).
4. Adapted from J. Galbraith, D. Downey, and A. Kates. *Designing Dynamic Organizations: A Hands-On Guide for Leaders of All Levels.* New York: AMACOM, 2001.
5. E. Goffman. *Strategic Interaction.* Philadelphia: University of Pennsylvania Press, 1969, pp. 12–13.
6. Cheryl Dahle. "Fast Start—Your First Sixty Days." *Fast Company*, June 1998.
7. "Organizational Learning as Cognitive Re-definition: Coercive Persuasion Revisited." Boston: MIT Sloan School of Management, 1999, p. 1.
8. E. Goffman. *Strategic Interaction.* Philadelphia: University of Pennsylvania Press, 1969, p. 47.
9. Adapted from J. R. P. French and B. Raven. "The Bases of Social Power." In *Studies in Social Power*, ed. D. Cartwright. Ann Arbor: University of Michigan, Institute for Social Research, 1959, pp. 150–167.
10. D. S. Reina and M. L. Reina. *Trust and Betrayal in the Workplace: Building Effective Relationships in Your Organization.* San Francisco: Berrett-Koehler, 1999. See Chapters 6–8.

11. J. J. Gabarro and J. P. Kotter. "Managing Your Boss." *Harvard Business Review,* May 1993, pp. 150–157.

12. S. D. Brookfield. *The Skillful Teacher.* San Francisco: Jossey-Bass, 1990.

13. Waldroop and Butler. "Guess What? You're Not Perfect." *Fortune,* 16 October 2000.

C H A P T E R S I X

Stage Three: Building

Coming Together

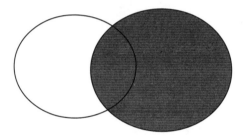

New Leader   Organization

I'd been at [my new company] for about nine months. I'd just finished a major proposal and submitted it to one of our most important clients. After a day, the client called me and told me that the proposal was great and that they were anxious to move forward. Naturally, I felt great. The project would be good for the company, my department, and it would help me meet several of my goals for the first year. It usually takes longer to successfully pitch such a major project, so I was feeling pretty confident when I sent a copy of the proposal and a summary of the response to my boss, Jean.

Jean called me in for a meeting the same day. "I can't believe you did this," Jean said. "The recommendations you're making here are completely contrary to the way we do business."

—Frank

What should Frank have done?

a. He should have made the changes required, informed his boss, and explained the situation to the client.

b. He had multiple stakeholders to please. He knew he was right and felt that his primary responsibility was to the client. He should have told his boss that it was too late because the client liked the proposal, and moved things forward.

c. He should have interpreted the situation as a signal that it was time to sit down with his boss and determine what he could do to preserve the client relationship while ensuring that standards were followed.

Any one of the options listed above sounds like it might address the issue. In Option a, Frank takes a conciliatory approach in his attempt to maintain good relations with both the boss and the client. However, if Frank's idea really was a good one, this option loses it entirely, and the clients who were excited with Frank's idea will find themselves disappointed. Disappointing a client when it can be avoided is never a good strategy.

In Option b, however, while Frank might maintain the client relationship, and might even bring a great deal of revenue into the business, he also alienates his boss. His boss, no doubt would feel dismissed and undermined. Option c is the best case scenario. Frank is potentially able to meet both his client's and his boss's needs and use this as a vehicle to learn from this experience.

THE NEW LEADER'S EXPERIENCE

At this point the new leader has been in place for six to nine months. While the initial entry into the organization is complete, the greatest challenge to the new leader's progress at this point is "The Big Dip," shown in Exhibit 6-1. The dip represents a strong emotional reaction to the difficulty of assimilating. It is often in response to something that

Exhibit 6-1. The emotional and intellectual journey: Stage Three.

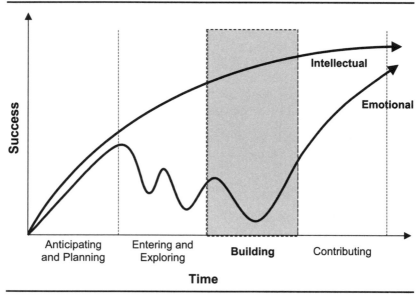

happens that is significantly at odds from what the new leader expected to happen—just around the time the new leader has been part of the organization long enough to think she had it figured out. Why does this happen? Often it is because the new leader is ready to act but realizes that the organization is not.

The cause of the dip usually falls into one of three categories:

- *Misunderstood relationships.* The new leader thinks someone is supportive and comfortable with what she is doing when he is not. Or the person she thought was friendly and a great colleague turns out to be neither. Usually some event triggers this awareness and the new leader may wind up feeling confused, and at times betrayed.

- *Misunderstood operating procedures.* The new leader thinks she has a decision or approval to do something, but in reality she doesn't.

- *Misunderstood task.* The new leader thinks she's supposed to be working on A, but the organization thinks she's working on B.

There is a predictable pattern to when people realize that the situation they entered may not be as receptive as they expected. Facing this emotional dip can challenge the confidence of even the most competent, experienced, and self-assured executive. It is often at this time that people reevaluate their decision and ask themselves whether they should stay with your organization. They seriously question whether they will ever be able to achieve what they were hired to do. Many of the emotional reactions have a lot to do with the relationships and the networks. It can help if the new leader focuses on which relationships really work and which do not and why. It is also a signal for the new leader to go back and test his understanding of the rules. It can be difficult for him to figure out if he has approval to do something or not. You can use your knowledge of the organization to check his understanding of the rules of engagement, the rules of decision making, and the rules of communication.

This dip is the point at which most of the turnover occurs. The ratio of people leaving organizations in less than two years relative to total turnover is about 85 percent, and this number is accelerating. The people who are leaving are doing so in very short cycles. Typically it is during the dip period that people say to themselves, "This isn't going to work for me." What is most likely happening is that the reciprocal impact of the individual and the organization, a central component of our definition of assimilation, is not occurring. The organization may not be change ready, and the new leader may have misunderstood the organizational signals, neglected to build the proper influence networks or solidify leadership prior to taking major action.

Recently, the news has been full of stories of people who hit the dip like clockwork and chose to leave the organization. Here are a few recent examples.

The *New York Times* ran an article on November 9, 2000, that outlined Heidi Miller's assessment of her recent career moves. Miller left her position of five years as CFO of Citigroup in February 2000 to take the position of CFO of Priceline. She resigned from Priceline in October 2000, only eight months later (the "big dip").

"A lack of authority was one of Ms. Miller's reasons for leaving Citigroup," according to the article. Miller went to Priceline expecting to have more authority than she did at Citigroup. She also expected that being a woman would not be a barrier to her ability to gain power and control in a start-up. The article quotes Miller as saying, "I know I've had a very good run [at Citigroup], but that doesn't excuse what I know to be a real bias [against women] . . . I thought a start-up like Priceline would be a better place for women to flourish." It sounds like what she found instead was that she was unable to have the degree of control she sought. She also described the organization's attitude toward women, "I don't think young men are any less biased than old men are." In that regard, she said, "Dot-coms are smaller versions of big corporations."[1]

On October 26, 2000, the *New York Times* reported that the U.S. Olympic Committee's CEO, Norm Blake, resigned "under pressure."[2] Blake, the USOC's first CEO, resigned after nine months (the big dip) in the post. Blake stood by his ambitious reorganization plan, despite resistance to a corporate model that called for sweeping staff cuts and funding reform that included cutting money for sports in which Americans rarely win medals. Blake was previously chief executive of U.S. Fidelity Guaranty, an insurance and financial company he led from the brink of bankruptcy in 1990 to a \$250 million profit in 1998. He also guided Promus Hotel Corporation to a lucrative merger with Hilton Hotels. His critics pointed to management techniques they said were better suited to the business world than the athletic field.

On November 10, 2000, the *New York Times* reported that the Maytag Corporation's Chief Executive, Lloyd D. Ward, resigned.[3] This announcement came fifteen months after his appointment as CEO. The company offered few details about Mr. Ward's abrupt departure except for a brief statement saying that the resignation resulted from differences between Mr. Ward and Maytag's board "over the company's strategic outlook and direction." Wall Street analysts said that they were unaware of the specifics behind Mr. Ward's resignation, but they thought it might have been tied to several factors: everything from possible disagreements between the board and Mr. Ward about trying to turn around the profit outlook in an increasingly competitive environment, to possibly moving the company's headquarters to Chicago from Newton, Iowa.

What can you do to help the new leader recover from the "dip"? You can coach him to acknowledge his feelings by encouraging him to be self-aware and utilize his cognitive abilities while retaining his focus and perspective. You can also support him as he reassesses his position in light of the new information he gained, and help him to be flexible as he redefines and reclarifies his goals and priorities and, as always, assesses the entire situation in terms of his hedonic "abacus." Rarely is nothing being achieved. If that truly is the case this is a time for both the organization and the individual to reevaluate their decision. Last, you can create organizational opportunities that support the building and strengthening of relationships and networks.

THE ORGANIZATION'S EXPERIENCE

As new leaders go through the Building stage, they experience a great deal of stress that can affect those around them. As one senior executive noted:

The most worrisome way that I have seen new leaders foul up is also perhaps the most prevalent way of getting into trouble— over the handling of stress. It is such an incredibly stress-filled time that the way you handle stress can really cause a problem. I have seen people lose their temper or they isolate themselves a little too much. They display such a high level of seriousness that they're not much fun. They are kind of prickly and that damages relationships. And they tend to get defensive if they get any feedback. They get wound up and refuse to take a vacation to cool off. They always do better when they just go with the flow and try not to get everything perfect.

By this time, though, the honeymoon is over. People in the organization no longer think of the new leader as the new person tending to his own business. He is now in a position to affect others' business—this can cause people to question their prior assumptions about his competence.

Because people no longer feel obliged to give the new leader any latitude, conflicts emerge that were previously buried. People now feel that they can be "real," without holding back any punches. The problem is that new leaders still have a long way to go. The dip is an emotional experience. It can go undetected by the rest of the organization—some people may even assume that the new leader is doing a great job and really contributing while he's really experiencing a new round of cognitive dissonance—debating whether to leave or stay.

Resentment of, or resistance to, a new leader is especially fierce in organizations with strong cultures. In these cases, any change that a new leader proposes feels like an assault on everyone in the organization. Because people identify so strongly with the organization's culture, the new leader's tweaks, however small, are perceived as disrespect. As one client recently said referring to a new leader who entered her team and destroyed what was left of team morale, "We wanted a shot in the arm, and she shot us in the leg." Blinded by its own paradigms, an organization rarely questions itself about its own culture. Look at the symptoms the organization is manifesting—is it consistently rejecting new leaders for the same reasons? Are these the right reasons, or did people's reactions to proposed changes, or real differences in style, contribute to the severity of their responses to these new leaders?

THE RECIPROCAL IMPACT

The Building stage is about consolidating the new leader's influence in order to allow her to begin to act. At this point, the new leader has been in the job for six to nine months. She already has clearly articulated goals and expectations, and now she's ready to start making decisions. As she begins to act, she will likely encounter cultural potholes—unexpected resistance and barriers. Stumbling against these unknown barriers is likely at each stage of the assimilation process. However, when new leaders finally begin to implement their achievement legacy, they trigger reactions that would have been difficult to anticipate. When a new leader is just talking about and planning action, it doesn't actually threaten any cultural sacred cows. It is different when a new leader takes action, because actions beget reactions.

The length of the Building stage depends on many different variables. While it is typically nine to eighteen months long, a self-aware new leader and an assimilation-savvy organization can accelerate the process considerably. As the new leader progresses through the Building stage, she should be having an impact on the organization in a more direct way by who she is, what she knows, what she can do—and often in ways that are different from the current operating procedures. In the two earlier stages, you helped the new leader focus on achieving small wins. Now is the time to help her to build on the relationships she's initiated by developing networks and beginning to act at multiple levels. Her actions will be sending signals to the rest of the organization about her trustworthiness and will determine whether or not people can believe what she's communicating. This is why it is especially important to continue to provide assistance to the new leader as she monitors and assesses herself, her relationships, networks, and the organization's reactions to her changes, as she is acting. Encourage her to utilize ongoing feedback loops—in which the new leader solicits feedback, modifies,

acts, solicits more feedback, etc.—this is time-consuming but will ultimately lead to more successful outcomes.

At this stage, the new executive should be fully utilizing the organizational support systems—the assimilation coach, the HR Touchstone,
the hiring manager, and the mentor. It is not always easy for senior
people to admit that they read the cues wrong, so they tend to hold back
from talking with others about it. We have found that the people who
navigate through the dip most successfully and continue to assimilate
aren't afraid to go to their boss or others and say, "What happened? I
don't understand." The benefit of reaching out for help is that it allows
the new leader to redirect energy quickly.

The primary focus of the Building stage is the implementation of
the new leader's achievement legacy. By now, many things have become
familiar to her. The basic routines require less conscious thought. This
is the phase in which she makes the tough decisions about her team,
solidifies her leadership and influence, and begins to test her strategy
within the strategy of the larger organization. As Exhibit 6-2 indicates,
the organization's and the new leader's activities at this stage should
support all of her assimilation goals.

Although the direct responsibility for successful assimilation now
falls more heavily on the shoulders of the individual, the organization
should still be playing an active role in supporting the new leaders in
their assessments and human resource decisions and helping them develop relationships by creating cross-organizational networking opportunities.

THE ORGANIZATION'S INTERVENTION STRATEGY

By this stage the new leader needs a trusted sounding board and ways
to broaden his scope beyond his area or department. The organization
can help to mitigate the extreme doubts that occur at this point by

- Sponsoring a new leader forum
- Utilizing the Assimilation Game
- Conducting an assimilation survey

INTERVENTION: SPONSOR A NEW LEADER FORUM

The new leader assimilation meeting outlined in the previous chapter is
designed for individual new leaders and their teams. The new leader

Exhibit 6-2. Stage Three: Key goals supported.

Goals / Stages	Create Achievement Legacy	Understand Organizational Dynamics	Build Influence	Assume Leadership	Align Systems
Stage IV: Contributing	Follow up on feedback	Formally integrate cultural changes	Create opportunities for organizationwide interaction	Provide developmental opportunities	Formally integrate changes to the system
Stage III Building	**Provide feedback mechanisms**	**Provide coaching**	**Create opportunities to build networks**	**Support personnel transitions**	**Establish parameters for change**
Stage II: Entering and Exploring	Help get industry experience	Facilitate cultural audit	Facilitate key relationships (act as a translator)	Facilitate assessment of team's skills and competencies	Act as a sounding board
Stage I: Anticipating and Planning	Prepare a developmental plan	Advise new leader; provide information about culture	Prepare key stakeholders for new leader's arrival	Prepare team for new leader's arrival	Provide access to systems information

forum, on the other hand, provides a group orientation experience for a number of new senior leaders. It is a high-level orientation, whose primary purpose is to provide cross-organizational networking opportunities. It also allows new leaders to learn about the business from the senior players who are already running it. The process and design of the new leader forum are further discussed in the Build Influence section of this chapter.

INTERVENTION: THE ASSIMILATION GAME

The Assimilation Game provides an opportunity for group learning while examining and legitimizing a new leader's reactions to the organization. Utilizing real-world vignettes and a scoring system based on the new leader's responses, the game illustrates how seemingly unimportant decisions can lead to negative consequences and alternately how prudent decisions can make significantly positive impacts organizationwide. A fully detailed description of the Assimilation Game is given in the Build Influence section in this chapter.

INTERVENTION: ASSIMILATION SURVEY

In order to determine how to best support the new leader at this sensitive time, you should be in touch with his feelings, his experience, and his organizational context. To help you gain this insight, we have included a sample assimilation survey (see Exhibit 6-3). This survey is used by a multinational financial services company with all new executives at the six- to nine-month point. We recommend you distribute it to new leaders as they enter the Building stage.

The following section discusses the assimilation goals of the Building stage, as summarized in Exhibit 6-4.

ASSIMILATION GOAL: CREATE AN ACHIEVEMENT LEGACY

The new leader has built relationships, conducted assessments, tested hypotheses, and incorporated feedback from multiple sources. At some

Exhibit 6-3. Sample assimilation survey.

1. When did you start this job? (Date)
2. Did you transfer from another area within the firm?   O Yes   O No
3. How many professional positions did you have prior to this job?
4. How long did you work at the prior job?
5. Please respond to the following items by indicating the degree to which you agree or disagree with the statement.

	Strongly agree	Agree	Neither agree nor disagree	Disagree	Strongly disagree
1. I understand the scope and breadth of my job responsibilities.	O	O	O	O	O
2. I understand my goals and objectives.	O	O	O	O	O
3. I understand how my performance is going to be measured and evaluated.	O	O	O	O	O
4. I know whom to go to for guidance and decisions about my work.	O	O	O	O	O
5. It has been easy for me to get clear direction and priorities.	O	O	O	O	O
6. I understand what authority and discretion I have to make decisions.	O	O	O	O	O
7. It is clear to me whom I need to communicate with frequently about my work.	O	O	O	O	O
8. I understand what I need to communicate to the people I work with.	O	O	O	O	O
9. I have a strong and positive relationship with the people who work closely with me on a regular basis.	O	O	O	O	O
10. The feedback I've been receiving has been very helpful in my adjustment to the new position.	O	O	O	O	O
11. Most of the people I work with have been very helpful and supportive in getting me oriented to the new position.	O	O	O	O	O
12. I have established a strong bond with someone who is acting as a mentor and sponsor to me.	O	O	O	O	O
13. There are occasions when I am not sure what I should be working on.	O	O	O	O	O
14. I clearly understand the basis upon which I will be compensated this year.	O	O	O	O	O
15. The culture and values at my prior employer were very similar to those at my new job.	O	O	O	O	O
16. At this time my manager is very satisfied with my performance.	O	O	O	O	O
17. My job is everything I expected it to be when I was considering the opportunity prior to joining the firm.	O	O	O	O	O
18. I feel that taking this job was definitely the right decision for me.	O	O	O	O	O

point she has to put herself on the line and take action. It is another first—perhaps the most visible and most public one. The new leader is also testing whether or not she'll get the organizational support she was promised.

Nearly every day, there is news of another new leader resigning from his position, citing the failure to execute his strategy as the reason. This is often the case of a leader who acted before he had the pieces of an enabling strategy in place, and who therefore was unable to execute a solid strategy.

Exhibit 6-4. Assimilation goals: Building.

Assimilation Goals	Organizational Role
Create an Achievement Legacy	
Set challenging but implementable goals.	Support/Coaching
Gather input from all stakeholders before executing plans.	Support/Coaching
Explain past change attempts.	Raising Awareness
Understand Organizational Dynamics	
Employ "protest absorption" techniques.	Support/Coaching
Build Influence	
Create cross-organizational network-building and boundary-spanning opportunities for the new leader.	Facilitation
Build networks.	Support/Coaching
Sponsor a new leader forum.	**Intervention**
Implement the Assimilation Game.	**Intervention**
Assume Leadership	
Make the difficult staffing decisions.	Support/Coaching
Build a leadership team.	Support/Coaching
Advocate for team members.	Support/Coaching
Align Systems	
Bridge the gaps between the current and future states.	Support/Coaching

On November 2, 2000, the *New York Times* reported that the chief executive of Newell Rubbermaid, Inc. (the maker of Levolor blinds and Rolodex office supplies) resigned. The chief executive, John J. Mc-Donough, was esteemed for his vision but criticized for failing to carry it out smoothly.[4]

SUPPORT/COACHING: SET CHALLENGING BUT IMPLEMENTABLE GOALS

Just as we suggested that you encourage the new leader to avoid getting involved in large-scale projects during the Entering and Exploring stage, we feel strongly that you should intervene to ensure that the new leader does not delay too long before acting. The new leader's goals should be

POTHOLE: FAILED EXECUTION

In the 70 percent of the companies in which a CEO fails, the cause of the failure is not a result of a problem with the ideas or the strategy itself, but rather it's bad execution. According to R. Charam and G. Colvin, failed execution comes down to such simple things as not getting things done, being indecisive, and not delivering on commitments. Their conclusions were based on careful study of several dozen CEO failures they've observed over the decades through their work as, respectively, a consultant to major corporations and as a journalist covering them.[5]

challenging, but also realistic. Research on high achievers suggests that success is predicated on the ability to set high but obtainable goals. In other words, leaders lose credibility when they set goals too high and console themselves when they are not completed by reminding others that they were probably not reachable from the beginning. The people who achieve most goals have the following attributes:

- An openness to feedback from the environment, which is translated into modifying and adjusting goals and plans to ensure success
- An ability to set high but achievable goals
- The ability to take responsibility for their actions
- An intrinsic motivation to achieve[6]

There is an experimental activity based on David McClelland's research in Motivation Theory[7] that is used to assess goal-setting style. In this exercise, senior executives are presented with a ringtoss game and placed in several competitive teams. Points are weighted based on the distance from the stake and number of rings that are successfully tossed. Some executives stand as far away from the stake as the game rules allow. This is indeed challenging. Others, in order to minimize their risk, stand almost on top of the stake. Both teams are given a trial round. Those teams most likely to win modify their strategy after the trial round is completed. Those that started far away move to a more moderate position and those that started too close do the same. They set high but achievable goals and moderate them based on feedback from their experience. Those concerned with saving face stay where they started. Those who are not achievement motivated do not change their position throughout the game.

Support/Coaching: Gather Input from All Stakeholders before Executing Plans

Regardless of how you approach the process of advising the new leader on her information gathering, the most important thing is that the information is gathered from multiple sources. Prior to finalizing any plan at any level, people need the input of their bosses at every step of the way. At a senior level, however, their agenda will affect many others throughout the organization. For this reason, the new leader should seek input from peers; their opinions can provide additional insight into some of the potential implications of derailers. Finally, those on the new leader's team should know all the possible implications of any proposed changes; most of them have been there longer than the new leader has and are more familiar with the organization. This makes their input critical. Besides, people won't work hard to implement what they don't own.

At this point in time, people still may not have a sense of how the new leader responds to negative information or information that doesn't support his initial thinking. While he may be asking his team for feedback, they may be wondering, "Does he shoot the messenger? Does he react in a punitive way? Does he get defensive and hostile? Or does he accept constructive criticism and modify his actions accordingly?" One wrong move and his source of information dries up. It is important for the new leader to be aware of his reactions to feedback so that he can clearly communicate his feedback style to others. You can support him in this effort by helping him frame his search for information by proactively raising issues and concerns and then encourage him to demonstrate consistently that he is able to hear the answers and take the appropriate actions.

Often, a new leader needs to make it safe to raise issues and concerns. One technique is to appoint someone on the team to play the role of critical evaluator. This is a role that needs to be rotated so that it becomes a normal part of the team process. Appointing someone on the team to play that role legitimizes the criticism. It is a technique used by President Kennedy after the Bay of Pigs debacle, because he determined that many of his key players failed to speak up about their reservations.

Your perspective is invaluable. As someone outside the new leader's team, you are able to provide a more organizationwide perspective, which can keep the new leader from making assumptions about how any proposed changes will affect others.

One way to ensure buy-in is to hold an offsite meeting whose objective is to ensure that all stakeholders understand the proposed strategy, proactively identify potential problems, and work collaboratively to develop an implementation plan. This type of offsite is a natural extension of the assimilation offsite conducted during the Entering and Exploring stage. However, the focus here is on the new strategy or proposed actions, additional expectations, and role changes. It provides an opportunity to problem solve and will impact the sequencing and form of later implementations. It can last from one to several days, depending on the scope of the organizational needs and the degree of change contemplated. It is best if members of HR work with an external consultant to plan and coordinate, to leverage outside expertise, and to ensure that the skill and knowledge begins to reside within the organization.

Depending on the degree of change and size of the senior leadership team, two meetings may be required: the first with the direct reports and the next with a broader audience. While the two offsites should have common outcomes—to allow a new leader to set norms, model openness and collaboration, gain input, and plan for implementation—the goal of the senior team offsite is for the new leader to enlist the support and buy-in of his leadership team so that they can actively champion the change. Whether you hold one or two meetings, these offsites provide invaluable opportunities for surfacing resistance and openly engaging it, solidifying the team, and supporting the formation of a group positioned for change.

As the new leader begins to implement her achievement agenda she will receive "feedback" from others in the organization. Some of the autonomy and support she was promised may not be there. Some people call this experience the "big lie." If the wall is too impermeable, she will make a judgement about whether or not she will be able to succeed in this organization. Part of this judgment process involves weighing her decision against her initial criteria to identify the disconnects. Sometimes adjusting to the realities is a matter of modifying expectations. Other times, there is too large of a disconnection between what she was told her job would be and what her job truly entails.

We hired someone as a marketing communications specialist. We recruited her for over a year. She came in believing this was a job reporting directly to the division head, and that she was going to be doing really strategic marketing communication. And it turned out that we wanted her to write copy. That was a big disconnect. And we had a manager unfortunately who was a little grandiose in some of the conversations. But this type of individual never recovered from the huge disconnect between what she thought the job was going to be and what it ultimately turned out to be. She went to take action and was told definitively that she could not do what she was proposing to do. And despite the fact that we also told her that if she continued to do the job we needed her in then there would be an opportunity for her to do the job she thought she would be doing eventually.

Several new senior managers who had recently gone from industry to a multinational consulting firm explained their reasoning to us when we interviewed them:

I was doing well in my past position and was ready for a new challenge, even though the challenge came with fewer guarantees. The excitement and glamour of consulting (or start-ups) and the potential upside was very tantalizing. What I did not see as an observer looking in was all the legwork that goes on behind the scenes. I encountered all of the usual problems a new hire faces—I did not have any networks or people I could trust. I arrived on site and found that I did not have any secretary, any private office, any help with travel arrangements. To make matters worse, I did not have any readily available resources and discovered that I had to scrounge for support. Because the organizational structure was relatively flat, I found that I had none of the support that a hierarchy provides. And I had sales pressure, with minimal access to my old client base. I was angry.

RAISING AWARENESS: EXPLAIN PAST CHANGE ATTEMPTS

If what the new leader is planning to do has already been attempted and failed, you will want to gather as much information as possible about that situation so that you can share the lessons learned with him. Inquire about the implementation history of the proposed changes: Ask people who were involved in the previous attempt: What kept it from being successful in the past? What were the barriers? What could have been done differently? What has changed in the environment between then and now that will either work for or against this next attempt? Probe for details so you can help the new leader learn from others' experiences.

ASSIMILATION GOAL: UNDERSTAND ORGANIZATIONAL DYNAMICS

While the new leader may be full of ideas and enthusiasm, his team is most likely cautious and reticent, still ambivalent about whether he is someone they want to follow. Because it takes time for teams to get to know a new leader, and for a new leader to demonstrate competence, teams may initially lack willingness to align themselves with the new leader's proposed changes. As a foreign entity entering a new system, a new leader experiences resistance to change as an "antibody problem."[8] It is common for the "antibody problem" not to surface until right before or right after the leader acts or executes his business strategy, because at this time he is stepping on people's political territory in a way that may force them to engage in defensive routines.

You helped the new leader initiate relationships during the Entering and Exploring stage, but these relationships have not yet been tested. It is easy for people to be on good behavior until the new leader makes a decision that affects their work or their role. Then all bets are off. Their reactions may be shocking. Your job is to prepare the new leader well enough that he can absorb these shocks and address their causes appropriately.

Failing to be aware of resistance and how to manage it can have devastating consequences, as the following story demonstrates:

At a large technology company a woman from an outside company was hired and received three quick promotions. She took charge pretty well in her first job—she was thought to be a real comer. She quickly got promoted to officer rank. Then the playing field changed because of the level. What happened was that she was done in politically. I think it had to do with the culture. There was still a lot of the previous company's culture in the new company although the merger happened a while back. There were tribal blood ties remaining. So when you're from the outside, even if you are from the company that acquired the original company, you have to kind of watch the old guard ties. I don't think she probably thought about that. And I guess the reason I say this is that I think they would have cut one of their own more slack than they did her.

And I think that her work was . . . actually she was excellent and I think she was a change agent in a change agent role. She was making some fair amount of progress at her job. So I think what she did showed judgment but I think she underestimated the politics. And the fact that she was really not letting people know what she had accomplished. When the company hit some choppy times the decision was made to make some officer level cutbacks. There was a meeting to determine which of the officers had to go. And I understand from her that what happened at that meeting was that she just didn't have strong support but nobody had anything bad to say about her either. Her really strong supporter, a very senior man, told her afterward that when he heard that she didn't have strong support from anyone other than him he was going to cut her position. He described his thoughts during the meeting, "I didn't express my strong support of you because I know you're young and you're good and I know this culture will kill you if you don't have more than just one supporter.

Support/Coaching: Employ "Protest Absorption" Techniques

When the new leader first arrived, he most likely faced resistance from his team because he was new and resistance to change is a typical response. At that point, the team would have been resistant to anyone new, irrespective of the individual characteristics of the leader and before any changes were made resulting from his arrival. Now, however, the new leader is beginning to take initiative, take action, and make decisions.

Although managing resistance is a large part of any leader's job, it remains one of the most challenging factors for any professional committed to innovation and reform. It is, in fact, the area that leaders have to spend the most time working through. There are proactive ways to manage the change process so that resistance may actually be used as a tool for professional development, growth, and reflection.

It is much easier to attribute resistance to change to incompetence in the people themselves than to probe for the specific reasons underlying the reaction. It is key that the new leader develop strategies to minimize resistance. By proactively helping stakeholders identify issues and blocks to the change process and providing guidance and explanation for the change, managers can minimize the risk of an incomplete change initiative. Protest absorption is a technique where the leader moves actively toward the resistance. He uses negative inquiry to determine what the concerns are and to harness the energy inherent in that resistance and to collaboratively search for solutions.

It is important to remind the new leader to validate and avoid negating past efforts. One leader in the Building stage describes the difficulty in the following narrative:

> *I think it has a lot to do with all of the changes that occurred over the last couple of years. And that people still do not feel trust in the organization. They seem to have come from a situation where there was a critical trust, loyalty amongst one another and now over the past couple of years all of that has changed and now new people are coming into the organization. And I think they feel very concerned for their personal situation. I think that there is a level of mistrust of the new people coming in and what their true intentions are. I think there is a tendency to be very cautious about teaming with these new individuals. I'm not quite sure how that has adversely impacted me.*

ASSIMILATION GOAL: BUILD INFLUENCE

By now you have helped the new leader to lay the groundwork to begin the process of initiating relationships. Now is the time for her to leverage these relationships and begin to build her own networks. It is through these networks that people are able to get to the real work in the organization. Reference the sources of power you identified earlier. To a large degree, these networks determine success. This process of replicating what was left behind in her old organization is one of the most difficult adjustments the new leader faces.

Establishing new networks prior to developing a reputation and in the absence of a secure power base is very challenging. Client networks the new leader worked so hard to build are now largely unavailable—they belong to another organization. Fortunately, the introduction of knowledge management databases has reduced the dependence on individual people for acquisition of knowledge. A senior vice president at one of the big five accounting firms describes it this way:

> *I kept waiting for my boss to grease the way. I guess you could say I was his willing slave—relying on him to pave the path. Several of my peers told me that I needed my own sources of information and that I wasn't networking upwards appropriately. In this project-based environment that meant no one really knew what I was capable of doing.*

FACILITATION: CREATE CROSS-ORGANIZATIONAL NETWORK-BUILDING AND BOUNDARY-SPANNING OPPORTUNITIES FOR THE NEW LEADER

Advise the new leader to look for opportunities to have an impact outside of her "official" role. Help her start to consciously look for special projects or other opportunities that provide links across organizational boundaries. Most of what happens in organizations is not reflected on an organizational chart. Rather, it is the work that lies between the boxes on the organizational chart (the white spaces). The way to manage the white spaces is to identify the needs that are not within anyone's role but that are needed for the organization to function more efficiently. Encourage the new leader to take these on as her responsibilities when she's ready. Sometimes these needs are brought to a new leader's attention—people reach out to them even when the work is outside of the new leader's role. At other times you will have to help the new leader identify the need and think about how she can proactively insert herself into the role. Regardless of the approach, this is an excellent opportunity to build influence, as well as expand the new leader's networks.

According to Morrison and Phelps, "Taking charge entails voluntary and constructive efforts by individual employees to effect organizationally functional change with respect to how work is executed within the contexts of their jobs, work units, or organizations. It is discretionary work, that is, it is not formally required. Taking charge is inherently change-oriented and aimed at improvement. It focuses on the inherent means for accomplishing organizational goals, such as work methods, policies and procedures."[9]

One executive shared the following story with us:

> One senior leader I knew had a limiting ability. For him, communication was an issue. It wasn't even as much communication as it was that people didn't understand what their career path was going to be and he didn't communicate with them about possibilities. This was a particularly big problem in that department because the department was a hybrid—it actually started as a cross-functional team and had burgeoned into a department. Because there was no other department like it within the entire organization, people within it couldn't look at others' career paths as a guide. This leader didn't see it really as his role to facilitate relationships and be an advocate for his team members with people outside the department (their peers or superiors) in order to help them determine possible next steps. As a result, people didn't feel good about staying in the department because they felt like, "Gosh, if I don't do something quick I might get stuck here and no one else will know me." There was greater turnover than normal in that team as a result of this guy not realizing that while helping people finding niches for themselves within the organization may not have been a part of his formal job spec, it was very much a part of his role as a leader.

SUPPORT/COACHING: BUILD NETWORKS

By now, the new leader has begun to develop trust and build relationships. He and his boss are now taking joint responsibility for the success of his area. The reporting relationship between the new leader and his boss should have evolved from High to Low supervision. At this stage he should be reporting on outcomes, not activities. The boss should be delegating more and more responsibilities. This is the time to begin to test that and if it is not happening, you will want to coach the new leader to raise the issue and think strategically about how to work more collaboratively with his boss.

POTHOLE: AVOIDING UNCOMFORTABLE RELATIONSHIPS

Responding to their emotional needs instead of to job demands, managers may avoid relationships that make them uncomfortable. Managers who are uncomfortable with people with greater power may neglect upward relationships. Managers may choose to associate with their subordinates out of distaste for the conflict and tension touched off by lateral relationships.[10]

The new senior leader must establish independent credibility. In the eyes of others in the organization, he's not that "new" anymore. To become a resource, the new leader needs to have networks in place across the organization. As Leonard K. Sayles defined it, "A network is a reciprocating set of relationships."[11] In other words, networks are webs of relationships among people with common interests who rely on each other as sources of information and data. They are built on a foundation of trust and respect and grow as each member of the network has shared positive experiences with another. The relationships gain strength as both parties show that they can and will come through for each other. It is particularly challenging for a new leader to create networks because it takes time for him and his peers to build mutual goals and agendas. A new manager has to create a successful history.

In order to form a network, each party must be viewed as a resource that possesses something that others need, and vice versa. A new leader needs things from other people because there will be things he cannot do or know without relying on others. But in order to get the things he needs, the new leader must have something to offer. These lateral relationships are as important as superior-subordinate relationships. They are the pathways through which much is accomplished.

Robert E. Kaplan uses the metaphor of "trade" to describe how networks operate: "Managers enter trade relationships with lateral network members for one compelling reason: they depend on these people and literally can't get their jobs done without them. Like nations, managers are not self-sufficient and must engage in 'foreign trade' to get what they need."[12] In order for a new leader's peers to engage in this kind of trade with him, they must see the adventures for themselves. He will have to use all the information he's gathered to date to be able to determine what others in the business think they need. "Managers trade power or the ability to get things done. They provide services to others in exchange for the services that they themselves require."[13] This is the basis of the principle of reciprocity.

The first step in supporting a new leader's network-building activities is to help him be honest with himself about how others in the organization perceive him. Help the new leader assess his attractiveness as a trading partner. Notice how frequently he is asked to be on a task force. How much access to power does he have? What common work history with others can you help the new leader build on? These will help you provide the new leader with a sense of how the organization views him. You also need to make the new leader aware of his reputation, whether others think he's building a successful track record, and what people are telling his boss about his performance.

One senior leader explained his feelings about his role in developing relationships when he was assimilating into a major insurance company:

> I knew that I had to be the one to make the efforts. Being on the leadership team I was on was very difficult, because I was one of the first new people to come into the organization at that level and everyone was very skeptical of me. I know a couple of them were resentful, and also somehow word got out as to my salary so people knew I was making considerably more than most of them and that just added to the tension. So it was really incumbent on me to reach out to them and create a comfort level and to help them understand, I was always very explicit about my respect for the past and that I felt very lucky to be a part of the organization. I also reinforced my awareness of the fact that I wouldn't be here if it wasn't for all the fine work that preceded me and I would always try to make them part of the process. After a lot of education and a lot of infor-

mation sharing early on I think over time the situation got much better.

Shell Oil provides a good example of trade networks in action. Shell's approach to identification and development of leaders is that the directors of the local operating companies conduct what can best be termed a series of swaps and negotiations in order to provide the best possible development opportunities for their people. One swap might necessitate eight others, and costs are assumed by the local company. One senior executive stated, "If I say to a director: 'I'm going to take one of your best people and give you an untested person. But you are still going to pay for your top person,' they know we're doing it for the right reasons." In this example, the senior executives swap and negotiate for resources. They engage in trades to obtain the specific competencies they need in one area, and try to make the trade more appealing by offering something the other party needs in return. It is a barter system.

This isn't always an easy process. It takes time for new leaders to educate people about the value they add. It is difficult to conduct business trades when dealing with interdepartmental interactions because there are functional differences among the different units, each of which has different goals, interests, cultures, reporting relationships, and different standards and means of measuring. Trade barriers are even higher when there is a level difference. "Trade barriers climb higher when the functional differences inherent in lateral relationships are augmented by hierarchical difference."[14] Managers of staff functions that line managers regard as inessential often run into this roadblock. A manager's influence is tied to how much the other person depends on him. Therefore, a manager must be in a position to reciprocate.

ORGANIZATIONAL INTERVENTION: SPONSOR A NEW LEADER FORUM

Organizations can't grant networks to managers. However, an organization can legitimize network building. We have found that the best way for an organization to approach network building is to provide a structured way for members of the organization to share ideas in order to develop common mind-sets, frameworks, and approaches. Often corporate-sponsored management programs fulfill this need. You can also sponsor a new leader forum—a high-level orientation for new senior leaders whose primary purpose is to provide cross-organizational networking opportunities.

One of our clients conducts such meetings several times a year. The goal is to provide an overview of the firm's business, organization, key players, and culture to recently hired VPs and managing directors. The objectives of this session are to accelerate the acculturation process of lateral hires into the firm by:

- Providing a common understanding of the business dynamics (products, competitive environment, clients) and strategy
- Introducing key players in the business and beginning a dialogue with new hires
- Beginning to build networks among recent lateral hires in different functions and at different levels
- Identifying the business topics and concerns important to new hires

The new leader forum is a meeting in which new leaders convene to learn about other parts of the business that will impact them. Senior players are invited to explain the roles, responsibilities, and strategies of their respective functions. They distribute information about the specifics of their business and illustrate their points with minicases and follow-up discussions. They might also go into detail about the history of relationships with long-standing clients and some of the nuances of these relationships and the members of the client organizations. Topics covered might include:

- Business strategy, direction, and priorities
- Overview of key business areas by business leaders
- Interdependencies among key areas
- Compliance issues unique to the division
- Strategies for operating in the organization and specific division environment: behaviors, expectations, tips on navigating the maze.
- Cultural values and potholes

The above topics can be addressed with a combination of lectures, discussions, and cases and provide the new leaders with a comprehensive view of the business realities of the organization as well as addressing cross-divisional issues.

The forum also creates opportunities for people from different parts of the firm to interact with one another, to network with their peers and possible mentors. It provides a structured approach to social opportunities in which aspects of the culture can be shared. Retired leaders and seasoned pros are invited to host a dinner and sit at the tables during the workshop to transfer knowledge of the organizational history, myths, and memories. The head of HR facilitates a version of the Assimilation Game described on the following pages.

Participants at these forums have reported that they felt more informed, involved, and better equipped to handle the challenges of their new job following the event. The comments below highlight the results of this type of forum:

- *Being a member of the division's financial group, I feel that I am now more aware of what the various revenue-producing groups do in the firm.*

- *The seminar has provided useful contacts through networked or presented material for future contact in my marketing functions. Much of it has already proved to be useful for reference and has been looked at by many of my team members.*

- *The forum made me more conscious of consensus-building approaches to my job.*

- *I have a greater respect for all of my peers and management of the firm.*

- *I found the insight from more senior players about how our division works and how to avoid "potholes" most useful.*

- *This forum will assist me in keeping all of our products in mind when speaking with clients and prospects.*

- *The seminar helped to increase my confidence. During the acculturation phase, there were senior speakers whom I found invaluable.*

- *The dialogue with the presenters was a good opportunity to question senior management about their views on strategic plans, growth, etc.*

- *The forum reinforced the firm's commitment to its people. I walked away with the feeling that my firm really cares about its people. This gesture strengthened my commitment to the firm.*

ORGANIZATIONAL INTERVENTION: IMPLEMENT THE ASSIMILATION GAME

The Assimilation Game is one way to actively engage an audience and provide an overview of the issues associated with the assimilation process in a relatively short period of time. The game's primary purpose is to provide an interactive learning experience that legitimizes the reactions new leaders have during assimilation process. Exhibit 6-5 illustrates one version of the game "board," which approximates the shape of the "Emotional and Intellectual Journey" graph (Exhibit 6-1). It can be customized to the specific circumstances of each particular organization.

The game can be played in teams or by one large group as a discussion catalyst. Individuals can also play the game at their own desktops, on their own time. Each "spot" on the game board corresponds to a story—similar to the stories that we use to begin each chapter in this book. Participants are presented with options for addressing the situation described in the story and are awarded points on the basis of their responses. The game can be used with large or small groups. One way to use the game with larger groups is outlined below:

- Participants are placed in small groups (at tables).
- Each table picks a number on the game board in each "zone."
- There are four zones for "Anticipating and Planning," "Exploring," "Building," and "Contributing."
- All tables must have at least one turn "in the zone" before moving on.
- Each number selected is represented by a "vignette" of an entry experience.
- The group discusses the vignette and "votes" on the best response.
- Responses to each of the vignettes are scored.

During the discussion that follows the scoring it often becomes apparent to new leaders that they are not alone in experiencing a sense

Exhibit 6-5. Assimilation Game board.

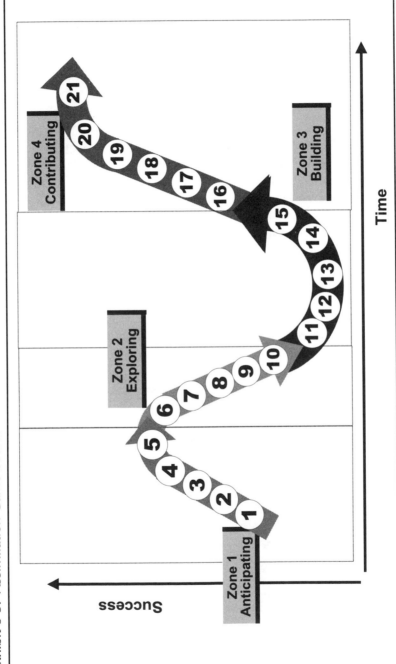

of loss of control and frustration. This often serves to validate their feelings and reduce the negativity. Sometimes the head of HR leads the meeting and facilitates the discussion by generating alternatives. His presence signals that the organization is not oblivious to the discomfort of the new leaders.

ASSIMILATION GOAL: ASSUME LEADERSHIP

In order for a new leader's team to understand his vision, he has to paint a picture of a future state that can be easily understood. To make it operational and real, the team will have to break down the high-level vision into its component parts. Involving the team in the strategic-mapping process increases their commitment, because the final vision will have been shaped by them, and to some extent, framed by their concerns, and planned according to their capabilities. This is especially important for new leaders, because working with their team provides an opportunity to get to know each individual and for them to get to know the new leader.

One executive reflected on his own abilities to involve others in planning when he first started in his new leadership role:

I guess initially I was a bit too quick to impose my view, my opinion of things, and I know that approach was not received well. Part of it was my eagerness, my knowledge of the fact that what I was suggesting was a proven tactic, that it could work and that I've seen it work other places. You know, been there, done that so what's the big deal? So, what was required of me was to be far more patient with individuals, to make sure that they are part of the solution and that it is not just my solution but that it is truly our solution. That requires a lot of dialogue, which is something that I find very frustrating. But a lot of dialogue about looking at the issue, getting everyone's input on it and then throwing out solutions in a very informal, comfortable way. And then talking through those solutions, seeing what they are comfortable with, where they see the risk. That's another thing in this organization—risk. That's everyone's starting point—What's the risk? And so it becomes this long, drawn out process and it may mean that you have to go back many, many times and have the same conversations over

*and over. But you cannot act until you recognize that people
are comfortable and they are really committed. It is a very
slow process.*

Support/Coaching: Make the Difficult Staffing Decisions

You have helped the new leader assess the organization, the team's competence, the dynamics, and the competencies that will be needed to implement the strategy. Now is the time to make difficult decisions. Making HR decisions can be one of the most uncomfortable facets of the new job. The new leader must consider whether skill gaps can be filled by training her existing team (retooling) or by replacing existing staff with others who possess the competencies needed (replacing).

One executive explained his approach to making this difficult decision:

> *I took the approach that we all took in terms of assessing that
> talent against the requirements for the new positions as we had
> defined them, and as a result we did ask some people to leave
> the organization. There were some people we deemed marginal
> and weren't sure of what their level of success would be, but we
> decided to go ahead and give them the opportunity. I think
> that was driven more by market situation and the lack of available
> talent than perhaps anything else. But in a couple of cases
> they proved us wrong and rose to the occasion. It was really a
> matter of putting them in the right job and providing them
> with the right resources and coaching, and they've done extremely
> well. And there were a couple of people after a year or
> so into this we've decided that they probably will have marginal
> careers here or we are in the process of counseling them
> out of the organization.*

The decision is often a blend of "retooling" and "replacing." Replacing can be one of the most difficult challenges a new leader faces and counseling someone out of a job is a delicate situation. As always, encourage the new leader to make fact-based decisions based on excellence and demonstrated performance. Use excellence as the standard to which each member of the team is compared. This way, the assessments that inform decisions about who on the team should stay and who should go are based on the same, clearly defined criteria. The organization should support the process of counseling the team members out of the team. It's sometimes possible to look for opportunities for these people in other parts of the organization. Some organizations help people find opportunities outside the organization as well.

You should publicly support the rationale behind such decisions in order to allay doubts about the new leader's competence in handling the situation. A new executive who makes these decisions often risks incurring the resentment and resistance of remaining team members, who may feel that he did not know enough to make such important decisions so early in his tenure. The remaining team members have bonds and friendships with the departing teammates that can result in a tremendous amount of anger toward the new leader and the organization. Productivity and morale typically diminish drastically after personnel disruptions. If the organization strives for fairness and caring in the dealings with the members of the team who are leaving, it will go a long way in preserving the morale of the remaining members—the often-overlooked "victims."

SUPPORT/COACHING: BUILD A LEADERSHIP TEAM

Creating a leadership team allows a new leader to delegate some of her responsibilities to the members of her own leadership team. This allows her to take on projects that are broader than her day-to-day management activities. It also increases productivity, employee commitment, and customer satisfaction. Additional benefits of a cohesive leadership team include:

- Presenting a united front to employees, customers, and other key stakeholders
- Increasing coordination across functions and activities
- Enhancing strategic and operational decision making
- Supporting the translation of decisions into actions
- Managing complexity

SUPPORT/COACHING: ADVOCATE FOR TEAM MEMBERS

Once the leadership team is in place, it is critical that you coach the new leader to become an advocate for the members of her team. As the team is assisting the leader in taking on some of her tasks, so can the leader assist her team by "going to bat" for them within the organization. One senior executive explained how not advocating for team members can negatively impact how a leader is perceived:

No one saw him as a manager or a leader. He had absolutely no impact even though he had technical knowledge of the functions that report in to him. Certainly he could have taken on the role of a leader to advocate for the needs of the people who report to him. To help pave the way for them. To be sure they have the resources they need to get their work done. And he has not done any of that and so people feel as though there is no value in interacting with him—there is nothing to be gained. So he has never forged any kind of a team, because he has never really demonstrated how he can be of service to the people who report to him and I just think that's so critical. I think that's the role of a manager or a leader. How you help people get their jobs done. And because he lacks the technical knowledge and the business knowledge he is not a particularly good strategist so he doesn't add value in that arena.

Compare this to the description of a leader who made successful efforts to advocate for her team members:

Her plans were sound. She was really the best I'd ever seen at assessing a problem, finding out all of its dimensions, and then inspiring people around a solution that they could all believe in. She was really amazing. She wasn't just a "plan it and pass it" kind of leader. She had other responsibilities to her peers and her boss, which she took very seriously, but she was also not afraid to really get her hands dirty—and as a result, she was more approachable, and people felt comfortable going to her. She was technically smart, very technically able, but she was also a good listener. People were fighting for resources, and she really heard them. She started to run their interference for them. And they really loved her because she really heard them. And then she began to apply what they really needed. So she added context and cut down bureaucratic nonsense for them.

ASSIMILATION GOAL: ALIGN SYSTEMS

Even the best plan will falter if other players in the organization are attending to a different agenda. Priorities and systems need to be congruent if the power of the organization is to be activated.

SUPPORT/COACHING: BRIDGE THE GAPS BETWEEN THE CURRENT AND FUTURE STATES

The new leader should have already looked at the current state, strategy, structure, people, processes, and rewards/metrics during previous stages. At this time, he should be focused on working collaboratively with those parts of the organization that directly impact his ability to execute his strategy. You should help him identify the disconnects between the current state functioning and the way that he will need things to be functioning. This will determine what must be modified in order for his plan to be implemented successfully.

As the new leader begins to implement his business strategy, it's a good idea to encourage him to step back and examine the resources he has at his disposal. You can advise him to incorporate the following elements into the planning process. This allows him to reduce the unintended consequences that occur in all situations, but more frequently with the uninitiated leader.

TRANSITION PLANNING
■ Will additional resources be required to proceed? How will they be secured?

- What approvals will be required?
- Do you anticipate any barriers in implementing changes?
- How will we measure success?

PLANNING COMMUNICATION AND COMMITMENT

- Whose support will be needed to successfully implement the plan?
- What is their stake in the proposed design?
- How do people in the organization prefer to communicate? What is(are) the best delivery method(s) for communicating the plan?

PLANNING FOR STAFFING NEEDS

- Is a mechanism for dealing with the resulting personnel issues in place?
- How will gaps in the staffing plan be filled?
- Will a new process of governance be required? At the minimum, the new leader must determine forums for decision making, create means of performance appraisal, and develop new communication channels.[15]
- What are the possible enablers and barriers within the organizational culture?
- Which organizational values support the structure? Which ones are in conflict with it?
- Which critical values are to be in place in the future organization that will require a shift in mind-set?

IS THE NEW LEADER READY TO MOVE INTO CONTRIBUTING?

The following questions will help you assess whether the new leader is ready to move to the next stage in the assimilation process. You can ask these questions during coaching sessions, or use them as a handout.

1. You discover that a number of meetings have been held relating to your area of responsibilities that you did not know about. Decisions have been made at these meetings that seriously affect your work. What happened? What should you do?

2. You receive a complicated request from a major client. You correctly answer the client's question and provide the information requested. But you soon discover that your boss and the corporate legal group are upset and angry. What did you do? What happened?

3. After evaluating the work in your department, a number of members on your team have pointed out—and you agree—that a long-service employee in the department has not been performing well for some time and is very negative and angry. You have had many years of experience as a manager and know that you need to speak with this individual and be very clear and direct about performance and the need to improve, or risk being terminated. You have the conversation and several days later get a call from corporate employee relations saying that you acted inappropriately. What happened?

4. You've been exceeding the sales objectives for your region. The people you've hired are also doing well. At the peer review meeting with your manager, you learn that your peers and colleagues have rated you below average in leadership and team collaboration. What happened? What should you do?

Notes

1. P. McGeehan. "Executive Assesses Her Adventure at a Dot-Com." *New York Times*, 9 November 2000, C1.
2. J. Longman. "Plus: Olympics: U.S.O.C. Chief Quits, Citing Lack of Support." *New York Times on the Web*, 26 October 2000, *www.nytimes.com*.
3. D. Barboza. "Maytag's Chief Executive Resigns, Citing Differences." *New York Times on the Web*, 10 November 2000, *www.nytimes.com*.
4. G. Winter. "Chief Who Put Newell Rubbermaid Together Quits." *New York Times on the Web*, 2 November 2000, *www.nytimes.com*.
5. R. Charan and G. Colvin. "Why CEO's Fail." *Fortune*, 21 June 1999, pp. 68–93.
6. D. C. McClelland and R. E. Boyatzis. "Leadership Motive Pattern and Long Term Success in Management." *Journal of Applied Psychology* 67 (1982): 737–743.
7. D. C. McClelland. "Motivation Theory." *Accel-team.com*, 9 November 2000, *www.accel-team.com*.

8. A. N. Korn. "Gotcha!" *Across the Board* 35, 8 (1998): 30–35.
9. E. W. Morrison and C. C. Phelps. "Taking Charge at Work: Extrarole Efforts to Initiate Workplace Change." *Academy of Management Journal* 42 (1999):403–419.
10. R. E. Kaplan. *Trade Routes: The Manager's Network of Relationships.* Greensboro: Center for Creative Leadership, 1983.
11. L. R. Sayles. *Managerial Behavior: Administration in Complex Organizations.* New York: McGraw-Hill, 1964.
12. R. E. Kaplan. *Trade Routes*, p. 5.
13. Ibid., p. 7.
14. Ibid.
15. Ibid., p. 99.

CHAPTER   SEVEN

Stage Four: Contributing

The Organization and New Leader: Assimilated

**New Leader within
Organization**

I'd been in my new job as head of communications and public relations for about eighteen months. For seven weeks, I'd been putting in over sixty hours, and I was exhausted, totally wiped out. But I was encouraged at the same time. It was beginning to look like all of this hard work would pay off. After three months of preparation, we were finally ready to launch our first major new campaign since I joined the organization.

Then one Monday morning shortly after I'd started to see the proverbial light at the end of the tunnel, the president of the company called me in for a meeting. He asked me to join a new task force for a corporatewide initiative that would require a huge time commitment over the next several months.

—Catherine

What should Catherine do?

a. Regretfully decline the invitation to work on the task force because successfully launching this campaign is one of her key goals for the year.

b. Agree to work on the task force, without hesitation, because she can delegate work on the campaign to her team.

c. Accept that she'll have to start working seventy-hour weeks.

Declining the invitation *seems* reasonable. If you're going to build credibility—and hence your influence in the organization—you have to meet established goals. However, by now Catherine has built a strong, competent team and has identified managers on her team who can manage aspects of the project in her absence. She should also have implemented clear systems and processes to monitor progress and ensure that an escalation process is in place so that she is informed of potential problems. This would allow Catherine to choose Option b, work on the task force, thereby fulfilling her obligations both to her team and to the organization as a whole. She might still have to work more hours, but she'll be able to focus more on her enterprisewide responsibilities.

THE NEW LEADER'S EXPERIENCE

By the Contributing stage, a successful new leader has solidified his team and agenda and begun to experience success. The new leader is not a "first-timer" anymore. He's had numerous chances to demonstrate competence and build the relationships he needs. It is hoped that by now he has built credibility, the currency he can use to help shape the organization as a whole. However, according to what senior leaders report, at this stage they are *still* assimilating. Now is the time to focus the new leader on broadening and deepening his presence in the organization—to move from a focus on his own team and agenda to a more enterprisewide view. Only after he has sought out ways to impact the organization on a broader level through mentoring others and through his presence on the executive team does he truly become an insider.

This success is apparent to others by virtue of the new leader's increasing influence and competence in the new organization. The new leader experiences this success as both an expanded sense of self-efficacy and an increased confidence in his ability to perform in the role. For this reason, the emotional and intellectual curves shown in Exhibit 7-1 begin to converge again.

THE ORGANIZATION'S EXPERIENCE

Especially in organizations with traditionally long-tenured employees, leaders who reach the Contributing stage may still be viewed as "outsiders" even though they've become competent in their new roles. Richard, an executive vice president, talks about his experience as an "outsider" over two years after entering a new organization:

> *I've been here over two years, and I still don't feel like an insider. And I've often given thought to that and my assumption is that a lot of that has to do with the fact that there are so many long service employees with this organization and they are extremely loyal and committed to each other, not the company. And you encounter a couple of different types. You know, the ones that are very exclusive, they let you know from the get go that you're not part of the group. And then you have the others that kind of give you the impression that they welcome*

Exhibit 7-1. The emotional and intellectual journey: Stage Four.

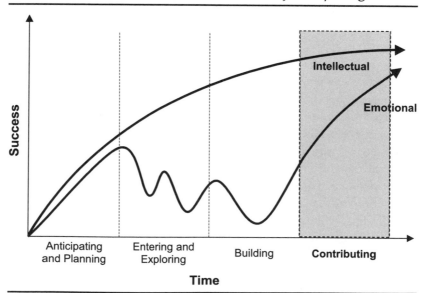

you and they welcome your input and opinions but its a strange kind of dynamic. People are not forthcoming. They say they are open and they're not willing to offer their opinions and so what happens is that in any type of interaction there is a lot of questioning and dancing around the issue, trying to understand what your point of view is on something before they are willing to offer you theirs.

If I go to one of my colleagues and ask for her input on a particular issue and say to her, "How do you think I should respond to this particular situation?" she will tend not to answer the question but she will engage in a line of questioning that really starts to cut at where I am on it and what I've done about it thus far. And all I've asked is a very simple question, but I'm having to provide all this detail around the situation, which from my vantage point is not germane to the question at all. It just needs to be answered and there is this begging for information. I think it's worse for me because I'm still considered an outsider.

They seem to have come from a situation where there was a critical trust, loyalty among one another and now over the past couple of years all of that has changed and now new people are coming into the organization. And I think they feel very concerned for their personal situation. I think that there is a level of mistrust of the new people coming in and what their true intentions are. I think there is tendency to be very cautious about teaming with those of us who are new.

THE RECIPROCAL IMPACT

The Contributing stage usually begins at around the eighteenth month. All research suggests that it takes at least this long for new leaders to:

- Fully understand how the organization really works.
- Build strong, supportive networks and relationships.
- Get to the point where success is visible.
- Gain a reputation of being an enterprisewide resource.
- Establish effective systems, processes, and control systems.

The focus in this phase is on creating alignment; modifying, broadening, and adjusting plans; and performing beyond formal role expectations. The new leader now has reputational power that she didn't have when she walked in the door. Maintaining a reputation for achievement and continuing success in the function, as well as at an enterprisewide level, requires constant realignment of the new leader and her strategy. By this stage, she should have her own house in order and focus on creating broader organizational impact. As Exhibit 7-2 indicates, your activities to help the new leader reinforce her status as a *fully functioning leader* during the Contributing stage support the achievement of the final goals of assimilation.

The shift in responsibility for the assimilation process culminates at the Contributing stage. At the beginning of assimilation, the organization and the individual are equal partners, sharing in the responsibility of the success of the individual's assimilation process. The organization's involvement in the assimilation process shifts gradually over time toward a less direct and less structured involvement. However, you should continue to contribute to the individual's success, in the role of a touchstone by providing coaching, feedback, and support to the individual as needed.

THE ORGANIZATION'S INTERVENTION STRATEGY

In this stage you should be working with the leader to broaden his horizons. Some areas of focus might be:

- Identifying opportunities to create impact in the organization
- Building a talent pipeline
- Developing high potentials
- Looking for ways to strengthen relationships with others

During the Contributing stage, you can also help the organization further advance the assimilation process by suggesting the use of a cross-evaluation system.

INTERVENTION: CONDUCTING A CROSS-EVALUATION

In a cross-evaluation system, an individual receives feedback from others in a position to assess job performance as it relates to meeting customer

Exhibit 7-2. Stage Four: Key goals supported.

Goals / Stages	Create Achievement Legacy	Understand Organizational Dynamics	Build Influence	Assume Leadership	Align Systems
Stage IV: Contributing	**Follow up on feedback**	**Formally integrate cultural changes**	**Create opportunities for organizationwide interaction**	**Provide developmental opportunities**	**Formally integrate changes to the system**
Stage III Building	Provide feedback mechanisms	Provide coaching	Create opportunities to build networks	Support personnel transitions	Establish parameters for change
Stage II: Entering and Exploring	Help get industry experience	Facilitate cultural audit	Facilitate key relationships (act as a translator)	Facilitate assessment of team's skills and competencies	Act as a sounding board
Stage I: Anticipating and Planning	Prepare a developmental plan	Advise new leader; provide information about culture	Prepare key stakeholders for new leader's arrival	Prepare team for new leader's arrival	Provide access to systems information

needs, no matter where they are placed in the organization. Typically, participants are in different functions that are highly dependent on one another for getting the work done. Feedback is focused on how an individual's job skills and behavior impact the ability of others to perform. A cross-evaluation system is tied to customer indicators rather than internal measures such as improved teamwork.

The primary purpose of cross-evaluation is to strengthen horizontal linkages by clarifying mutual expectations and providing feedback on actual performance among highly interdependent functions and areas. This is achieved through individuals providing evaluative comments and ratings to other members in the cross-evaluation group. The feedback should be focused on how the others' job skills and behavior impacts their own ability to perform. Each individual, in turn, is assessed by all other members of the group.

The feedback component of the process allows the new leader to check for gaps in alignment of his functional area with the rest of the organization while at the same time empowering each of the individual members of his team with feedback on how to improve handoffs to colleagues in other functions for organizational effectiveness. It is designed to:

- Assess individual business contribution based on job-specific performance criteria (i.e., quantifiable or "objective" indicators).

- Define performance attributes so that they can be observed by others (i.e., observable behaviors or "subjective" indicators).

- Highlight those dimensions that reflect collaborative behavior, promote the "organizational team," and dovetail with the business strategy.

Cross-evaluation differs from peer evaluation in that peer evaluation focuses on teamwork whereas cross-evaluation deals with business results and is linked to customer indicators. It is commonly used when there are interdependencies between functions and/or a manager is not in the position to observe and assess all performance factors. It is a powerful feedback tool to promote collaboration between business units and functions.

How well a team functions is not solely determined by the capabilities of its members. Equally important determinants of team effectiveness are how clearly specific roles and responsibilities on the team have been articulated and to what degree specific functions and tasks of individual members have been linked to their impact on larger organizational outcomes. Another critical factor is how well members of the team understand what each person needs from the other in order to effectively carry out their job function. It is up to you, in conjunction with the new leader, to discover the team's expectations and clarify the handoffs.

A cross-evaluation workshop provides the new leader with a way to get to know new functions, shape the organization and the work flow, and understand how the team is positioned in the value-added chain. It allows him to see who needs what from whom. We find that the ongoing matrix of communication built by the cross-evaluation process is as important an outcome as the actual ratings themselves. Even the process of designing a cross-evaluation system can serve as a valuable tool by surfacing fundamental organizational strengths and barriers.

Cross-evaluation systems are particularly useful in strengthening horizontal links in a matrixed environment. Setting up a process whereby a group of individuals with common goals provide each other with periodic feedback builds a safe environment for people to share information and ideas, and to begin collaborating through a legitimized, *business-related* mechanism. The focus on business results is critical. Many senior executives, who have the most to benefit from tools that help them negotiate complex matrix systems, are resistant to spending time in activities that seem the least bit "soft."

Exhibit 7-3 is an example of a cross-evaluation worksheet that was used by an international organization.

In this next section we discuss the assimilation goals of the Contributing stage, which are summarized in Exhibit 7-4.

ASSIMILATION GOAL: CREATE AN ACHIEVEMENT LEGACY

COACHING/SUPPORTING: MODIFY STRATEGY BASED ON FEEDBACK

No matter how successfully new leaders navigate the first three stages of the assimilation process, they have inevitably made mistakes. The actions the new leader took early on may have been appropriate at the

Exhibit 7-3. Sample cross-evaluation worksheet.

Division/Unit Name_____

Instructions: For each division/unit listed, please list key needs, deliverables, expectations, and success measures.

Division/ Unit	What we need from this division/unit to do our job effectively	What key deliverables/ support/info we need from this division/unit	What key expectations we have of this division/unit	Success measures
Division #1				
Division #2				
Division #3				
Division #4				

time, but given that change is a constant, the organization may look and feel very different by the time he reaches the Contributing stage. This is to be expected. Perhaps they made decisions early on that were not made with the right information or understanding. Even if someone gave a new leader every possible piece of information he might need during those early stages, he may not have fully developed a frame of reference that would have allowed him to process that information correctly. By helping him to face this reality head on and to acknowledge that he may have made mistakes, you can give him the chance to correct them before they become insurmountable barriers.

Fifty percent of the executives we've interviewed had a new boss within two years of their hire. If this is the case, you can play a critical role in helping the new leader think about what to do differently and

Exhibit 7-4. Assimilation goals: Contributing.

Assimilation Goals	Organizational Role
Create an Achievement Legacy	
Modify strategy based on feedback.	Support/Coaching
Understand Organizational Dynamics	
Reshape the organizational culture.	Support/Coaching
Build Influence	
Expand the span of influence.	Support/Coaching
Become a more strategic contributor to the executive team.	Support/Coaching
Mend relationships that were neglected.	Support/Coaching
Carefully choose the issues to focus on.	Support/Coaching
Understand the importance of coalitions.	Support/Coaching
Assume Leadership	
Broaden the scope of leadership by empowering others.	Support/Coaching
Solidify diagnostic and interactive control systems.	Support/Coaching
Align Systems	
Identify the disconnects that require broader organizational change.	Support/Coaching

understanding how the organization itself is different. Given the changes, he may want to retest his assumptions about:

- The relative strategic importance of various business functions
- Staffing needs
- Which potential initiatives best align with current strategic priorities
- Sequencing of strategic initiatives
- The skills and abilities needed
- Necessary adjustments to their management style and the expectations you have of your team

ASSIMILATION GOAL: UNDERSTANDING ORGANIZATIONAL DYNAMICS

By this time, the process of day-to-day decision making and relationship building within the organization should be a more intuitive and routine process for the new leader. He should have developed *unconscious compe-tence* in managing his own function and understanding the dynamics of the organization. With this unconscious competence, certain aspects of his job become easier because he has become attuned to the organization and knows what early warning signs to look out for. With this organizational knowledge now under his belt, he no longer needs to be told that something is not working because he has learned how to read between the lines. He is able to anticipate problems because he now has the experience to envision the broader organizational implications of his actions, as well as those of others. Although new leaders will have had considerable exposure to the organization's dynamics by the Contributing stage, many are often surprised by unexpected difficulties encountered in this area.

Support/Coaching: Reshape the Organizational Culture

Given the increased breadth and depth of her influence, the new leader is in a position to have an impact on how the culture of the organization is shaped, in addition to how the organization operates. Throughout her interactions with others, as she has implemented a strategy to create a legacy of achievement and aligned her team with her vision, she has had multiple opportunities to observe the ways in which cultural barriers can impede progress. At this stage, she should have developed the credibility and stature to address any interpersonal, procedural, or cultural dysfunctions. She can exert the influence she has as a leader, along with the credibility she has earned, to identify these problems and mobilize the necessary resources required for finding solutions.

ASSIMILATION GOAL: BUILD INFLUENCE

Throughout the previous stages of the assimilation process, the new leader has been building networks up, down, and across the organization. Every interaction with a peer, superior, or client has been seen as an opportunity to win trust, build relationships, and expand one's potential for exercising influence. Increasing one's effectiveness and impact within an organization requires a broader view of one's span of influence, responsibilities, and networks.

SUPPORT/COACHING: EXPAND THE SPAN OF INFLUENCE

At the Contributing stage, the new leader's ability to broadly define her role to include activities not specified in her job description is critical. She must be ready to both broaden her understanding of the kinds of actions required while at the same time demonstrating a keen political understanding of the context in which these tasks must be carried out. Instead of thinking primarily in terms of her own function, she may need to consider the perspectives of, and impact on, other areas of the organization.

One avenue for expanding her influence is to develop a network and understanding of relationships and functions throughout the organization. Seeking out a broader perspective will allow the new leader to develop a more nuanced understanding of the complex web of interrelationships and increase her value as a resource to her colleagues in other areas. Not only will the leader be better equipped to frame the issues facing her own function but she will enhance her credibility among her colleagues by serving as a linking pin between areas of the organization.

SUPPORT/COACHING: BECOME A MORE STRATEGIC CONTRIBUTOR TO THE EXECUTIVE TEAM

A primary vehicle for organizational influence is through active participation on the executive team. The executive team provides the opportunity for the new leader to have organizational impact and to influence the future of the organization. The role of the executive team is to consider the "whole enterprise," combining a strategic, external focus that utilizes collective business knowledge with an operational focus that leverages the team's technical expertise.

In our experience, executive teams don't come together easily. As the new leader begins to develop increased influence among her peers, it will become easier for her to offer feedback about how the executive team functions. If there is no formal executive team, she can begin advocating for one. The absence of a fully functioning executive team often stems from some combination of the following causes:

- Functional leaders have been chosen because of their subject matter expertise and naturally prefer to devote their energies to the development and enhancement of their own products or services.

- The visionary and strategic role has traditionally been concentrated in one person—the CEO, president, or other leader with the greatest seniority.
- Team members do not know enough about the unique perspectives of others on the team to be able to establish common ground.
- Those on the team are conflict-adverse, resulting in a failure to engage and make decisions about critical business issues.

Because of their varied functional perspectives, members of an executive team will often disagree on fundamental issues but may be uncomfortable surfacing them, fearing they may damage their relationships with each other. In a fully functioning executive team, members are able to engage this contention directly, recognizing the validity of others' perspectives and opinions and maintaining respect for each other personally.

Advise the new leader to consider the following issues as she talks to people about how the executive team functions:

- What is the current strategy, as you understand it?
- How does your area contribute to implementing the strategy?
- What falls between the cracks? What isn't occurring that should be?
- In what ways do you work together?
- Are there regular meetings? Who is involved?
- What does the team do best and where are its weaknesses? Some possibilities include:
  - Achieving high profitability and efficiency
  - Enhancing product capabilities
  - Effectively leveraging business opportunities
  - Building a high-performing culture and organization
  - Enhancing service quality

Many people have difficulty seeing their world from other than a functional perspective. To move from being a leader of a function to a fully contributing member of an organization's leadership team requires a shift in perspective. The leadership team perspective requires:

POTHOLE: NEGLECTING TO WEAR AN ORGANIZATIONAL HAT AS WELL AS A FUNCTIONAL HAT

This mental shift from a functional perspective to taking an organizational one is a difficult transition to make. Until this point, the new leader has focused his attention on achieving successes in his own functional area and on influencing and winning over his own team. In order to have organizational impact it is necessary to step outside of the comfort zone of having a discipline-specific leadership role to a more complex role where he is required to "wear multiple hats." He will find himself at times having to advocate the interests and positions of his own function while still reflecting a broader, enterprisewide view.

- Making trade-offs to optimize the portfolio rather than individual business strategies
- Making decisions for the "corporate good" rather than narrow functional interests
- Changing the focus from "how can we do this" to "can we make money"—business over functional results

SUPPORT/COACHING: MEND RELATIONSHIPS THAT WERE NEGLECTED

During the early stages of the process, there were activities the new leader had to set aside in favor of more pressing needs. There were relationships that weren't pursued aggressively because others were more important. Encourage the new leader to think about these relationships now. Be a bridge to help the new leader repair or build relationships and demonstrate that he is committed to hearing others' views and providing support.

There may also have been process issues that were closed or covered up. Perhaps a previous boss may have said, "This is how we do things around here, end of story." The new leader may now be ready to address issues that he wasn't ready to touch earlier because he hadn't built the necessary trust within the organization. The most successful new leaders continue expanding their networks and power bases outside their immediate team environments.

SUPPORT/COACHING: CAREFULLY CHOOSE THE ISSUES TO FOCUS ON

Time is often the largest resource constraint for a leader. You can help a leader assess her return on management time by looking at how she spends her days. Does she choose the meetings she goes to or does she say yes to all she is invited to? Is she choosing which activities to get involved with or only reacting to those that are presented to her? Is she continually responding to the immediate urgent items and neglecting the long-term important issues? It is impossible to have impact on all issues in all areas. Maximizing one's impact (as well as feeling in control of one's schedule) means choosing and focusing on those issues where one brings unique skills and talents and where there is likely to be the highest return on effort. You should advise the new leader to pick the issues where she wants to make her mark on the organization with these factors in mind:

- *Seize the opportunities that are likely to have the highest return.* The new leader should avoid reacting to an opportunity without strategically thinking through its likely impact and success. This will guard against her falling into the trap of picking hollow opportunities with little likelihood of success. Opportunities that are pursued and then produce minimal impact have the adverse effect of building skepticism among her colleagues about the value of her contribution to the team.[1]

- *Seek to increase your individual self-awareness and those of the team.* Team effectiveness depends on the skills and talents of the individual members and how these skills and talents are collectively harnessed. A good leader is one who is self-aware of his own unique strengths and weaknesses as well as those of individual members of the team and can create strategies for

POTHOLE: ASSUMING THAT GREAT IDEAS STAND ON THEIR OWN

Achievement-oriented people tend to assume that great ideas stand on their own merit, that people will agree on the ideas without any preselling or consensus building. Exercising influence requires convincing people to support an idea that they wouldn't have necessarily supported because a persuasive argument has been made linking the new idea to the individual's self-interest.

complementing and leveraging these to maximize efficiency, competence, and talent.

SUPPORT/COACHING: UNDERSTAND THE IMPORTANCE OF COALITIONS

Coalitions are built by leveraging existing networks in the service of a specific goal. They emerge around specific issues and specific plans and are usually strategic in focus. Members of a coalition don't necessarily share similar philosophies or even agree on most things—think of the peacemaking coalitions in Northern Ireland or the Middle East.

It is easy to win the support of those who are like-minded. It is an art form and, in many cases, a necessity for a leader to win the support of those who have different views. Developing an inclusive agenda that incorporates people's knowledge and an understanding of organizational dynamics will ensure a new leader broad support and heightened credibility.

In organizations in which one has "grown up," coalitions develop naturally. To consciously promote them may seem artificial and manipulative to some. In your role as an organizational representative, you can legitimize their use to the new leader. Explain that coalitions provide a vehicle to shape a consensus for action—and great ideas without broad support do not get implemented. Here are some tips you can share with the new leader for winning support for his ideas:

- *Gather information, assess where you will find support and where you will face resistance, and take time to understand why.* Be conscious and aware of individual agendas and the motivations behind the support and the resistance, how individuals define their self-interests, and incorporate this knowledge into your strategy. This knowledge will help strategize how to convince those who are undecided, ensure that supporters aren't taken for granted, and win over your naysayers. Gathering complete information also guards against making any premature assumptions.

- *Solicit and incorporate the input of others to strengthen ideas.* Ensuring that the proposal reflects the input of others is critical to success. Different people offer different perspectives and expertise, knowledge of details and specifics (including potential barriers and derailers) that can add value not only to the conceptualization but the implementation of an idea.

- *Presell ideas to ensure ownership and buy-in.* While the easiest way to build a coalition is to enlist the support of people who are already in agreement with you, this may not be sufficient consensus for action. Often broad support of like-minded people, as well as those who may not normally support such ideas or initiatives, is required to ensure successful implementation and broad organizational impact. The process of asking for input, in itself, is a powerful tool for building support. One is more likely to support an idea if one's input has been solicited. Also, there is a lag time between hearing a new idea and general receptivity toward the idea.

ASSIMILATION GOAL: ASSUME LEADERSHIP

From the first day the new leader walked through the door and sat behind her new desk, she has the positional authority of "leadership." The early stages of the assimilation process for a new leader form the testing ground for how well she adapts to the new environment, how quickly and skillfully she builds the credibility, trust, and relationships required to go from "positional" authority to "actualized" authority. Over this critical period, you have helped the new leader adapt to the new environment—learning about the organization and the industry, understanding the organizational dynamics and culture, laying the foundation for how her team will operate. At this stage, if the leader is assimilating successfully, she will have established and maintained dialogue with her team, developed and communicated a vision incorporating their input into her action plans, and determined resource requirements and staffed appropriately. In other words, she has set the framework for delegating greater responsibility to her team and can now turn her attention to assuming broader leadership within the organization. To fully assume leadership, the new leader still needs to bring the team up to a level of capability that will allow them to self-manage their day-to-day operations.

SUPPORT/COACHING: BROADEN THE SCOPE OF LEADERSHIP BY EMPOWERING OTHERS

Your role is to remind the new leader that the talent assessment that was conducted earlier in his tenure was done not only to determine whom to keep. It should also have identified people who needed developmental opportunities. This assimilation action is a "two-fer." It enables the new leader to extend his influence while at the same time building loyalty and capacity within his own team.

You can be of great value as the new leader begins to branch out into the organization. He will need your help to ensure that his team is self-sufficient enough to allow him to pursue more organizationwide opportunities. As the new leader begins to demonstrate success in his functional role and becomes a more valued resource across the organization, he's increasing the likelihood that other opportunities will arise for him to use his skills beyond his functional area. These often come in the form of invitations to join strategic-planning groups, task forces, or committees. Even with highly skilled team members, he cannot move into a broader, more strategic role if he does not have a team that is able to assume more responsibility. Without control systems in place that support an empowered team, he may end up feeling trapped in his role. Regardless of his success, he will be limited by the competence of his team.

Andrew, a senior executive from a premier computer company, knew he'd be able to contribute more once his team started *asking* to take work off of his plate. He was comfortable handing off work to them.

I ensure that they [members of my team] have what they need to serve their clients. Where I serve them the most is identifying opportunities for them, helping them work through ideas and solutions, and helping them to structure the intervention. Where I get more involved is with the organizational effectiveness issues and how to work with their clients in addressing those. So I do a lot on the more strategic, diagnostic end. I ask things like: What is really at play here, below the surface? What are the ways we can respond? And then I coach them through their conversations with their clients and get their buy-in and ensure that they have the resources to implement. After that, they update me, might come back with a question or two, but really the ball's in their court and they've been set up to deliver. I feel very comfortable about that, and so do they.

You can also help the new leader begin to identify and create opportunities for people to apply their new learning or to fill developmental gaps through on-the-job experiences. Remind the new leader that it's important not to delegate to others until they are ready. She should know that the payoff for her will be the security of knowing that she has a function that runs well enough to give her the time she needs to pursue her assimilation into the larger organization. You can either partner with the new leader to do this work, connect her with other people in the organization who can help to develop her people, or provide external referrals, such as private training vendors or consultants.

To the extent possible, ensure that the new leader schedules regular coaching sessions with members of her team focusing on developmental areas, to talk about progress and learning opportunities, and to provide an opportunity for questions and candid conversation. People need opportunities to test their assumptions with their boss, and to have an environment in which to ask her the tough questions without fear of losing face. Make sure the new leader understands that these meetings should provide a "safe place" where she and her team member can talk openly about what they've learned, what improvements still need to be made, and how they can best leverage new knowledge and experience.

Support/Coaching: Solidify Diagnostic and Interactive Control Systems

Empowerment cannot succeed without the proper control mechanisms in place. Managers must be able to rely on the efforts and initiative of employees within their teams in order to attend to broader duties. Employees throughout the organization must understand the business's strategy and their role in achieving strategically important goals. As managers face increasing demands on their time, they must use their scarce resources wisely, and employees must be empowered. The way to safely achieve employee empowerment is to help the new leader define boundaries and controls that will allow him to monitor progress and communicate what is and is not acceptable. Without proper clarification and without these systems in place, employees will not be armed with enough information to make their own decisions.

Robert Simons[2] identifies two kinds of control systems: diagnostic and interactive.

- *Diagnostic control systems* are designed to ensure the efficient and effective achievement of goals without the kind of constant monitoring that could be a distraction to leaders. These systems focus people and provide a basis for decision making. Their parameters are understood by everyone in the function, and they are linked to rewards and recognition measures. For example, a diagnostic control system in a claims-processing center would be designed to automatically track the number of claims handled and the time it took to handle each claim, and to generate a report summarizing this information at specified intervals.

- *Interactive control systems* are designed to provide managers with information about changes in the competitive environment and the activities of their subordinates so that they can respond proactively. They allow a leader to engage his team personally in strategic discussion and debate, which in itself provides opportunities for coaching and development.

As you advise the new leader during the implementation of his achievement agenda, ensure that he reexamines the systems and measures that are currently in place and asks himself the following questions:

- What are they measuring?
- What is important to the strategy?
- Are the systems tracking what I need them to track?

Have the new leader distinguish between the lagging and leading indicators he is using. Using lagging indicators as sole measures is like driving while looking in the rearview mirror. By the time you see the image in the mirror, it is too late—it is already behind you. Instead, one must look at the factors that will contribute to getting to the goal (leading indicators) and measure those. For example, if the new leader's strategy involves building a sales culture, the leading indicator would be a process measure that would look at what he needs to do to achieve certain sales goals, such as generating leads, while a lagging indicator would be actual sales. If one only measures the lagging indicator—the sales goal itself—and it is not achieved, then it is too late to put a corrective action in place. If factors have been identified all along the way that will indicate whether or not the sales target will eventually be hit, then the feedback provided by those measures will indicate what has to be altered in order to be successful.

This is the time to begin putting control systems in place that will allow the new leader to empower his people while still providing them with the guidance they need to make decisions that are aligned with the team's agenda and with the organizational agenda. However, it's important to ensure that these measures do not put the new leader and his team at odds with others in the organization.

ASSIMILATION GOAL: ALIGN SYSTEMS

The new leader has had some successes and has made positive changes within her function. This has enhanced her reputation and influence throughout the organization. To allow her to begin acting on an organizationwide level, it's important that she turn her attention to bringing systems and processes throughout the organization into alignment with her agenda. By now, her team should be self-sufficient enough to support her in this effort.

SUPPORT/COACHING: IDENTIFY THE DISCONNECTS THAT REQUIRE BROADER ORGANIZATIONAL CHANGE

One of the common derailers to successful strategy implementation is the lack of proper alignment of strategy with structure, people, processes, and metrics. As the new leader begins to assume a more strategic leadership role at this stage in the process, he needs to assess what are the potential systemic and procedural obstacles to achieving his business objectives. Thinking strategically about how to proactively assess the broader organizational changes that need to occur becomes a new function for him.

It is easy for new leaders at this stage to let enthusiasm about possibilities cloud their vision of the larger, systemic changes that are required for successful strategy implementation. During the 1999 holiday season, for example, many Internet companies fell prey to this derailer. They had an enticing sales proposition, they had the merchandise, they had robust order fulfillment processes, and they even had credit policies that could accommodate the Christmas rush. However, many of these companies did not have distribution centers that could hold up under the weight of the additional traffic. Therefore, their distribution centers were inundated and they couldn't get the merchandise out in time. The result was that many customers did not receive their merchandise in time for Christmas.

Your role at this stage is to encourage the new leader to utilize and expand on his understanding of the complexities of organizational operations—from both a tactical and interpersonal perspective—to anticipate what in the greater organization will have to be changed in order to be able to fully achieve an achievement legacy. One method for helping the new leader achieve organizational alignment is through the use of the cross-evaluation system that was previously discussed.

IS THE NEW LEADER ASSIMILATED?

In those who successfully assimilate, we observe a series of continuums that build over time. In order to progress from one stage to the next, there are certain actions and thought processes that both the new leader and the organization must participate in. Taken together, they form the following continuums, as previously discussed:

- Create Achievement Legacy
- Understand Organizational Dynamics
- Build Influence
- Assume Leadership
- Align Systems

THE ASSIMILATION PROCESS:
A DUAL PERSPECTIVE

As Exhibit 7-5 shows, the organization and individual each have important and mutually constructive roles throughout the assimilation process.

Exhibit 7-5. The dual roles in the assimilation process.

Achievements

Fully Performing Assimilated Leader

Months	Role	Create Achievement Legacy	Understand Organizational Dynamics	Build Influence	Assume Leadership	Align Systems
18 Months	New Leader: *Contributing*	Modify strategy based on feedback	Shape the culture	Build coalitions	Utilize your resources effectively	Influence others to make changes that will support strategy
	Organization: *Create Opportunities*	Follow up on feedback	Formally integrate cultural changes	Create opportunities for organizationwide interaction	Provide developmental opportunities	Formally integrate changes to the system
6–18 Months	New Leader: *Building*	Execute business strategy	Attribute meaning within the context	Build networks	Make team changes	Identify potential dependencies and derailers to executing your strategy
	Organization: *Support/Coach*	Provide feedback mechanisms	Provide coaching	Create opportunities to build networks	Support personnel transitions	Establish parameters for change
0–6 Months	New Leader: *Entering and Exploring*	Develop a business strategy	Assess the culture	Build relationships	Set expectations; establish norms	Test hypothesis, learn about the organization as it will impact your achievement legacy
	Organization: *Facilitate*	Help get industry expertise	Facilitate cultural audit	Facilitate key relationships (act as a translator)	Facilitate assessment of team's skills and competencies	Act as a sounding board
Day One						
Pre-hire	New Leader: *Anticipating and Planning*	Develop an entry strategy plan	Gather info about the culture	Determine with whom to build relationships	Self-assess leadership style	Develop hypothesis
	Organization: *Preparing*	Prepare a developmental plan	Advise new leader, provide information about culture	Prepare key stakeholders for new leader's arrival	Prepare team for new leader's arrival	Provide access to systems information

The five key goals of this process benefit and require the input and actions of individual new leaders and of those who support them.

Over time, and with the right organizational enabling systems and structures in place, a new leader builds toward the achievement of these goals in the following ways:

- *Create Achievement Legacy:* Beginning with developing an entry strategy and a preliminary business plan, moving into developing the business plan, and evolving to executing the plan and, eventually, to collecting feedback and modifying it accordingly

- *Understand Organizational Dynamics:* Beginning with gathering information about the culture, moving into assessing the culture, and evolving to attributing meaning to what is observed within the context of the organization and, eventually, to actively shaping the culture

- *Build Influence:* Beginning with determining with whom to build relationships, moving into building relationships based on competence, commitment, and communication, and evolving to the cultivation of networks and, eventually, to developing coalitions

- *Assume Leadership:* Beginning with self-assessing for leadership style, moving into assessing the team's skills and competence while setting expectations and establishing norms, and evolving to making changes within the team and, eventually, once the team is settled, developing a self-empowered team

- *Align Systems:* Beginning with developing hypotheses about the strategy, structure, people, processes, and metrics, moving into testing these hypotheses and learning about the organization to determine the impact on the achievement legacy, and evolving to identifying potential dependencies and derailers and, eventually, to identifying organizationwide changes that will support the success of the achievement legacy

As we hope that this book has shown, assimilation is an ongoing process, and the lessons learned by new leaders—as well as by those who work with them—provide the foundation for continued growth and development throughout their tenures. In the current environment of rapid growth and integration of new ideas and technologies, organizations exist in a constant state of change, continuously adjusting their strategies and structures to support new ways of working. New leaders who join assimilation-savvy organizations will be better equipped to manage transition and change in this increasingly volatile environment.

Notes

1. J. R. Katzenbach. "The Myth of the Top Management Team." *Harvard Business Review,* November/December 1997, p. 90.
2. R. Simons. "Control in an Age of Empowerment." *Harvard Business Review,* March/April 1995, pp. 80–88.

APPENDIX A

The New Leader's Handbook

INTRODUCTION

This Handbook is addressed specifically to the new leader and is focused on the activities that the new leader can do *prior* to his first day in a new job. This Handbook should be copied and distributed to a prospective new leader as early in the assimilation process as possible. In order to gain a full understanding of assimilation, and the actions that an assimilation-savvy organization should take in anticipation of a new leader's arrival, this Handbook should be read in conjunction with *Assimilating New Leaders: The Key to Executive Retention*, by Diane Downey et al. (AMACOM, 2001).

When they enter a new organization, most new leaders understand that they are going to have a lot to learn about an organization and how it functions. Intellectually, new leaders experience continued and growing success as they learn more and more about how the organization operates and begin to have an impact on shaping the world they have entered. Most people anticipate the process of conquering the intellectual challenge or "learning curve" that comes with each new situation. It is widely accepted that this process will take some time. What people tend not to anticipate, however, is the range of emotional experiences that accompany the assimilation process as shown in Exhibit A-1.

New leaders are often caught off-guard by their emotions. Senior executives who have been successful in their careers and have strong professional identities may have a difficult time dealing with their feelings of discomfort and disorientation. They are used to being in control

Exhibit A-1. Assimilation: The emotional and intellectual journey.

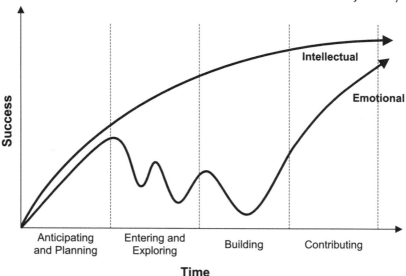

and to having their competence recognized. They are used to setting the pace in the environment around them, not having to adjust to the pace of others. The lack of "mooring" that results after entry is unexpected and unsettling and is often compounded by a combination of several factors:

- There is less authority and discretion than expected.

- The scope and expectation of the role does not match what was promised.

- The capabilities of the team are different than expected.

- Operating practices and procedures are counterintuitive.

- Loss of a network is destabilizing.

- There is uncertainty about whom to trust.

- Everything takes longer than expected.

Clearly, many of these factors relate to mismatched expectations. The emotions new leaders experience as they enter an organization follow a fairly predictable pattern. They often experience extreme highs and lows (or dips). The dips are usually a result of new leaders realizing that there is a huge gap between what they expected and what the reality is, leading them to question their suitability for the job. The first dip typically occurs after about four weeks, followed by another after six months on the job. Almost without exception, new leaders experience another "big dip" shortly after they enter the Building stage (at roughly nine months).

Thorough due diligence prior to accepting and careful preparation prior to beginning a job can provide a clear, objective view of the organization. The Handbook begins with the moment an executive decides to pursue a new job and covers the time up to "Day One" of employment. Traditionally, the period of interviewing, evaluating job options, and preparing for a new job is considered to be a time when the organization is holding all the cards while the individual does not have much control. In reality, an informed prospective new leader has an immense amount of power during this process, and *knowledge* is the key to unleashing it.

We suggest that new leaders engage in comprehensive research about the organization—about what it is like from the inside out. What do people think about working there? How does this organization treat new leaders who enter from the outside? Who in the organization does this role interact with? What are the resources available in the new organization that will solidify or prevent success in the role?

In order to uncover the answers to these and more questions, you will have to investigate and assess a large amount of information about the organization, yourself and your fit during a small period of time. Following the advice outlined in the Handbook will guide you through the steps you should take to avoid making the wrong decision and to position yourself in the best possible way for a successful organizational entry.

For more information, see the New Leader Assimilation Web site, accessible at executiveassimilation.com, leaderassimilation.com, and newleaderassimilation.com.

The Assimilation Journey. Section 1.
Determining the Assimilation Potential

In most of the literature on decision making, the focus is on "the decision." Deciding whether or not to accept a job offer is no exception.

The cognitive dissonance that you feel prior to making a decision is uncomfortable. People find it uncomfortable to be in limbo. They want to avoid their discomfort and deal with the consequences later. In other words, they want to resolve the dissonance by making a decision, *any* decision. To avoid making a decision that you'll regret later, it's crucial that you remain conscious of your rush to decision, and that you *methodically* engage in the process, no matter how tedious it may seem. Many people use a career counselor or trusted adviser who can provide a neutral sounding board and support them through the evaluation process. In order to gather enough information to decide whether to take the job, you should focus on the following key goals:

- Assess yourself.
- Assess the organization.
- Assess the position.
- Assess the culture.
- Make an educated decision.

PRE-HIRE GOAL: ASSESS YOURSELF

ACTION: DETERMINE MULTIPLE CRITERIA

Picture this scenario: A recruiter has assured you that this is a "once in a lifetime" opportunity. You think to yourself that the recruiter has a good reputation, and you haven't heard of many jobs that will offer the same possibility for financial remuneration, and prestige. There's a danger that, if you haven't been actively looking elsewhere, you will tend to believe the recruiter, because it is your only frame of reference. Before rushing to a decision, determine if you have searched for other alternatives. Have you risked asking for what you really want?

When people are being seriously considered for a position, they may feel an emotional high. The recruiting process often resembles a courtship, so each side presents its best face to the other. It is often difficult to ascertain what the organization is really like. Depending on your current situation, you may not want to look for disconfirming information, choosing instead to "believe the hype." A new leader shared her experience of being wooed by the courtship:

The recruitment and selection process was very seductive and flattering for me. In my own experience, it was very difficult to separate out the hype from the reality. I guess that self-deception is a uniquely human quality that can easily take over and badly skew judgment. It also probably diminished my natural due diligence process. I would say, in spite of my training in such matters, I chose to rely on intuition rather than research.

To facilitate the decision-making process, people often use short-cuts, or judgmental heuristics. These allow you to make decisions that build on your previous experience without having to exhaustively study each and every possible option. People often rely on the "anchoring and adjustment" heuristic wherein an initial piece of information acts as an anchor, or starting point, for subsequent thoughts.[1] For example: when buying a car you are often presented with a very expensive model first. By comparison, any lower-priced car will appear to be a great bargain. The definition of what is possible has been determined, but not by you. Anything you suggest that is not "anchored" in the initial suggestion may appear to be inappropriate. The salesperson provided the anchors by which you will judge all additional information.

The most effective way to avoid bias due to anchoring or selective vision (seeing only what you want to see while disregarding disconfirming information) is to determine clear, predefined criteria that will allow you to evaluate your options dispassionately. Making a criteria-based decision provides you with a referent point that allows you to avoid such selective visioning and anchoring. You want a new job to meet as many of your criteria as possible, and it's crucial that you prepare these criteria *before* you begin the interview process!

It might help to use a decision-making matrix as shown in Exhibit A-2. Every job is a "mosaic" of positive and negative qualities: Until you step back to examine them collectively, it's difficult to tell what the big picture looks like. The "Decision Support Matrix" is a tool that assists decision makers in ranking the options under consideration. Consider all aspects of the job—responsibilities, expectations, challenges, and relationships. Decide on the criteria to use in rating your concepts. Examples of such criteria might be "I will be able to use my change management skills," or "I will be allowed to pursue new markets." *Use as many criteria as possible!*

If there are gaps or deficiencies in the current offer, see if you can

Exhibit A-2. Decision support matrix.

#	Option Description	Criteria Rank 1 (low) – 5 (high)			Total Points	Rank
		A	B	C		

discuss these with your potential boss. Determine whether it is possible to modify the situation to align more closely with your criteria. Do not bend on your nonnegotiable job criteria! Too often, people don't realize they've made a mistake until they've been in their new jobs for months. It's better to realize early that assimilating into this organization will not be easy.

PRE-HIRE GOAL: ASSESS THE ORGANIZATION

ACTION: MAKE "DEMANDS" FOR ACCESS TO INFORMATION AS NEEDED

In order to gain the knowledge you need to unleash the power you have during this time, you should demand access to the appropriate information and the key players. The people you talk to *expect* to be asked for information, and *failing* to ask can actually make you seem arrogant or unable to understand the complexities of the issues at hand. In all likelihood, the answers you get will provoke more questions. The result will be a much broader sense of the dynamics of the organization and challenges facing your team. Put yourself in your future job and take into consideration your increased responsibilities and positional power. This may be uncomfortable, especially if you are making a large leap into a more senior role. One aspect of this comes down to asking the tough questions and making demands for access to information as needed. This is no time to be reticent. In fact, you are in the ideal

---

POTHOLE: DECIDING ON THE BASIS OF ONLY ONE OR TWO CRITERIA

Asenior vice president of a product line in the retail banking division of a global bank seems to have decided to leave her job based solely on her need for advancement:

> *I wasn't really unhappy at my previous job. I'd been there twenty years, and I had a pretty successful career there. I had good relationships with my peers—we worked well together as a leadership team. But with at least fifteen years left ahead of me, there wasn't really anywhere left for me to go within that organization. I really felt I was ready to run my own business line. I had the experience, I had the ideas—I just wasn't going to get the opportunity in the foreseeable future. My boss wasn't that much older than I was, and she didn't have any plans to leave. It was a tough decision, and it took me awhile to make it. But I finally decided to leave. The pay at this job isn't that great anyway. I know I could do better. And I never have liked the way decisions were made here.*

position to ask questions—you've got a license to ask for as much information as you need to know, without running the risk of undermining your own credibility as a knowledgeable leader. You'll also have a much better chance of avoiding any dangerous misinterpretations about expectations, which is a major cause of executive turnover.

ACTION: DETERMINE THE STRATEGIC POSITION OF THE ORGANIZATION

Before deciding whether to take the job, you need to understand what the organization's strategy is. How does the organization intend to achieve its goals and objectives? For example, does it plan to differentiate itself by product, service, cost, or growth? Is it clear what business it won't take and why? Does the strategy appear to be able to support the organization's goals? To what degree is technological change reshaping the industry? Are the goals, reward systems, structure, and human resource systems aligned? What are the gaps in the organization that your hire is meant to fill?

You need to determine whether you can thrive and flourish within the organization's current environment. Over time you will be able to make changes, but it is more important that you feel comfortable operating within the boundaries of the existing strategy and that you believe in the direction of the organization. Use the following questions to begin to get a sense of the strategic position of the organization:

- What are the business problems facing your unit and the organization as a whole?

- What is turnover like throughout the organization? Have they determined what the retention levers are that will address turnover? What are they?

- Are the performance management systems designed to weed out the deadwood?

ACTION: DETERMINE WHERE THE ORGANIZATION IS IN ITS LIFE CYCLE

In determining where the organization is in its life cycle, consider whether this is a start-up mostly focused on building credibility and product, or a business experiencing growing pains that must put energy into building its infrastructure, control environment, and growing its talent base? In *Growing Pains*, Eric C. Flamholtz identifies seven stages of growth in a company's life cycle:

ENTREPRENEURSHIP
- New venture
- Expansion
- Professionalization
- Consolidation

PROFESSIONALLY MANAGED FIRM
- Diversification
- Integration
- Decline and revitalization[2]

All organizations pass through various stages of development. The stages are determined in part by the organization's size as measured by its annual revenues.[3] An entrepreneurship is a business that has been created where none previously existed. Organizations in this phase of their life cycle are often lacking in formal management, systems, and procedures. In professionally managed organizations, on the other hand, management and management systems are in place and routinized.

As a potential newcomer, it will be important for you to identify where in the life cycle the organization in question lies, because the implications for you vary depending on the answer. For example, in an early stage of an entrepreneurship, you can expect that you may receive little support as a newcomer. Almost everybody will be new themselves and there most likely is no formal assimilation process in place. You can also imagine that in order to succeed in such a new environment, you would have to be able to tolerate ambiguity and be able to create order out of disorder. Generally, the proper probing can help you determine where in the life cycle the organization is. After you have this information, compare the organization's needs to your own skill and comfort level to determine whether there is a match.

Action: Determine Whether the Structure Supports the Strategy

The organizational structure can determine whether you will be able to successfully execute your strategy down the road. You will want to assess the structure before you accept the position. You should be considering the following:

- Will the structure of your new organization allow you to make innovations independently? For example, if you are one of six SBUs, can you change strategy or focus for your region or do you need to ensure that the change is made in concert with the other heads of the business?
- Where does your function fit in the pecking order? Is this a marketing-driven organization? Does the finance function have disproportionate influence?
- How is information shared throughout the organization?
- How important or influential is the governing body—the executive team? How do they operate?

PRE-HIRE GOAL: ASSESS THE POSITION

ACTION: STRIVE FOR CLARITY ABOUT THE JOB DESCRIPTION

You need to examine the job description carefully—for what it *doesn't* say, as well as for what it says. Get a clear sense of what others will expect of you in your new job—your boss, your team, and your other key stakeholders. Considering your role only in terms of what *you* have to do, instead of in terms of how you provide for and depend upon others in the organization, will make it very hard to convince others of your competence. At the same time, if you don't recognize the importance of the interrelationships among functions and between your team and its stakeholders, you'll miss out on valuable sources of information about the organization. Use the following questions to gain a better sense of the relationships surrounding the position:

- Whom will you rely on for success?
- Who are your stakeholders going to be?
- To what degree will you be empowered to address issues, and how will you be expected to prioritize your commitments to various stakeholder groups?

Unfortunately, most job specifications fail to provide these answers. In that case, you *must* take it upon yourself to ensure that you and those hiring you develop a shared understanding of the expectations of the role. This will require a lot of talking and asking questions. Make sure that the agreed-upon specifications are put in writing.

Another way to gather information is to find out who your key stakeholders are and what they will expect of you. Different people view the organization from different frames of reference, from the perspective of their function, as well as their particular roles within the organization. Once you are hired you will be entering multiple teams, all of which you will be counting on for your success.

A job spec only tells you about what *you* have to do. Every person, or every group, in the organization sees your role through a unique frame, and you should focus on "collecting" as many of these frames as possible. Closely reviewing these perspectives and expectations will help you determine which activities affect the largest number of constituencies and which groups require more specialized attention. As you listen to each perspective, think about the following two questions: How *similar* are they? Where are the disconnects? Once you identify the disconnects, you will want to probe further into the areas of disagreement to obtain clarity. During your interviews, you can begin to obtain information about these multiple frames and about the multiple points at which your role connects to others in the organization. Use the following questions as a framework to gather information about the position:

- Is the organization structured to enable you to do what you need to?
- How much sponsorship is there for your mandate?
- How much autonomy/control will you have?
- How would your accountabilities be structured? How would they be measured?
- Why did your predecessor leave?
- What is the strategic position of your team? Are they well placed for success?
- How does the organization expect your team to contribute to the achievement of its strategic goals?
- How will you be supported, in general and throughout the assimilation process?

PRE-HIRE GOAL: ASSESS THE CULTURE

ACTION: OBSERVE HOW YOU ARE TREATED DURING THE RECRUITING PROCESS

When trying to get a sense of the organization's culture, it's important to take a close look at how you're treated during the recruiting process. Try to consider the cultural dynamics that you witness during the interview process as an advance warning, and do not assume that what you see is an anomaly. Take it all in as data. We have worked with many senior executives who have been frustrated by contentious issues after entering, when the existence of these issues was not a well-kept secret and probably could have been observed in a number of interactions with the company before the hire. Since you most likely have significant experience and have learned how to handle a variety of adverse situations, it is easy to feel that these issues will not characterize your professional relationships. Remember that you will not be exempted from current norms and behaviors.

The following story from Greg, a senior executive at a Fortune 100 company, deals with his observations through the interview process:

This place seemed crazy. Other places I'd interviewed at were much more organized. There was an interview schedule that was strictly followed: I'd meet with several of my peers, with my proposed boss in the morning, and then later in the afternoon after I'd met everyone else. I felt that they were concerned about my feelings and respectful of my time. Then at the last company I went to, they really kept me waiting. Finally I met with the senior guy. Midway through the interview his assistant came in and pulled him out of the room. He explained that this was an emergency and left. One of his other subordinates joined me. The whole day was like this. Nothing went as planned. It was very chaotic. I don't think a single one of those interviews lasted as long as they were supposed to, and most of them were cut short by half. While I know this is routine in more dynamic industries, it struck me as unprofessional.

Which interview was best? Actually, the interviews at the last company probably provided a fairly realistic representation of what the culture was really like. The "business as usual" environment gave Greg an insider's view that the first interview did not. Greg was presented with many cultural clues even in his very first meeting.

You want to determine your compatibility with the organization in advance of accepting a job because if you feel uncomfortable with an organization during the recruiting process, it is unlikely that you would be able to stay long enough to facilitate long-term change. If you decide that you would be able to thrive in the environment, understanding the dynamics in advance will allow you to anticipate potential problems and plan accordingly. You can use the following questions to determine your compatibility:

- What was your gut reaction to the people you met with?
- What information did you gain from conversations with people in both formal and informal situations?

- Did that information match or clash with what you found in reference materials, press releases, etc?

- Has this information given you a good sense of the industry?

- If so, do the cultural values mesh well with your own?

ACTION: DEVELOP A COMPREHENSIVE VIEW OF THE CULTURE

All organizations possess assumptions, values, and norms that are as much a real part of the life of the organization as the building it is housed in and the people that work there. These assumptions, values, and norms are rooted in the organization's history—where it began, how it evolved, and the challenges it has faced. They provide the basis for how members of the organization make sense out of everyday life. As a leader, you will be called upon to publicly live and articulate the organization's values. If you don't share these values, it will be difficult for you to assimilate. The interview process is the time to uncover details about the organization's values and how they manifest themselves so that you can determine whether of not you will be able to live and promote them. The success rate of the blending of your style with the organization's style will depend, in part, on the malleability of both entities and the degree of overlap between the two styles.

A Procter and Gamble executive described the impact of culture as follows:

> People on the outside might portray our culture as imposing lock step uniformity. It doesn't feel rigid when you are inside. It feels like it accommodates you. And best of all, you know the game you're in—you know whether you're playing soccer or football; you can find out very clearly what it takes to succeed.[4]

In addition to the cultural audits described in Chapter Five of *Assimilating New Leaders*, there are many different possible approaches to gaining an understanding of the culture. At the very least, you should assess the organization's work/life balance, resource allocation, openness to change, and attitude toward newcomers. Consider the following kinds of questions as you assess how receptive to change your new organization is:

Work/Life Balance

- Is the new organization a "workaholic" environment?
- Whether a workaholic environment or not, what kind of flexibility does the organization allow?

Resource Allocation

- Are staffing decisions based on preexisting headcount or on workload and profitability?
- Will you have adequate support or will you be expected to do everything yourself?

Openness to Change

An analysis of the history and the current state of an organization as they relate to change can indicate the degree to which the organization in question is ready to accommodate and accept change in the future. In assessing your organization's willingness to change, some of the things you might want to consider include:

- Has the organization changed strategy recently? Was it successful?
- How are new products and services suggested and developed?
- Is there a process for generating and presenting new ideas?
- What is the organization's reputation where change is concerned? Is it viewed as cautious or progressive, and what evidence do you have to support this conclusion?

Attitude toward Newcomers

- Are there many newcomers currently in the organization? At what levels?
- Do newcomers tend to stay? How long?
- Is there evidence that the ideas of newcomers are incorporated?
- How long has the top management been in place?
- How diverse is the experience of top management? (e.g., other companies? other roles?)

The organization's attitude toward newcomers will play a large role in determining your ability to assimilate.

For example, one senior executive at a well-known entertainment firm realized the implications of joining an organization with a history of long tenure:

> *As any appointments were named, an e-mail would go out that would really give a whole litany of the background and history of the promoted person. During the time I was at Company X, I don't think there was any person who got named even just to director or a key level who hadn't been with the company for less than fifteen to twenty years. One day when I was reading my e-mails I thought to myself, "Oh my god, I am going to die here!" They were truly looking for people who remained with the company for that long. Even if people had come into the organization from pretty high-powered jobs somewhere else, they would have to work at Company X for a long time before they would get that type of recognition or promotion.*

In the story above, the practice of only promoting people with a long track record with the company could certainly be a barrier to opportunities for a newcomer.

PRE-HIRE GOAL: MAKE AN EDUCATED DECISION

ACTION: MANAGE YOUR COGNITIVE DISSONANCE

You may experience cognitive dissonance, a feeling of discomfort caused by holding two or more inconsistent cognitions, or ideas, at the same time.[5] A common example of cognitive dissonance is that it's difficult to make the decision to take a new job when, in reality, both your current job and the proposed one have positive attributes. The tendency is to magnify the problems of one's current job while unrealistically viewing the proposed new job as an ideal alternative.[6] The fact that a person can see the benefits of both sides creates cognitive dissonance. Because this is an uncomfortable state to remain in for very long, the tendency is to remedy this internal conflict by demonizing one's current job. This often manifests itself as enhancement of the positives of one situation and exaggeration of the negative aspects of the alternatives. Often, the exaggeration of positive aspects through cognitive dissonance can deter an individual from performing thorough due diligence, which usually ends in an underinformed decision. Cognitive dissonance should be managed in order to avoid excessive enhancement or exaggeration during the decision-making process. Avoid the tendency to "make a decision—any decision" to eliminate the discomfort. Reframe your dilemma in positive terms. It is good you have options. You are in control.

ACTION: WEIGH THE CHALLENGES THE JOB PRESENTS

As you begin to get information about the job and the expectations people will have of you, keep track of the problems and challenges you hear. Which of these will impact your probability of successful assimilation? Which will you be expected to be a part of solving? Given what you have learned about yourself, about the organization, and about your compatibility with the organizational culture, which of the challenges are insurmountable, if any? You should be ready to synthesize all the information you have gathered and begin to draw conclusions. Armed with your research, ask yourself the following questions, and answer them as honestly as you can:

- Are you comfortable with the inherent cultural aspects in the job, given what you've learned?
- Do you have the skills to execute the tasks and strategies that will be expected of you?
- What are the (potential or existing) obstacles to your success? Are they manageable? Do you have the skills to work around these obstacles?
- If there are skill gaps, can you fill them, or will they present insurmountable barriers to your success in this job?

Charting Pluses, Concerns, and "Fixes"

To help you put this information in a context that will help you make a decision about joining the organization, you can use a simple grid like the one shown in Exhibit A-3 to evaluate the positive or negative dimensions of each challenge or aspect of the job, as well as identify whether they are "fixable."

Exhibit A-3. Challenge of the job: Worksheet.

Pluses	Concerns	Fixes

Use a separate chart for each idea or cluster of ideas, as follows:

1. List all of the "pluses" of this position in light of your multiple criteria and career trajectory. Think of all of the benefits, advantages, and merits of this position.

2. List all of the concerns about the position. Think of all of the disadvantages, downsides, and problems.

3. Next to each concern, list a way to fix, minimize, or neutralize the cons. If there is no fix, then write "no fix" in the "fixes" column next to the concern.

4. On a scale of 1 to 10, rate your ability to implement each "fix." To support your rating, list the key experiences that you feel you can draw on in order to effect solutions.

You will come to one of two conclusions: that it *can* or *can't* be worked around or fixed. But the fact that something *can* be fixed doesn't mean that you want to expend the energy. Weigh each of the fixes carefully—how much energy are you willing to spend on each or any of them? Use what we call your "hedonic abacus," that internal mechanism by which you balance the potential pain of a situation against its possible benefits. If too many things slide to the "pain" side of the abacus as you're evaluating one of your fixes, and aren't offset by other things that you expect to gain, you've identified a significant barrier to accepting the job.

Your obligations and, consequently, the actions you need to take in order to prepare yourself, are different before and after you accept a job offer. When senior leaders decide to join a new organization, it's usually because they want to pursue new opportunities. What they usually find is that, while they encounter new norms and new values, pursuing new opportunities and implementing new changes is not always as easy—or as welcome—as it may at first seem. The next step in the process is to prepare yourself for the new opportunity.

The Assimilation Journey. Section 2.
Anticipating and Planning

To develop an entry strategy, you will focus primarily on activities that support three of your overall assimilation goals: Creating an Achievement Legacy, Assuming Leadership, and Building Influence. The components of an entry strategy are:

- Acquisition of knowledge and subject matter expertise about the industry and business
- Honest delineation of developmental needs
- Identification of key influence relationships
- Specification of preliminary priorities and approaches

ACQUISITION OF KNOWLEDGE AND SUBJECT MATTER EXPERTISE ABOUT THE INDUSTRY AND BUSINESS

ACTION: CONDUCT AN ASSESSMENT OF KNOWLEDGE GAPS

If you are entering a new industry, as well as a new job and new organization, the Anticipating and Planning stage is the time to learn everything you can about this new business environment—the products, marketplace, and competitive history that inform your organization's current strategy. You're going to be entering a "new land," and this means learning to speak a new language. After you enter, you won't have enough time to develop all of the in-depth industry knowledge that you need.

ACTION: HIRE AN INDUSTRY SPECIALIST TO BRING YOU UP TO SPEED

An important aspect of the control you have over your assimilation at this stage is your ability to determine not only what you need to learn but *how* you go about learning it. In many cases, there isn't enough time to learn everything you need to know between the time you take the job and the day you enter the organization. Why not take advantage of external subject matter experts who can bring you up to speed in a fraction of the time? Although this will cost you something, consider it an investment in your future. Once you enter the organization this can be funded out of your departmental budget. Nothing builds credibility as quickly as industry knowledge.

One executive, faced with a short anticipating and planning stage, hired an external consultant to help bring her up to speed on current research that was crucial to her new job:

> *I only had about three weeks between taking this new job as head of communications for a major food and beverage company. I hadn't worked in this industry before. I was hired primarily because of my track record in public relations and corporate communications in other industries. I knew there was a lot I'd have to learn on the job, but if I was going to have any kind of impact in the first few months I was there, even in small ways, I had to know more about the industry. So I hired a consultant who had done a great deal of work over the past ten years in the entertainment, hospitality, and food and beverage industries. He shared some very thorough reports on market trends over the last five years, and what the experts were saying about what was likely to happen in the industry over the next five years. We had several two- or three-hour meetings in which we talked about these reports, and she answered my questions. As a result, I ended up looking pretty damned knowledgeable and forward-thinking—some of my colleagues hadn't read up on industry projections, so I was able to establish credibility early. It was well worth the money.*

HONEST DELINEATION OF
DEVELOPMENTAL NEEDS

ACTION: IDENTIFY PERSONAL DEVELOPMENTAL GAPS

Try to find out why you were hired. It seems like a simple question to ask, one that should have a simple answer. But you'd be surprised by how your assumptions about why you were hired can differ from the true reasons behind the organization's decision. In all likelihood, you weren't the only candidate they were looking at seriously. Find out what your perceived desirability is—that is, why didn't they hire the other person, or people? What did they lack that the organization assumes you have? What is the organization assuming you can do better? Clearly, you were hired because the organization believed that you have the skills and experience to do the job. When you find out what the other candidates lacked, ask yourself whether these are things that you can provide, strengths that you can truly leverage in order to succeed.

If you find out that key aspects of your role require skills or abilities that aren't among your key strengths, plan for how to compensate for your weaknesses. No one is good at everything; needing help doesn't make you an imperfect leader. *The best leaders, in fact, are those who know their own weaknesses and are able to put structures in place that compensate for them.* To do this, you will need a sense of your individual team members' competence levels. Based on the information you have been able to glean from others and your preliminary assessment, determine who might be able to provide support in a given area, and plan to assign responsibilities accordingly. As always, this plan will be tentative, and will continue to evolve after you enter the organization. The key here is to become conscious of these issues so that you can begin to plan for how you will ultimately address them.

IDENTIFICATION OF KEY INFLUENCE RELATIONSHIPS

ACTION: UNDERSTAND THE KEY INFLUENCE RELATIONSHIPS

One component of the entry strategy is the identification of key influence relationships. It is important to identify and understand the key people your position will interact with, because your success in your new role will rely on them once you begin your job. You should make efforts to meet with each of them prior to beginning your job or within a short time following your arrival.

There are a couple of ways to uncover the key influence relationships connected to the new position. You may need to enlist the help of others to do either of them. One way is to map out each key process that your team is involved in. The HR Touchstone can often be an invaluable resource for such an exercise.

You will want to understand:

- How your role fits into the new team
- How the new team fits into the overall structure of the organization
- What the new role will require from others
- What others will require from the new role

Another way to identify key influence relationships is depicted in Exhibit A-4, which shows the basic organizational relationships of a CFO.

Exhibit A-4. Example: Stakeholder relationships.

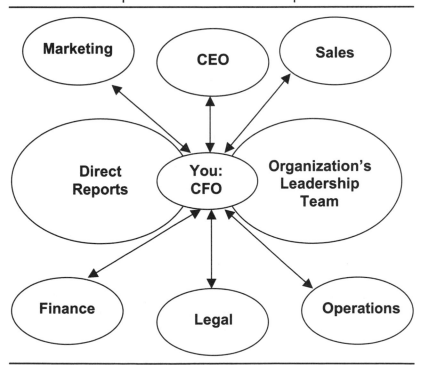

Making a chart like this for your new role allows you to visually record various key relationships. This can enable you to proactively anticipate their needs. As you begin to develop a complete picture of how your role supports other roles and how they support yours, you should begin to develop hypotheses about the problems that must be solved and begin to prioritize stakeholder needs. The following is a framework that can help you prioritize:

- Whose needs are more important from a practical perspective?
- Whom must I please before I can begin implementing any of his changes?
- Whose support will I need the most?

Once these people are identified, part of your entry strategy should include plans to meet with and begin a dialogue with those people who are considered to be key to the position. You may want to ask your HR Touchstone to help you set up meetings with them if you do not have easy direct access on your own.

SPECIFICATIONS OF PRELIMINARY PRIORITIES AND APPROACHES

ACTION: IDENTIFY AN APPROPRIATE MANAGEMENT STYLE

Before you enter, you'll also have to define a management approach that *works* in the new context, and one that is probably different from other contexts you've encountered. Look back over your past experience as a leader. What behaviors or leadership "flat sides" have derailed you in the past? And, of course, what contributed to your success? What kinds of leadership challenges did you face in your last job? If when you look back, you see themes emerging over your career, this is a clear indication that you'll need to consciously create some compensatory mechanisms to help you prevent past mistakes from recurring. For example, if you realize that people have often complained that you are not a good listener, you can bet that this will be a problem in your new job. It doesn't matter if you *think* you're a good listener. Maybe you are—what this information is telling you is that other people aren't *feeling* listened to. To compensate for this, you might have to remind yourself to summarize verbally what others have told you, so that they know that you understand and have been taking them seriously. And since "listening" happens virtually, as well, you might have to make time every day to respond to the memos and e-mails from people who are sending you their ideas and giving you feedback.

There are ways in which people in the organization are used to operating. It will be especially important for you to understand your new boss's management style because in part that will dictate how you adapt yours.

One of our interviewees explains how he and his boss have different management styles and how that impacts on his ability to be effective in the new role that was created for him within his new organization:

> *I think [my boss] was uncomfortable with the new position, uncomfortable with me. I think I represented the new regime and so I think he was somewhat distrustful of me. I don't think he liked the idea that I was matrixed to him. I think he felt that it would have guaranteed more loyalty or trust if I was a direct report. But in fact I am very loyal and confidential and I would never do anything to violate his trust. I think we are very different types of individuals. Very simply, he is a lawyer, he is very analytical and detail oriented. He has loyalty and commitment to individuals, whereas I see myself as being more focused on the good of the organization. I think people count and you have to factor people into your decisions but I don't think you should make decisions based on friendships or on past loyalties or commitments to anyone. I think I tend to be more conceptual than he is. I tend to look more at the big picture and not delve into the details.*

This executive had clues to these fundamental differences from the first time he and his boss sat down to speak. The Anticipating and Planning stage is the optimal time to begin to identify the differences in management style and to look inward to begin to understand the ways in which you can and cannot adjust your management style to work with your boss and your new team. There are some things about your previous experience that you probably would have liked to have done differently—now is the time to plan to make those adjustments, preferably in the direction of the organization and the boss you will now be connected to.

ACTION: INTERVIEW YOUR PREDECESSOR TO GAIN HIS PERSPECTIVE

If your predecessor is still around and open to talking with you, make every effort to sit down with him and discuss the challenges that are facing your team. When the predecessor is available and disposed to provide this information—in other words, if he hasn't been fired and thus is filled with bad feelings about the organization—there are few better sources. The departing leader has nothing to lose by helping you. More important, this is a person who has been in the trenches— somewhere the recruiters *and your boss* haven't been. You're likely to get a much more comprehensive perspective of the problems facing your team from someone who's already faced them. Interviewing the previous leader becomes especially important in situations where your tenure and that of the departing leader will overlap.

A military captain we spoke with took a proactive approach to learning about his company from his predecessor prior to taking command—but within limits:

> *I wanted to know some of the problems of the company. He was honest with me—you don't lie about your company. You can talk about strengths and weaknesses. You can also talk about strengths and weaknesses of people, but he told me, and I strongly agree, that you don't talk bad about the other officers or enlisteds in the company because maybe this next commander coming in is going to be the one who turns them around. The word to my last incoming commander about me was that I was immature. Well, guess what, I blossomed. Luckily this guy didn't prejudge me based on that assessment he got. If he came in with a predisposed attitude against me, would I have turned around? Probably not. He wouldn't have taken the time.*

The captain and his predecessor recognized that an incoming commander needs to get an honest assessment of the strengths and weaknesses of the team. What these two officers also recognized was that differences in leadership style and circumstances of the mission can affect perceptions about the *potential*, as well as the performance, of individual team members. If you hear judgments of this sort from your predecessor, don't disregard them, but seek confirming—or disconfirming—information of your own. The last leader's poor performer might become your protégé.

ACTION: DEVELOP A "COMMAND PHILOSOPHY"

Writing a "command philosophy" is a technique new leaders in the military use for communicating expectations to their new teams. Here is how one captain in the U.S. Armed Forces described his use of the command philosophy to communicate values and expectations:

> *In my command philosophy, I'm going to lay out for my company, in detail, where I want to take them. I'm going to lay out what I expect of them. I'm going to make sure they know that when they don't meet expectations, I am going to counsel and let them know that they are not meeting the standard. I don't care what the last guy did—maybe Lieutenant X was the golden boy for the previous captain and he had a review that said he's the best, but maybe the truth is he's drinking buddies with that guy or pulled the wool over his eyes. That's fine, I'll find out, because I'm going to lay out the standards and judge everybody fairly by them. And they're going to know that up front; they're going to hear from me that there's not going to be any favoritism, and I'm going to follow that up with actions that demonstrate that fact.*
>
> *The command philosophy outlines what's important to me. It starts out: Know your job. Be technically and tactically proficient because people rely on you. And I go into reasons why you have to know your job. And its got to apply to every level, its got to apply to the guy who's just come here from Fort Knox, Kentucky with just six weeks of basic training. "Know your job" is standard. The next piece is about discipline—discipline in everything you do: in physical fitness training, in how you salute, and in how you conduct yourself with superiors and subordinates. I talk about how I won't ever reprimand you for taking initiative as long as you're demonstrating a certain level of integrity. If you break rules and tell me you were taking initiative, you're saying the wrong thing. And then I talk to them about character and why it's important to me. And*

then the last thing is integrity. We count on each other, people above us count on us and people below us count on us. So, we have to understand that integrity is critical in our job and that if you don't have trust within an organization then you don't have a successful organization. The organization, especially a military unit, can't function without a degree of trust that's continuous throughout the unit.

Developing and distributing a command philosophy is a common expectation for good leaders.

Using a command philosophy goes a long way toward mitigating the team's anxieties about your arrival. It allows you to:

- Be clear about your expectations.
- Let people know whom you are.

In private industry, the language of command philosophy is not in common use, but many leaders develop their leadership visions. This is not a pro forma activity for them. For many, it is the first time they have really thought through their own credo. As is true in the military, it often contains their values, standards, and expectations—of them- selves and for others.

Notes

1. M. H. Bazerman. *Judgment in Managerial Decision-Making*, 3rd ed. New York: Wiley, 1994, pp. 31–32.
2. E. G. Flamholtz. *Growing Pains: How to Make the Transition from an Entre- preneurship to a Professionally Managed Firm.* San Francisco: Jossey-Bass, 1990, pp. 32–33.
3. Ibid., p. 32.
4. Pascale, R. "Fitting New Employees into the Company Culture." *Fortune,* 28 May 1984.
5. L. A. Festinger. *A Theory of Cognitive Dissonance.* Stanford, Calif.: Stanford University Press, 1957.
6. Ibid.

Organizational Checklists: Overview of the Assimilation Process

Exhibit B-1. Stage One: Anticipating and planning.

Assimilation Goals	Organizational Role	
Organizational Intervention Strategies		
Hire an assimilation coach.	**Intervention**	❑
Appoint people within the organization to support the leader.	**Intervention**	❑
Create an Achievement Legacy		
Provide feedback and design a development plan.	Facilitation	❑
Legitimize access to information and key people.	Facilitation	❑
Build Influence		
Understand key stakeholder relationships.	Support/Coaching	❑
Prepare key stakeholders for new leader's arrival.	Facilitation	❑
Assume Leadership		
Identify the competencies of the surrounding team.	Raising Awareness	❑
Prepare the leader's team for his arrival.	Facilitation	❑
Gain the outgoing leader's support of the new leader's entry.	Facilitation	❑

Exhibit B-2. Stage Two: Entering and exploring.

Assimilation Goals	Organizational Role	
Create an Achievement Legacy		
Set priorities.	Support/Coaching	❑
Focus on "small win" activities.	Support/Coaching	❑
Conduct an organizational assessment.	**Intervention**	❑
Understand Organizational Dynamics		
Be aware of the dynamics of first impressions.	Support/Coaching	❑
Be aware of paradigm conflicts.	Raising Awareness	❑
Be aware of unique cultural cues.	Raising Awareness	❑
Conduct a cultural audit and identify cultural dynamics organizationwide.	**Intervention**	❑
Build Influence		
Utilize power and influence.	Support/Coaching	❑
Establish trust.	Support/Coaching	❑
Build a collaborative relationship with the boss.	Facilitation	❑
Plan for the "dips."	Support/Coaching	❑
Build relationships with peers.	Facilitation	❑
Conduct a stakeholder analysis.	**Intervention**	❑
Assume Leadership		
Act "as if."	Support/Coaching	❑
Help the new leader to clarify roles and expectations within the team.	Facilitation	❑
Manage resistance to change.	Raising Awareness	❑
Assess the team for skills and competencies.	**Intervention**	❑
Help new leaders hire "their own people."	Raising Awareness	❑
Schedule a new leader assimilation meeting.	**Intervention**	❑

Exhibit B-3. Stage Three: Building.

Assimilation Goals	Organizational Role	
Create an Achievement Legacy		
Set challenging but implementable goals.	Support/Coaching	❑
Gather input from all stakeholders before executing plans.	Support/Coaching	❑
Explain past change attempts.	Raising Awareness	❑
Understand Organizational Dynamics		
Employ "protest absorption" techniques.	Support/Coaching	❑
Build Influence		
Create cross-organizational network-building and boundary-spanning opportunities for the new leader.	Facilitation	❑
Build networks	Support/Coaching	❑
Sponsor a new leader forum.	**Intervention**	❑
Implement the Assimilation Game.	**Intervention**	❑
Assume Leadership		
Make the difficult staffing decisions.	Support/Coaching	❑
Build a leadership team.	Support/Coaching	❑
Advocate for team members.	Support/Coaching	❑
Align Systems		
Bridge the gaps between the current and future states.	Support/Coaching	❑

Exhibit B-4. Stage Four: Contributing.

Assimilation Goals	Organizational Role	
Create an Achievement Legacy		
Modify strategy based on feedback.	Support/Coaching	❑
Understand Organizational Dynamics		
Reshape the organizational culture.	Support/Coaching	❑
Build Influence		
Expand the span of influence.	Support/Coaching	❑
Become a more strategic contributor to the executive team.	Support/Coaching	❑
Mend relationships that were neglected.	Support/Coaching	❑
Carefully choose the issues to focus on.	Support/Coaching	❑
Understand the importance of coalitions.	Support/Coaching	❑
Assume Leadership		
Broaden the scope of leadership by empowering others.	Support/Coaching	❑
Solidify diagnostic and interactive control systems.	Support/Coaching	❑
Align Systems		
Identify the disconnects that require broader organizational change.	Support/Coaching	❑

Bibliography

Abelson, R. "A Growing Corporate Challenge: The Empty Executive Suite." *New York Times,* 16 November 2000.

Allen, N. J., and Meyer, J. P. "Organizational Socialization Tactics: A Longitudinal Analysis of Links to Newcomers' Commitment and Role Orientation." *Academy of Management Journal* 33, 4 (1990): 847–858.

Andrasik, F. "Organizational Behavior Modification in Business Settings: A Methodological and Content Review." *Journal of Organizational Behavior Management* 10, 1 (1989): 59–77.

Argyris, C. *Knowledge for Action: A Guide to Overcoming Barriers to Organizational Change.* San Francisco: Jossey-Bass, 1993.

Aronson, E. *The Social Animal.* 8th ed. New York: Worth, 1999.

Ashforth, B. E., Saks, A. M., and Lee, R. T. "Socialization and Newcomer Adjustment: The Role of Organizational Context." *Human Relations* 51, 7 (1998): 897–926.

Ashkenas, R., Jick, T., Ulrich, D., and Paul-Chowshury, C. *The Boundaryless Organization Field Guide: Practical Tools for Building the New Organization.* San Francisco: Jossey-Bass, 1999.

Ashkenas, R., Ulrich, D., Jick, T., and Kerr, S. *The Boundaryless Organization: Breaking the Chains of Organizational Structure.* San Francisco: Jossey-Bass, 1995.

Associated Press. "For Many Workers, a Season of Worry." *New York Times,* 24 December 2000, sec. B, p. 8.

Austin, M. J., and Gilmore, T. N. "Executive Exit: Multiple Perspectives on Managing the Leadership Transition." *Administration in Social Work* 17, 1 (1993): 47–61.

Bandler, R., and Grinder, J. *Reframing: Neuro-Linguistic Programming and the Transformation of Meaning.* Moab, Utah: Real People Press, 1982.

Bandura, A. *Social Learning Theory.* Upper Saddle River, N.J.: Prentice Hall, 1977.

Barboza, D. "Maytag's Chief Executive Resigns, Citing Differences." *New York Times on the Web,* 10 November 2000, *www.nytimes.com.*

Barker, J. A. *Paradigms: The Business of Discovering the Future.* New York: HarperCollins, 1992.

241

Barnett, C. K., and Tichy, N. M. "Rapid-Cycle CEO Development: How New Leaders Learn to Take Charge." *Organizational Dynamics* 29 (Summer 2000): 16–32.

Bazerman, M. H. *Judgment in Managerial Decision Making.* 3rd ed. New York: John Wiley & Sons, 1994.

Becker, H. S. "Notes on the Concept of Commitment." *American Journal of Sociology* 66 (July 1960): 32–40.

Beckhard, R., and Harris, R. T. *Organizational Transitions: Managing Complex Change.* Reading, Mass.: Addison-Wesley, 1977.

Beer, M., and Gibbs, M. *The Challenge of Commitment.* Boston: Harvard Business School Press, 1993.

Bennis, W. G., Kenneth, B. D., and Chin, R. *The Planning of Change.* 4th ed. New York: Holt, Rinehart & Winston, 1985.

Blau, G., and Boal, K. "Using Job Involvement and Organizational Commitment Interactively to Predict Turnover." *Journal of Management* 15, 1 (1989): 115–127.

Braddock, D., and Gibbs, N. H. "Occupational Employment Projections to 2008." *Monthly Labor Review* [Employment Outlook: 1998–2008], November 1999, 51–77.

Breuer, N. L. "Even in High-Turnover Industries, Not Everyone's a Quitter." *Workforce,* 22 August 2000, *www.workforce.com.*

Bridges, W. *Surviving Corporate Transition: Rational Management in a World of Mergers, Start-ups, Takeovers, Layoffs, Divestitures, Deregulation and New Technologies.* New York: Doubleday, 1988.

Brookfield, S. D. *The Skillful Teacher.* San Francisco: Jossey-Bass, 1990.

Buckingham, M., and Coffman, C. *First Break All the Rules.* New York: Simon & Schuster, 1999.

Buckley, M. R., Fedor, D. B., Carraher, S. M., Fink, D. D., and Marvin, D. "The Ethical Imperative to Provide Recruits Realistic Job Previews." *Journal of Managerial Issues* 9, 4 (1997): 468–484.

Bureau of Labor Statistics, U.S. Department of Labor. "Employee Tenure in 1998." News Release. September 23, 1998.

Burke, R. J., and McKeen, C. A. "Facilitating the New Manager Transition: Part I." *Executive Development* 7, 2 (1994): 16–18.

———. "Facilitating the New Manager Transition: Part II." *Executive Development* 7, 4 (1994): 10–12.

Business Issues Research Group. *Avoiding the Brain Drain, What Companies Are Doing to Lock in Their Talent.* Kepner-Tregoe, January 1999.

Cappelli, P. "A Market-Driven Approach to Retaining Talent." *Harvard Business Review,* January 2000, 103–111.

Carrison, D., and Walsh, R. *Semper Fi: Business Leadership the Marine Corps Way.* New York: AMACOM, 1998.

Catlette, B., and Hadden, R. "Prepare Employees for Their Next Job and They'll Stick Around." *Workforce,* 22 August 2000, *www.workforce.com.*

Center for Creative Leadership Home Page, 26 September 2000, *www.ccl.org.*

Chambers, E. G., Foulon, M., Handfield-Jones, H., Hankin, S. M., and Michaels, E. G. III. "The War for Talent." *McKinsey Quarterly* 3 (1998): 48–57.

Ciampa, D., and Watkins, M. *Right from the Start: Taking Charge in a New Leadership Role.* Boston: Harvard Business School Press, 1999.

Conner, D. R. *Managing at the Speed of Change: How Resilient Managers Succeed and Prosper Where Others Fail.* New York: Villard Books, 1993.

Corcoran, E. "The E Gang." *Forbes,* 24 July 2000, 145–172.

Cummings, T. G., and Huse, E. F. *Organization Development and Change.* 4th ed. St. Paul: West, 1989.

Dahle, C. "Fast Start—Your First 60 Days." *Fast Company,* June 1998, 182.

Davis, M. G., and Clark, L. A. "Changing of the Guard." *Across the Board,* September 1993.

Davis, S., and Meyer, C. *Blur: The Speed of Change in the Connected Economy.* Reading, Mass.: Addison-Wesley, 1998.

De Lisser, E. "More Entrepreneurs Take Help of Executive Coaches." *The Wall Street Journal,* 5 September 2000.

Deutsch, Claudia H. "Management: Companies Scramble to Fill the Shoes at the Top." *New York Times on the Web,* 1 November 2000, *nytimes.com.*

Dobbs, K. "Train Your Managers." *Training,* August 2000, 62–66.

Dobrzynski, J. H. "Online Pioneers: The Buzz Never Stops." *New York Times,* 21 November 1999.

Downey, D. "Cross-Evaluation as an OD Tool." *MetroNews,* May 1996.

Egan, G. *Working the Shadow Side, a Guide to Positive Behind-the-Scenes Management.* San Francisco: Jossey-Bass, 1994.

"Employee Turnover Depresses Earnings, Stock Prices 38%, Nextera Research Study Shows," 8 August 2000, *e-cruiter.com.*

Fairhurst, G. T., and Sarr, R. A. *The Art of Framing: Managing the Language of Leadership.* San Francisco: Jossey-Bass, 1996.

Feldman, D. C. "A Contingency Theory of Socialization." *Administrative Science Quarterly* 24 (1976): 433–453.

Ferris, G. R., Perrewe, P. L., Anthony, W. P., and Gilmore, D. C. "Political Skill at Work." *Organizational Dynamics* 28, 4 (2000): 25–37.

Festinger, L. *A Theory of Cognitive Dissonance.* Stanford, Calif.: Stanford University Press, 1957.

Flamholtz, E. G. *Growing Pains: How to Make the Transition from an Entrepreneurship to a Professionally Managed Firm.* San Francisco: Jossey-Bass, 1990.

French, J. R. P. Jr., and Raven, B. "The Basis of Social Power." In *Studies in Social Power,* edited by D. Cartwright. Ann Arbor, Mich.: Institute for Social Research, 1959.

French, W. L., and Bell, C. H. Jr. *Organization Development: Behavioral Science Interventions for Organization Improvement.* Englewood Cliffs, N.J.: Prentice Hall, 1995.

Gabarro, J. J. *The Dynamics of Taking Charge*. Boston: Harvard Business School Press, 1987.

———. "When a New Manager Takes Charge." *Harvard Business Review*, May/June 1985, 110–123.

Gabarro, J. J., and Kotter, J. P. "Managing Your Boss." *Harvard Business Review*, May 1993, 150–157.

Galbraith, J. R. *Competing with Flexible Lateral Organizations*. 2nd ed. Reading, Mass.: Addison-Wesley, 1994.

Galbraith, J. R., Downey, D., and Kates, A. Designing Dynamic Organizations: A Hands-On Guide for Leaders at All Levels. New York: AMACOM, 2001.

George, M. A., and Miller, K. D. "Assimilating New Employees." *Training and Development*, July 1996, 49–50.

Ghemawat, P. *Commitment, The Dynamic of Strategy*. New York: The Free Press, 1991.

———. *Competition and Business Strategy in Historical Perspective*. Boston: Harvard Business School Publishing, 2000.

Gladwell, M. *The Tipping Point: How Little Things Can Make a Big Difference*. Boston: Little, Brown, 2000.

Goffman, E. *The Preservation of Self in Everyday Life*. New York: Doubleday, 1959.

———. *Strategic Interaction*. Philadelphia: University of Pennsylvania Press, 1969.

Goleman, D. *Emotional Intelligence*. New York: Bantam Books, 1997.

———. *Vital Lies, Simple Truths: The Psychology of Self-Deception*. New York: Simon & Schuster, 1985.

———. "What Makes a Leader?" *Harvard Business Review*, November–December 1998, 93–102.

———. *Working with Emotional Intelligence*. New York: Bantam Books, 1998.

Greiner, L. E., and Schein, V. E. *Power and Organization Development: Mobilizing Power to Implement Change*. Reading, Mass.: Addison-Wesley, 1989.

Hamel, G., and Prahalad, C. K. *Competing for the Future*. Boston: Harvard Business School Press, 1994.

Hammond, J. S., Keeney, R. L., and Raiffa, H. *Smart Choices: A Practical Guide to Making Better Decisions*. Boston: Harvard Business School Press, 1999.

Harmon-Jones, E., and Mills, J., eds. *Cognitive Dissonance: Progress on a Pivotal Theory in Social Psychology*. Washington, D.C.: American Psychological Association, 1999.

Heskett, J. L., Sasser, W. E. Jr., and Schlesinger, L. A. *The Service Profit Chain*. New York: The Free Press, 1997.

"Hindery Out, Casey In as Global Crossing CEO." *New York Times on the Web*, 11 October 2000, *www.nytimes.com*.

Hirsch, P. M. *Pack Your Own Parachute: How to Survive Mergers, Takeovers, and Other Corporate Disasters*. New York: Addison-Wesley, 1987.

Horney, N. F., and Koonce, R. "Using Competency Alignment to Shape, Drive, and Sustain Change Efforts." *National Productivity Review* 15, 3 (1996): 41–53.

"How the Human Resource Function Can Create Value and Drive Strategic Success." *Balanced Scorecard.* Report based on presentation by David Ulrich. Boston: Harvard Business School Publishing, 2000.

Hultman, K. *Making Change Irresistible: Overcoming Resistance to Change in Your Organization.* Palo Alto, Calif.: Davies-Black Publishing, 1998.

Hymowitz, C. "How Cynthia Danaher Learned to Stop Sharing and Start Leading." *The Wall Street Journal,* 16 March 1999, sec. B, p. 1.

Jablin, F. M. "Organizational Entry, Assimilation, and Exit." In *Handbook of Organizational Communication,* edited by F. M. Jablin, L. L. Putman, K. H. Roberts, and L. W. Porter, 679–741. New York: Sage, 1987.

Jablin, F. M., and Krone, K. J. "Organizational Assimilation." In *Handbook of Communication Science,* edited by C. R. Berger and S. H. Chaffel, 711–746. Newbury Park, Calif.: Sage.

Janis, I. L., and Mann, L. *Decision Making: A Psychological Analysis of Conflict, Choice, and Commitment.* New York: The Free Press, 1977.

Janis, M. "Shhhhh, the Dragon Is Asleep and Its Name Is Resistance." *Journal of Staff Development* 19, 3 (1998): 13–16.

Johnson, D. W. *Reaching Out: Interpersonal Effectiveness and Self-Actualization.* 6th ed. Boston: Allyn & Bacon, 1997.

Johnson, H. T. *Relevance Regained: From Top-Down Control to Bottom-Up Empowerment.* New York: The Free Press, 1992.

Jones, G. R. "Psychological Orientation and the Process of Organizational Socialization: An Interactionist Perspective." *Academy of Management Review* 8, 3 (1983): 464–474.

———. "Socialization Tactics, Self-Efficacy, and Newcomers' Adjustments to Organizations." *Academy of Management Journal* 29, 2 (1986): 262–279.

Jordan-Evans, S. *Love 'Em or Lose 'Em: Getting Good People to Stay.* San Francisco: Berrett-Koehler, 1999.

Kaplan, R. E. *Trade Routes: The Manager's Network of Relationships.* Greensboro, N.C.: Center for Creative Leadership, 1983.

Kaplan, R. S., and Norton, D. P. "The Balanced Scorecard—Measures That Drive Performance." *Harvard Business Review,* January–February 1992, 71–79.

———. "Putting the Balanced Scorecard to Work." *Harvard Business Review,* September–October 1993, 134–147.

Katzenbach, J. R. "The Myth of the Top Management Team." *Harvard Business Review,* November–December 1997, 83–91.

Kodish, S. P., and Kodish, B. I. *Drive Yourself Sane: Using the Uncommon Sense of General Semantics.* Rev. 2nd ed. Pasadena, Calif.: Extensional Publishing, 2001.

Kofodimos, J. R. "Teamwork at the Top: The Need for Self-Development." *Issues & Observations* 11, 1 (1991): 1–3.

Kolbe, K. *Pure Instinct: Business' Untapped Resource.* New York: Times Books, 1993.

Korn, A. N. "Gotcha!" *Across the Board* 35, 8 (1998): 30–35.

Kotter, J. P. *The General Managers.* New York: The Free Press, 1982.

————. *Leading Change.* Boston: Harvard Business School Press, 1996.

Koudsi, S. "Down and Out." *Fortune,* 2 October 2000, 42–43.

Kroll, L. "Survivor." *Forbes,* 7 August 2000, 94–98.

Kruger, P. "Stop the Insanity!" *Fast Company,* July 2000, 240.

Kuhn, T. S. *The Structure of Scientific Revolutions.* 2nd ed. Chicago: University of Chicago Press, 1962.

Laporte, L. J. "Leadership Succession in the Military." Carlisle, Pa.: U. S. Army War College, 31 March 1989.

Lawler, E. J. "Affective Attachments to Nested Groups: A Choice Process Theory." *American Sociological Review* 57 (June 1992): 327–339.

"Leadership (2): Horses for Courses." *Business Europe,* June 1999.

Lee, R. J., and King, S. N. "Executive Effectiveness and Fulfillment: A Leadership Factor." *Leadership in Action* 19, 5 (1999): 1–7.

Lee, T. W., Ashford, S. J., Walsh, J. P., and Mowday, R. T. "Commitment Propensity, Organizational Commitment, and Voluntary Turnover: A Longitudinal Study of Organizational Entry Process." *Journal of Management* 18, 1 (1992): 15–32.

Leger, D. E. "Behind Every Great Man Is a Great Manager." *Fortune,* 16 October 2000, 403–420.

Libove, L. R. *Chart Your Start: The New Employee's Role in Orientation.* King of Prussia, Pa.: Human Resources Development Quarterly, 1996.

Lieber, R. "Leadership Ensemble." *Fast Company,* May 2000, 286–302.

Lombardo, M. M., and Eichinger, R. W. "High Potentials as High Learners." *Human Resource Management* 39 (Winter 1998): 321.

————. *Preventing Derailment: What to Do before It's Too Late.* Greensboro, N.C.: Center for Creative Leadership, 1995.

London, M. "Overcoming Career Barriers: A Model of Cognitive and Emotional Processes for Realistic Appraisal and Constructive Coping." *Journal of Career Development* 24, 1 (1997): 25–38.

Longman, J. "Plus: Olympics; U.S.O.C. Chief Quits, Citing Lack of Support." *New York Times on the Web,* 26 October 2000, www.nytimes.com.

Louis, M. R. "Acculturation in the Workplace: Newcomers as Lay Ethnographers." In *Organizational Climate and Culture,* edited by B. Schneider, 85–129. San Francisco: Jossey-Bass, 1990.

————. "Surprise and Sense-Making: What Newcomers Experience in Entering Unfamiliar Organizational Settings." *Administrative Science Quarterly* 25 (June 1980): 226–251.

Lowenstein, R. "Alone at the Top." *New York Times Magazine*, 27 August 2000, 32–64.

Lubatkin, M., Schweiger, D., and Weber, Y. "Top Management Turnover in Related M&A's: An Additional Test of the Theory of Relative Standing." *Journal of Management* 25, 1 (1999): 55–73.

Luchins, A. S., and Luchins, E. H. *Rigidity of Behavior: A Variational Approach to the Effect of Einstellung.* Eugene, University of Oregon Books, 1959.

Lussier, R. N. "Startup Business Advice from Business Owners to Would Be Entrepreneurs." *S.A.M. Advanced Management Journal* 60, 1 (1995): 10.

Maanen, J. V. "People Processing: Strategies of Organizational Socialization." *Organizational Dynamics* 24 (Summer 1978): 539.

Macionis, J. J., and Benokraitis, N. V., eds. *Seeing Ourselves: Classic, Contemporary, and Cross-Cultural Readings in Sociology.* 5th ed. Upper Saddle River, N.J.: Prentice Hall, 2001.

Mackoff, B., and Wenet, G. *The Inner Work of Leaders: Leadership as a Habit of Mind.* New York: AMACOM, 2000.

Mael, F., and Ashforth, B. E. "Loyal from Day One: Biodata, Organizational Identification, and Turnover among Newcomers." *Personnel Psychology* 48, 2 (1995): 309–333.

Major, D. A., Kozlowski, S. W. J., Chao, G. T., and Gardner, P. D. "A Longitudinal Investigation of Newcomer Expectations, Early Socialization Outcomes, and the Moderating Effects of Role Development Factors." *Journal of Applied Psychology* 80, 3 (1995): 418.

"Manchester Consulting Executive Coaching Survey." *Manchester Consulting Executive Briefing* 1, 1 (2000): 1–4.

Manchester Inc. *Retention and Staffing Report.* Bala Cynwyd, Pa.: Manchester, Inc., 1998.

Marchand, D. A., Kettinger, W. J., and Rollins, J. D. "Information Orientation: People, Technology and the Bottom Line." *Sloan Management Review* 41 (Summer 2000): 69–80.

Max, K. "Priceline Names Its CFO—Citi's Heidi Miller." *The Street.com,* 3 November 2000, *www.thestreet.com.*

Mayer, J., and Salovey, P. "What Is Emotional Intelligence?" In *Emotional Development and Emotional Intelligences: Educational Implications,* edited by P. Salovey and D. Salovery. New York: Basic Books, 1997.

McCall, M. W. Jr., and Lombardo, M. M. *Off the Track: Why and How Successful Executives Get Derailed.* Greensboro, N.C.: Center for Creative Leadership, 1983.

McCauley, C. D., Moxley, R. S., and Van Velsor, E., eds. *The Center for Creative Leadership Handbook of Leadership Development.* San Francisco: Jossey-Bass, 1998.

McClelland, D. C. "Motivation Theory." *Accel-team.com,* 9 November 2000, *www.accel-team.com.*

McGeehan, P. "Executive Assesses Her Adventure at a Dot-Com." *New York Times*, 9 November 2000, sec. C, p. 1.

————. "Web Concern Hires Officer of Citigroup." *New York Times on the Web*, 24 February 2000, *www.nytimes.com*.

Meglino, B. M., Denisi, A. S., and Ravlin, E. C. "Effects of Previous Job Exposure and Subsequent Job Status on the Functioning of a Realistic Job Preview." *Personnel Psychology* 46, 4 (1993): 803–822.

Merton, R. *Social Theory and Social Structure*. New York: The Free Press, 1968.

Meyer, G. D. "An Upper Echelon's Perspective on Transformational Leadership Problems in High Technology Firms." *Journal of High Technology Management Research* 1, 2 (1990): 223–242.

Meyer, J. G. Jr. *Company Command, the Bottom Line*. Washington, D.C.: National Defense University Press, 1990.

Miller, V. D., and Jablin, F. M. "Information Seeking during Organizational Entry: Influences, Tactics, and a Model of the Process." *Academy of Management Review* 16, 1 (1991): 92–120.

Mohrman, S. A., Cohen, S. G., and Mohrman, A. M. Jr. *Designing Team Based Organizations: New Forms for Knowledge Work*. San Francisco: Jossey-Bass, 1995.

Morrison, A. M. *The New Leaders: Leadership Diversity in America*. San Francisco: Jossey-Bass, 1996.

Morrison, E. W., and Phelps, C. C. "Taking Charge at Work: Extrarole Efforts to Initiate Workplace Change." *Academy of Management Journal* 42, 4 (1999): 403–419.

Morrow, P. C., and McElroy, J. C. "Work Commitment and Job Satisfaction over Three Career Stages." *Journal of Vocational Behavior* 30, 3 (1987): 330–346.

Mowday, R. T., and Porter, L. W. "The Measurement of Organizational Commitment." *Journal of Vocational Behavior* 14 (1979): 224–247.

Mowday, R. T., Porter, L. W., and Steers, R. M. *Employee Organization Linkages*. San Francisco: Academic, 1982.

Muchinsky, P. M. *Psychology Applied to Work: An Introduction to Industrial and Organizational Psychology*. Stamford, Conn.: Wadsworth Thomson Learning, 2000.

Mueller, C. W. "Reduction of Power Differences in Practice: The Power Distance Reduction Theory and Its Applications." In *European Contributions to Organization Theory*, edited by G. Hofstede and M. S. Kassem, 79–64. Assen, Netherlands: Van Gorcum, 1976.

Mussen, P. H., Conger, J. J., and Kagan, J. *Child Development and Personality*. 3rd ed. New York: Harper & Row, 1969.

Nadel, S. J. "Welcoming Employees Properly Can Give Strategic Advantage to Savvy Employers." *Human Resources Report* 16, 39 (1998): 5–6.

Nadler, D. A. *Feedback and Organization Development: Using Data-Based Methods*. Reading, Mass.: Addison-Wesley, 1977.

Nadler, D. A., and Spencer, J. L. *Executive Teams*. San Francisco: Jossey-Bass, 1998.

Nextera Enterprises, Inc. "Employee Turnover Depresses Earnings, Stock Price by 38%, Nextera Research Study Shows." 8 August 2000, *www.sibson.com.*

Nicholson, N. "A Theory of Work Role Transition." *Administrative Science Quarterly* 194, 29 (1984): 172–191.

Numerof, R. E., and Abrams, M. N. "Integrating Corporate Culture from International M&A's." *HR Focus* 75, 6 (1998): 11–12.

Oakland, S., and Ostell, A. "Measuring Coping: A Review and Critique." *Human Relations* 49, 2 (1996): 133–155.

Olsen, S. "Priceline Cutting 87 Jobs; CFO Stepping Down." *New York Times on the Web*, 3 November 2000, *www.nytimes.com.*

O'Reilly, C. A. III, and Caldwell, D. F. "The Commitment and Job Tenure of New Employees: Some Evidence of Postdecisional Justification." *Administrative Science Quarterly* 26, 4 (1981): 597–616.

O'Reilly, C. III, and Chatman, J. "Organizational Commitment and Psychological Attachment: The Effects of Compliance, Identification, and Internalization on Prosocial Behavior." *Journal of Applied Psychology* 71, 3 (1986): 492–499.

"Organizational Learning as Cognitive Re-definition: Coercive Persuasion Revisited." Boston: MIT Sloan School of Management, 1999.

Pascale, R. T. "Fitting New Employees into the Company Culture." *Fortune,* 28 May 1984, 662.

———. *Managing on the Edge: How the Smartest Companies Use Conflict to Stay Ahead.* New York: Simon & Schuster, 1990.

Pearson, C. A. L. "The Turnover Process in Organizations: An Exploration of the Role of Met-Unmet Expectations." *Human Relations* 48, 4 (1995): 405–420.

Petrock, F. "Planning the Leadership Transition," *Journal of Business Strategy* 11 (November/December 1990): 14–16.

Pfeffer, J. *The Human Equation: Building Profits by Putting People First.* Boston: Harvard Business School Press, 1998.

———. *Managing with Power: Politics and Influences in Organizations.* Boston: Harvard Business School Press, 1992.

Pitts, R. A. "Diversification Strategies and Organizational Policies of Large Diversified Firms." *Journal of Economics and Business* 28, 3 (1976): 181–188.

Porter, L. W., Lawler E. E. III, and Hackman, J. R. *Perspectives on Behavior in Organizations.* New York: McGraw-Hill, 1975.

Porter, L. W., Steers, R. M., Mowday, R. T., and Boulian, P. V. "Organizational Commitment, Job Satisfaction and Turnover among Psychiatric Technicians." *Journal of Applied Psychology* 59, 5 (1974): 603–609.

Porter, M. E. *Competitive Strategy: Techniques for Analyzing Industries and Competitors.* New York: The Free Press, 1980.

Powell, G. N. "Reinforcing and Extending Today's Organizations: The Simultaneous Pursuit of Person-Organization Fit and Diversity." *Organizational Dynamics* 26, 3 (1998): 50–61.

Prahalad, C. K. and Hamel, G. "The Core Competence of the Corporation." *Harvard Business Review,* May 1990, 79–90.

Price, J. L. "The Impact of Turnover on the Organization." *Work and Occupations* 16, 4 (1989): 461–473.

Pulley, M. L. "Beyond the Corporate Box: Exploring Career Resilience." *Dissertation Abstracts International: Section B: The Sciences & Engineering* 57, 2-B (1996): 1427.

Reichheld, F. F. *The Loyalty Effect: The Hidden Force behind Growth, Profits, and Lasting Value.* Boston: Harvard Business School Press, 1996.

Reina, D. S., and Reina, M. L. *Trust & Betrayal in the Workplace: Building Effective Relationships in Your Organization.* San Francisco: Berrett-Koehler, 1999.

Ross, L., Amabile, T. M., and Steinmetz, J. L. "Social Roles, Social Control, and Biases in Social-Perception Processes." *Journal of Personality and Social Psychology* 35 (1977): 485–494.

Saks, A. M. "The Relationship between the Amount and Helpfulness of Entry Training and Work Outcomes." *Human Relations* 49, 4 (1996): 429–451.

Salancik, G. R., and Pfeffer, J. "Who Gets Power—And How They Hold on to It: A Strategic-Contingency Model of Power." *Organizational Dynamics* 5 (Winter 1977): 3–21.

Sayles, L. R. *Managerial Behavior: Administration in Complex Organizations.* New York: McGraw-Hill, 1964.

Schein, E. H. *Career Dynamics: Matching Individual and Organizational Needs.* Reading, Mass.: Addison-Wesley, 1978.

———. *Coercive Persuasion.* New York: Norton, 1961.

———. *Organizational Culture & Leadership.* San Francisco: Jossey-Bass, 1985.

———. "Organizational Learning as Cognitive Re-definition: Coercive Persuasion Revisited." Working paper. Boston: MIT Sloan School of Management, 1996.

Schlesinger, L. A., and Heskett, J. L. "The Service-Driven Service Company." *Harvard Business Review,* September–October 1991, 71–81.

Senge, P. M., Kleiner, A., Roberts, C., Ross, R. B., and Smith, B. J. *The Fifth Discipline Fieldbook.* New York: Doubleday, 1990.

Sheehan, E. P. "The Effects of Turnover on the Productivity of Those Who Stay." *Journal of Social Psychology* 133, 5 (1993): 699–706.

Simons, R. "Control in an Age of Empowerment." *Harvard Business Review,* March–April 1995, 80–88.

Simons, R. *Performance Measurement & Control Systems for Implementing Strategy: Text & Cases.* Upper Saddle River, N.J.: Prentice Hall, 2000.

Slater, R. *The GE Way Fieldbook: Jack Welch's Battle Plan for Corporate Revolution.* New York: McGraw-Hill, 1999.

————. "Jack Welch and the GE Way." *Soundview Executive Book Summaries* 21, 1.1 (1999): 1–8.

Smart, B. *Topgrading: How Leading Companies Win by Hiring, Coaching and Keeping the Best People.* Paramus, N.J.: Prentice Hall, 1999.

Smith, P. M. *Taking Charge: A Practical Guide for Leaders.* Washington, D.C.: National Defense University Press, 1986.

Sonnenfeld, J. *The Hero's Farewell: What Happens When CEOs Retire.* New York: Oxford University Press, 1988.

Stack, J. "The Next in Line." *Inc.com,* 11 October 2000, *www.inc.com.*

Stanley, S. M., and Markman, H. J. "Assessing Commitment in Personal Relationships." *Journal of Marriage and the Family* 54 (August 1992): 595–608.

Stanley, S. M., Lobitz, W. C., and Dickson, F. C. "Using What We Know." In *Handbook of Interpersonal Commitment and Relationship Stability,* edited by J. M. Adams and W. H. Jones, 379–392. New York: Kluwer Academic/Plenum, 1999.

Stein, N. "Winning the War to Keep Top Talent." *Fortune,* 29 May 2000, 132–138.

Stewart, T. A. "Whom Can You Trust? It's Not So Easy to Tell." *Fortune,* 12 June 2000, 331–334.

Stringer, R. A. Jr., and Uchenick, J. L. *Strategy Traps and How to Avoid Them.* New York: Lexington Books, 1986.

Sullivan, G. R., and Harper, M. V. *Hope Is Not a Method: What Business Leaders Can Learn from America's Army.* New York: Broadway Books, 1996.

Sweeney, P. "Teaching New Hires to Feel at Home." *New York Times,* 14 February 1999.

Taylor, G. S., and Zimmerer, T. W. "Voluntary Turnover among Middle-Level Managers: An Analysis of Perceived Causes." *Journal of Managerial Issues* 4, 3 (1992): 424–437.

"Trust: How to Build It, Earn It—and Reestablish It When It's Broken." *Harvard Management Update* 5, 9 (2000): 1–3.

Tyler, K. "Take New Employee Orientation off the Back Burner." *HR Magazine* 43, 6 (1998): 49–54.

Van Maanen, J. "Breaking In: Socialization to Work." In *Handbook of Work, Organization and Society,* edited by R. Dubin, 67–120. Chicago: Rand McNally, 1975.

————. "People Processing: Strategies of Organizational Socialization." *Organizational Dynamics* 7 (1978): 18.

Virany, B., Tushman, M. L., and Romanelli, E. "Executive Succession and Organization Outcomes in Turbulent Environments: An Organization Learning Approach" *Organization Science* 3, 1 (1992): 72–91.

Wagner, W. F. "All Skill, No Finesse." *Workforce,* June 2000, 108–116.

Waldroop, J., and Butler, T. "Guess What? You're Not Perfect." *Fortune,* 16 October 2000.

Wanous, J. P. *Organizational Entry: Recruitment, Selection and Socialization of Newcomers.* Reading, Mass.: Addison-Wesley, 1980.

Weick, K. E. "Small Wins: Redefining the Scale of Social Problems." *American Psychologist* 39, 1 (1984): 40–49.

What Keeps 'Em? A Report of Retention Drivers. Jacksonville, Fla.: Beverly Kaye & Associates, 2000.

Winkler, K., and Janger, I. "You're Hired! Now How Do We Keep You?" *Across the Board,* July–August 1998, 16–23.

"Winning the War for Talent." *Inc.com,* 11 October 2000, *www.inc.com.*

Winter, G. "Chief Who Put Newell Rubbermaid Together Quits." *New York Times on the Web,* 2 November 2000, *www.nytimes.com.*

Worchel, S., Jenner, S. M., and Hebel, M. R. "Changing the Guard: How Origin of New Leader and Disposition of Ex-Leader Affect Group Performance and Perceptions." *Small Group Research* 29, 4 (1998): 436–451.

"Workforce Trends." *Manchester Consulting,* 17 August 2000, *www.manchester us.com.*

Wurman, R. S. *Information Anxiety.* New York: Doubleday, 1989.

Yoon, J., Baker, M. R., and Ko, J. "Interpersonal Attachment and Organizational Commitment: Subgroup Hypothesis Revisited." *Human Relations* 47, 3 (1994): 329.

Young, H. P., ed. *Negotiation Analysis.* Ann Arbor: University of Michigan Press, 1991.

Zemke, R. "Why Organizations Still Aren't Learning." *Training,* September 1999, 40–49.

Index